The Language of Baklava

A MEMOIR

FIRST ANCHOR BOOKS EDITION, MARCH 2006

The Library of Congress has cataloged the Pantheon edition as follows:
Abu-Jaber, Diana.
The language of Baklava / Diana Abu-Jaber.
p. cm.
1. Cookery, Middle Eastern. 2. Jordan—Cookery. I. Title.
TX725.M628A28   2005   641.5956—dc22   2004056828

Anchor ISBN-10: 1-4000-7776-1
Anchor ISBN-13: 978-1-4000-7776-2

www.anchorbooks.com

Printed in the United States of America
10   9   8   7   6

FOR MY PARENTS,
PAT AND GUS ABU-JABER

Contents

Foreword

My childhood was made up of stories—the memories and recollections of my father's history and the storybook myths and legends that my mother brought me to read.

The stories were often in some way about food, and the food always turned out to be about something much larger: grace, difference, faith, love. This book is a compilation of some of those family stories as it traces the ways we grew into ourselves. I believe the immigrant's story is compelling to us because it is so consciously undertaken. The immigrant compresses time and space—starting out in one country and then very deliberately starting again, a little later, in another. It's a sort of fantasy—to have the chance to re-create yourself. But it's also a nightmare, because so much is lost.

To me, the truth of stories lies not in their factual precision, but in their emotional core. Most of the events in this book are honed and altered in some fashion, to give them the curve of stories. Lives don't usually correspond to narrative arcs, but all of these stories spring out of real people, memories, and joyously gathered and prepared meals.

I offer my deepest gratitude to the friends and family I write about in these pages and give thanks to everyone who knows that each of us has a right to tell our stories, to be truthful to our own memories, no matter how flawed, private, embellished, idiosyncratic, or improved they may be. I also offer apologies to anyone whose experiences I may have shared and recorded here without asking permission. I offer up these memories in hopes that others will feel invited or inspired to conjure up and share their own. Memories give our lives their fullest shape, and eating together helps us to remember.

The Language of Baklava

ONE

Raising an Arab Father in America

It's a murky, primordial sort of memory: a cavelike place, bright flickering lights, watery, dim echoes, sudden splashes of sounds, and—hulking and prehistoric—TV cameras zooming in on wheeled platforms. A grown man in a vampire costume clutching a microphone to his chest is making his way through rows of sugar-frenzied, laugh-crazed kids. He attempts to make small talk with the children through a set of plastic fangs. "Hello there, Bobby Smith!" He chortles and tousles a head. "How are you, Debbie Anderson!" I'm sitting in a television studio in a row full of cousins and sisters, not entirely sure how I got here—this was my aunt Peggy's idea. She'd watched *The Baron DeMone Show* for years and finally decided to send away for studio tickets.

He stalks closer and closer: I can see tiny seeds of sweat sparkling along his widow's peak. He squints at our oversize name tags: "Farouq, Ibtissam, Jaipur, Matussem . . ." I see his mouth working as he walks up our row of beaming, black-eyed kids. Eventually he gets to me. "Diana!" he cries with evident relief, then crashes into my last name. But apparently once this man starts going, he must see the thing through. He squints, trying to sound it out: "Ub-abb-yuh-yoo-jo-jee-buh-ha-ree-rah . . ." This guy's a scream! I can't stop laughing. What an idiot! I've got green eyes and pale skin, so evidently he feels I must speak English, unlike the rest of the row. He squats beside me, holds the big mike in my face, and says, "Now, Diana, tell me, what kind of a last name is that?"

This guy slays me! I can barely stop laughing enough to blast, "*English, you silly!*" into his microphone.

He jumps, my magnified voice a yowl through the studio, then starts laughing, too, and now we're both laughing, but at two different jokes—which must happen quite a bit on children's programming. He nods approvingly; they love me and my exotic entourage—later we'll be flooded with candy, passes, and invitations to return to the show. But at the moment, as the Baron stands to leave, I realize I'm not quite done with him yet. I grab him by the back of his black rayon cape and announce on national television, "I'm hungry!"

I'm six and I'm in charge; the sisters are just getting around to being born. Bud, my father, carries me slung over one shoulder when he cooks; he calls me his sack of potatoes. Mom protests, pointing out safety issues, but Bud says it's good for me, that it'll help me acclimate to onion fumes. I love the way his shoulder jumps and his whole back shakes as he tosses a panful of chopped tomatoes over the flames while the teeth rattle in my head.

My father is a sweet, clueless immigrant—practically still a boy. He keeps getting fooled. He saw TV for the first time when his boat stopped in Italy en route to Ellis Island. It was flickering in a hotel lobby. On the screen he saw a lady in a pretty blue dress singing to a cat dressed in a tuxedo. "Look at that," he marveled to his brother. "They've got a whole theater inside that box!" After he'd been in America a couple of months, a door-to-door salesman convinced him to spend three weeks of pay on a TV that didn't have any working parts. He told Bud it needed some time to "warm up." Bud hopefully switched it on and off for weeks before an American friend visited and explained that this TV would never be warm.

Bud learns English not from books, but from soaking in the language of work, of the shops and restaurants after he arrives in this country. I don't know where he learns how to hail strangers, but whenever my father needs directions—which is frequently—he flags down men and women alike with the same greeting: "Hey, bud!" I grow up thinking of all Americans as Bud—and even though my father's name is Ghassan Saleh Abu-Jaber, he becomes the original Bud.

I learn early: We are Arab at home and American in the streets. The streets are where Bud speaks English in a loud voice, swaggers, wears hard-soled shoes. Sometimes he slips and haggles with the clerk at Sears over the price of ties. He'll ask me in Arabic if I think the man is a big moron or just a little idiot. After considering my assessment, he'll formulate the appropriate bid—perhaps grudgingly offer to pay the price on the tag—minus two dollars! Plus an extra tie! Usually the clerk looks befuddled or calls for a manager, but every now and then, Bud'll find one who turns sharp-eyed and pleased, who throws out an unauthorized counteroffer—extra tie, but full price! Their voices flash in the flat mall light.

On Saturdays Bud is in the kitchen. The old houses along our elm-lined streets seem to sigh, screen doors ease open, the air sweetens, and the sky leans back on one elbow. First my father will make breakfast. After that, any one of a number of miraculous things can happen:

Go to Diplomat-Uncle Jack's house and have stuffed grape leaves.

Go to Professor-Uncle Hal's house and have kibbeh.

Go to Businessman-Uncle Danny's house and have stuffed squash.

Go to Crazy-Uncle Frankie's house and have roasted leg of lamb.

Go to Fair Haven Beach with everyone and have shish kabob.

Those aren't their real names: Uncle Hal is really Uncle Hilal, Jack is actually named Jaffer, Danny is Hamdan, and Frankie is short for Qadir. They are the uncles who, along with my father, came to America. Somehow, after they bought their new winter coats at Robert Hall in downtown Syracuse and changed the part in their hair, they all seemed to have new American names as well. Almost everyone I know has two names—one from Before and one from After. Even I have two names—for some reason, Bud calls me Ya Ba, which means "Little Daddy," but this name seems to belong between the two of us.

I love to be in the kitchen and watch my strong father at work in his undershirt, baggy shorts, and sandals. He's singing along with the radio and not getting a single word right. But what he lacks in accuracy he makes up for in gusto and verve. He slides a whole side of lamb out of the refrigerator, hoists it up for me and my friend Mer-

ilee to admire, and says, "Here he is! Here's Marvin." Bud likes to
name all big cuts of meat—usually Tom, Dick, Harry, or Marvin. I
stand close beside him, four feet high in flip-flops, bony shoulders
poking through the crossed straps of my sundress, plastic heart-
shaped sunglasses propped on my head, and watch as he centers the
meat on his chopping block and *whomps* his cleaver down. My friend
Merilee, with her freckles and straw yellow pigtails, shrieks and clatters out the back door. I happily tote the bloody kabobs from the
block to the marinade of garlic, rosemary, vinegar, and olive oil. Bud
tells me that someday I will make a fantastic butcher.

Next, Bud pushes the big, glistening chunks of beef and onion and
tomato onto skewers. The skewers are iron, with round hoops at one
end and cruel, three-sided points on the other, so heavy that once
they're threaded with meat, I can carry only one at a time to the
refrigerator.

Shish kabob means that there will be coolers and ice chests, blankets and salads, pita bread, iced tea, salty braided cheese, hummus,
maybe a visit to Rudy's stand, where they dip the scoops of ice cream
into a kind of chocolate that hardens into a shell. Maybe our mother
will bring frozen pound cake, because who wants to bake anything in
this heat?

There will also be sisters and cousins and aunties and uncles and
even more cousins, because there's no telling who's just "comeover,"
meaning come over from the old country. You never know when suddenly a second cousin you haven't seen in years will be standing in
the living room, asking for a little cup of coffee. They'll be hungry
because everyone who "comesover" is hungry: for home, for family,
for the old smells and touches and tastes. If we're not at the park,
sometimes these cousins and noncousins and friends and strangers
will drop by the house. Coincidentally, they always come at dinnertime. Always at the moment we turn on the stove.

Bud says that today we children need to be extra pleasant, polite,
and cute. Today Cousin Sami (Samir) will be with us. He is newly
arrived, twenty years old, sensitive, and willowy as a deer. He walks
tentatively in this new country, looking around himself as if about to

break into flight; his eyes glisten, eternally on the verge of tears. I overhear Bud telling Mom that he doesn't know if Sami will "make it." Mom blows a filament of hair out of her face; she's twenty-six years old and tall, but she doesn't have much more meat on her than I do. Her reading glasses are smart and serious. I can tell that she's thinking, What is it with these sensitive, crazy men?

We pack up the family and drive the road to the north, over tiny wooden bridges, past taverns with names like Three Rivers Inn and gurgling minute creeks, up to Fair Haven Beach on Lake Ontario, thirty miles from Syracuse. After we arrive and roll along behind people walking to their car in order to secure the best parking spot, it will take an even longer time to unpack the trunk and find the exact picnic tables and get out the bags and coolers and cousins and sisters. We cover several tables with red-checked tablecloths, paper plates, plastic containers full of everything. Bud piles briquettes into three different grills, and Uncle Hal adds more and more lighter fluid—usually while it's burning—so the flame roars right up at him in a fabulous arc. I draw in the rich chemical aroma: Barbecues are the smell of lighter fluid, dark and delicious as the aroma of gasoline.

Another car pulls up and there is Cousin Sami unfolding from Uncle Danny's Volkswagen. Sami holds out his hands as if testing the gravity on this new planet. He looks as if he might topple over at any moment. I adore him. Big, hearty Businessman-Uncle Danny, who's looking after him because his full-time father, Rich-Uncle Jimmy, lives in Jordan, laughs and calls him "a poet." I know immediately that's what I want to be, too, and I say this to my father as he's carrying a platter full of shish kabob. He looks unhappy at this news, but then Uncle Hal shouts, "Oh yes, there's a lot of money in that," and the adults laugh for inexplicable reasons and then forget about me.

The cousins—except for Sami—and sisters and I run in the frothy surf along Fair Haven's pebble beach. The water is electrically cold, threaded with mysteriously warm currents. We go in up to our necks and the waves lift us off our feet. We can do just this, standing in ice water and bobbing, for hours. A game for lunatics. We don't ever want to come in, even when our mother and one of the aunties wade out and says, "Your lips are purple, time to come in." First we make Mom demonstrate her ability to float in the water so that her shoulders submerge and her pink toes bob up and she looks as if she's sitting in a recliner. This, I assume, is a talent innate to all Americans. We all try, and our chicken-bone bodies just sink. Dad and his too many brothers don't even own bathing suits.

There's a commotion on shore. My father and the uncles are shouting and waving their arms: Shish kabob is ready! Uncle Hal is ferrying the sizzling skewers—we call them sheeshes—to a big platter on the table. Bud is turning more of them on the fire.

The shish kabob comes like an emergency. It sizzles at the table, and Uncle Hal pushes the chunks of meat off the skewers with a piece of pita bread. They all go to one central plate. He says, "This piece is for you and this one for you." It's best to wait for the second sheesh because for some reason the meat on the first always looks scrawny and shriveled and smells of uncooked lighter fluid. But there's no time to wait! You have to eat the lamb when it's hot enough to burn your fingers and scald your tongue.

"Eat it *now*," Uncle Hal says. "It's good right this second."

This is one of the secrets of shish kabob: how quickly it dries and hardens on the skewer. Not like a roast leg of lamb or breasts of chicken that fall off the bone when you cook them long and ruthlessly enough. Shish kabob is fierce. It comes charred and crusty outside and pink, almost wet red inside, richly redolent, in its special way, of marrow and pepper. It sizzles in your mouth and tastes faintly of the earth.

In the midst of all this drama and pageantry, however, I notice that Sami hasn't left his perch on the far end of the most distant picnic bench. His eyes are glowing as he watches us with both curiosity and aloofness. I pluck a morsel from the plate and run to him while it burns my fingertips. To my mind, this is the best way to show love— to offer food from your own hand. But he only closes his eyes and shakes his head dolefully.

Because I am six, I am typically the one being fed—I've never tried to feed anyone from my own hand like this before. But I've never had a cousin like this before. Usually my older Jordanian cousins arrive resplendent in polyester bell-bottom slacks—this being the late sixties—tall and strapping and hungry for America. With big mustaches, huge laughs, wild eyes, and big—very big—plans. Not Sami, though. Earlier that morning, Bud talked about it on the phone with one of his brothers. Sami didn't even want to come to America. In our family, we assume that everyone is simply dying to come here. It's like a law of nature: Grow up, go to America. I learn from sitting at the kitchen table, helping Bud poke kabobs onto skewers while he talks on the phone, that Uncle Jimmy sent Sami to America to "cure him" of something or other. When I ask Bud later what Uncle Jimmy wants to cure him of, he thinks about his answer for a while before he decides to say, "Of being a poet."

I stand before Sami, watching and admiring him, the lamb cooling in my hand. Finally I say, "What's a poet?"

He turns that vivid, astonished look back on me again and says, "I'm not a poet." He rubs the back of his neck and sighs. Then he murmurs, "I embroider shawls. Would you like me to make you one?"

I nod vehemently.

Uncle Hal overhears us. He laughs and shouts, "He's not a poet! *I'm* a poet—listen: 'If white is the color of mourning in Andalusia / It is a most fitting color. . . .' "

"You didn't write that," Uncle Danny says, and a new fight percolates among the brothers.

For some reason, then, Sami changes his mind and takes the piece of meat from my hand. It is cool now, and it won't be as good, but he eats it anyway, his luminous eyes fixed on me. His features undergo an alteration, as if a transparent veil has lifted from his face. It is the first time I've seen him smile. He says quietly, "It's good."

At the end of the day at the beach, about to drive home, we might stop at Ontario Orchards, a big farm produce stand, and buy a bag of fresh cherries, black with sugar. We pass them around during the ride and spit the pits out the windows. Then my sisters and I fall asleep. I'm so deeply asleep when we get home that I hope I'll get carried in.

But lately I've grown arms and legs that hang and dangle and might knock over just about anything.

"EAT IT NOW" SHISH KABOB

4 tablespoons olive oil
½ cup red wine
2 tablespoons red vinegar
4 cloves garlic, crushed
2 teaspoons dried oregano
2 teaspoons dried rosemary
Salt and freshly ground
   pepper

2 pounds boneless leg of
   lamb, cut into small
   cubes
1 large onion, cut into
   chunks
1 large tomato, cut into
   chunks

Whisk together the oil, wine, vinegar, garlic, and spices in a large bowl. Add the meat and stir to coat it thoroughly. Cover and refrigerate overnight; turn occasionally.

Thread the cubes of lamb on skewers, occasionally adding a piece of onion or tomato. Grill over hot coals, turning once. Cook to medium rare and eat while still sizzling.

SERVES 6.

The next day is the long, dull blank of Sunday. My mother sits on the couch reading one of her textbooks, studying to become a *master*. I once asked her: How much college is there? Does it end, or does it go on and on? She told me there's a bachelor, a master, and a doctor. I reeled at the thought of such infinite education but was most impressed by the idea of becoming a *master*.

Today I am aimless and a little bit lost. I drape myself over her long lap and trace invisible animals on her leg. Something is bothering me. I keep thinking about the way my uncles used the word *poet* as if it meant something different from what it was, as if they might as well have been calling Sami a pencil sharpener or coffee table. I listen to the soft, slow tick of my mother's pages. Finally I say, "Wh everyone call Sami a poet if he's not a poet?"

The pages stop. Mom puts her finger in the book and lowers it, and her cheeks are pink. I'm startled to see what an interesting question this has turned out to be. She doesn't always answer my questions. I know she hears them because she will lift her eyes from the page (there is always a page to be looked at) and her eyes will go unfocused with thinking. And then sometimes she will remember to answer, but I can't count on it.

Finally, Mom sighs and says, "Well, they don't exactly know what . . . else . . . to call him."

"Why? Why do they call him anything besides Sami?"

"Well, sometimes . . . sometimes . . ." Her voice wavers, and she looks around as if to find the right words somewhere in the living room. "Sometimes . . . some men—they get a little funny."

I nod. Uncle Jack, for instance, he's a scream!

"The thing is, okay, your cousin Sami—he wasn't—acting normal—with other men," she says.

I frown. I go back to tracing invisible animals. Things have gotten murky. This is a jigsaw puzzle of words. The more Mom talks, the more I sense a difference between the words themselves and what they mean. And gradually, slowly, an image takes shape in my mind—it comes to me quite clearly. I laugh out loud and say, "I know!"

Mom holds the book up to her chest. "You do?"

"He's funny because he embroiders shawls!"

Mom looks at me a moment longer. Her eyebrows lift. Then they relax. She says, "That's right."

One day, the shish kabob goes a little differently.

Professor-Uncle Hal and his wife, Writer-Auntie Rachel, and my favorite American-born cousins, rangy, roustabout Jess and Ed, live in a big country house right down the road from Ontario Orchards. Uncle Hal lives in a library filled with leathery historical books, selected for their carved covers and the heft and density of their language: He prefers lengthy books written in very small type. His library is filled with the Ottoman Empire, Boswell, Australian Aboriginals, Oliver Goldsmith, Southeast Asia, and James Fenimore Cooper. Though he teaches international politics, he has a broad, eclectic scope, and his dinnertime stories are as likely to include the details of the Oneida Indians as the intricacies of the medieval Arabs or the war in Vietnam.

They have chickens and a goat and a water-gray barn that my professor-uncle has filled with things like oil paintings in immense gilt frames, junked toys, battered pots, ancient clothes, unidentifiable tools and broken farming implements, Persian rugs, sacks of grain, silver coins and jewelry, rusted watering cans, abandoned birds' nests, and so on. It is a place stuffed with all the history in the world, the stories of ten thousand strangers, all living together here with all their separate textures and dusts and smells, along with the musty grain of the hayloft. I am obsessed with the barn and plan to live there someday.

My cousins are jumping up and down in the driveway as our car pulls up. "There's something so great," Ed gasps. "It's in the barn, come on!" We run to the barn, and as we get close my breath snags in my throat. There, in the open doorway of the barn, stands an ivory-colored lamb with dense fur, a piercing, plangent bleat, flipping ears, and rolling black eyes. I am stricken, paralyzed with love. I want to name him Harry, but Jess says no, this is Lambie, even though Mom and all the aunties are saying don't do that, that this kind of lamb doesn't like names. We surround Lambie, admiring him. Cousin Sami arrives and I want to introduce him to Lambie. They remind me of each other because of their gentle eyes and the way they turn away from things, their entrancing skittishness. But Sami pulls his fish-soft hand out of my grip and says no, he doesn't want to look at the lamb, and neither should I, for that matter. I find this notion so perverse as to be hilarious, and I run away from him, laughing.

The children cozy right up to Lambie, hug his hot neck, feed him handfuls of grass that we tear out of the lawn. He breathes his sweet, grassy breath on our faces; there are long canopies of lashes around his eyes. Ed comes running out of the kitchen with some string cheese and leftover spaghetti and meatballs he found in the refrigerator, and we try to feed it to him. Uncle Danny keeps jingling his change and looking around; Uncle Danny doesn't like a lot of monkey business. He clears his throat and says, "You know what, kids, it's going to be a while until dinner's ready. Why doesn't Auntie Yusra drive you to the ice cream stand?"

Fantastic! Let's go! We pile into the Beetles—Auntie Yusra will drive one, Auntie Jasmine will drive the other. Too many children climb in; we spill over one another's laps. Before we leave, Auntie Jasmine tries to coax Sami into joining us. "It'll be fun," she says. "You can help distract the children—teach them some of your poetry."

His delicate features contract. "I don't know any poetry," he says.

Auntie Jasmine folds down the Beetle's canvas convertible top, and we children are astonished to discover that three of us can fit into the pouched pleats of the folded-back top, which bends and sways under our weight. "I'm not positive that's safe," Auntie Jasmine says to Auntie Yusra. But they shrug and we set off, the canvas top thumping us wildly.

On the way there, I have a thought, and the thought is this: We are never. Under any circumstances. Ever. Allowed to have ice cream before dinner.

I start to formulate this curious and very interesting thought out loud, but right in the middle of my sentence, Auntie Yusra says energetically, "Hey, kids, why don't I teach you some Arabic drinking songs?" Fantastic! We learn the words to "Ah Ya Zain" ("Oh, You Beauty!") and "Ridi Ha" ("I Want Her") and even "Gameel Gamal" ("Beautiful Beauty"), which we belt out, lifting our voices over the rush of wind.

Rudy's is a tar-paper shack perched on the gravel lip of Lake Ontario. It leans a bit to the east, and the sticky black roof sits at a drunken angle on top. There's just a window with an apple-cheeked blond girl waiting in it with her pad of paper and a chewed stub of pencil. This lumpy little place with its ice-crusted freezers produces a lovely, buttery-satin ice cream. And even though we already know what we want, we still all study the lists of flavors, toppings, and nov-elties chalked onto the blackboard. I agonize over chocolate malts, root beer floats, and tin roof sundaes, but in the end I always get the scoop of vanilla dipped in the chocolate shell. The ice cream softens and slips, and the chocolate shellac stays semi-rigid and glossy, a minor miracle.

By the time we get back, a curious lethargy hangs over the house. The men are all asleep in the backyard or on the living room floor, and my mother and the aunties are murmuring at the kitchen table. There's been a change of plans, my mother tells us, we're not having shish kabob after all, we're having chicken and stuffed squash for din-ner. The kitchen stove is covered with burbling, lid-ticking pans; the air is towel damp and heavy with mystery.

None of us is really hungry anymore, anyway. We're dozy and full from the ice cream and the sunshine and the hearty, full-lunged singing. My sisters settle down to nap, and my cousins and I play game after game of Parcheesi on the wool Persian carpet in my uncle's library. The walls of old brown books seem to mutter and sit up, star-ing. Somewhere in the middle of the seventh or eighth game, my cousin Jess, who at nine is the oldest and shrewdest of any of us, Jess of the Cleopatra eyes and shining black hair like patent leather— suddenly looks up and says, "Let's go see Lambie!"

We clatter down the back steps, calling for the lamb, and we acci-dentally wake Uncle Jack, who sits up in the grass outside the barn. "Ah . . . oh . . . well, Lambie had to go visit his grandmother," Uncle Jack says.

Among our black-eyed, black-haired uncles and father, Diplomat-Uncle Jack was rumored to have somehow had ineffable red hair as a boy. Whenever he acted up, my Palestinian grandmother would put her hands on her hips and say, "That's the Irish devil in you!" Even though he is the oldest of the brothers in America, he acts like the youngest. He is the clever *mishkeljee*—the "troublemaker," with a fondness for stirring things up, spreading rumors, sprouting argu-ments, then disappearing.

"Lambie has a grandmother?" my cousin Ed asks skeptically. "Where?"

"Ah, yes, okay, um . . . she lives in Wisconsin. On a lovely lake filled with swans, in a house with glass doorknobs on every door."

"I doubt it," Ed says, though somewhat less incredulous now. It happens that Jess and Ed have glass doorknobs in their house. And I myself have heard of Wisconsin. I glance at the barn and think I see, moving quick and lithe as a lizard, the long slim arm and leg of Sami disappearing around the corner.

Dinnertime comes and we eat our chicken and stuffed squash, though the ice cream has dampened our appetites. Everyone does his or her usual. The grown-ups pile our plates with too much food. And there's the customary struggle with Uncle Hal, who likes to feed the children gaping mouthfuls of food from his own hand. He even tries to feed our mother and our aunties, who roll their eyes and bat his hand away, preferring to eat their own dainty American portions on forks. Uncle Jack offers me some important life advice, which is, he says, to never start drinking before noon or I'll grow up to be a bum. Auntie Rachel eats all the toasted pine nuts off the rice. Cousin Sami sits trembling with his hands on either side of his plate, eyes closed, not leaving the table. None of the adults seem to be comfortable with looking at him, and no one tries to coax him into eating. Their eyes roam toward him, then veer away; the mere sight of him is like an accusation. Even I can feel it, and I feel terribly guilty, though I don't know what I'm guilty of. Uncle Hal spears a few stuffed squashes and puts them on my plate. And then something very strange happens: Bud reaches over and plucks the squashes from my plate. I blink and look at him. This is such an oddity, so counter to all I know of my father, that I don't even have the words to comment on it.

That evening, after the frozen pound cake has been produced, the coffee brewed with cardamom, the dishes washed; after Auntie Rachel teaches us something in Russian that she says means "Require the children to work"; after the evening news has been watched and discussed, and the children have been quizzed on world geography and political history—I am sitting alone on the slanting back steps with my cousin Jess. We sit listening to the high, white chiming of crickets in the fields when she suddenly says, "We ate Lambie today."

I, however, at age six, am already showing a real aptitude for not believing inconvenient truths. "That's not scientifically possible," I say, using a phrase I have picked up from *Monster Movie Matinee*. "Lambie was a lamb," I state. "We had chicken and squash."

Jess stares at me with the direct, remorseless gaze that will carry over into her adulthood and eventually strike fear into the hearts of men. "Squash stuffed with ground lamb," she says. I gaze at the darkened barn, crammed with its boxes and piles of junk. Never before has it struck me as being quite so empty. I don't dare to venture any closer.

When we leave that evening, Bud, as usual, is the first out the door, waiting behind the wheel, the car engine murmuring in the lavender night. The women linger over their farewells. There is no sign of Sami, although as we walk down the long gravel driveway past the barn, I think I hear someone weeping behind the wall of the hayloft.

This story had to wait twenty years or so for its ending. I was already done with graduate school, already moved away from home, teaching and living on my own in another state. But one day I came home for a visit and something reminded me of that lamb, and I said to my father, "Remember Lambie, the little lamb at Uncle Hal's house? What really happened to him?"

Bud shook his head and said exactly what he has so often said over the years, which was, "Ya Ba, where on earth did you ever get this memory of yours from? You know, most men won't like having a wife with such a big memory."

Then he fell back into his bottomless recliner—his favorite and most auspicious place for storytelling and philosophizing, and began at the beginning before the beginning:

On that day, the day of the lamb, Bud and his brothers were all still young men, in their late twenties and early thirties, none of them all that far away from their childhood in Jordan. When they were children, their parents had owned orchards of olive trees, figs, and lemons and fields of corn, thyme, and jasmine, watering holes and greenhouses, herds of horses, goats, and lambs. They drew their silvery drinking water from a well, baked bread in a stone oven, and in the desert nights my father and his eight brothers had liked to sleep under a sky scrawled with stars or inside the billowing goat-hair tents that the Bedouins used.

Half my father's brothers stayed in Jordan, but the other half came to America, for education or money or some sense of promise that was the opposite of homesickness. They thought, even after ten or fifteen years away, that they were still the same wiry, tough-skinned wild boys running barefoot through briars and hardscrabble land. When Uncle Hal saw the runty lamb in his neighbor's fields, he thought of the feather-light springtime in Jordan when the countryside was filled with new lambs and of the scent of freshly grilled meat and the way he and his brothers stood between these two events, birth and food, though they were only boys; so much responsibility for a miraculous, sacred transformation. How could he help himself? Even though he knew better, even though he told himself not to, Uncle Hal bought the runty lamb from the farmer. Then he called his brothers. Together, they decided they would butcher the lamb the way they used to when they were children and their parents were still alive and nobody knew anything about the bright grocery stores of America or the way meat appeared, bloodless, gleaming with cellophane, stacked in cold rows.

This was the way it was supposed to happen: Four of the brothers would hold the lamb still, and with one powerful, swift stroke, Crazy-Uncle Frankie would cut its throat. Uncle Frankie was nominated for this unpleasant task by virtue of being the youngest brother in America as well as having the least exciting job (washing school buses) and because none of the brothers wanted to slaughter the lamb after seeing the children cozying up to it. Uncle Jack, it seems, had a change of heart and wanted to return it to the farmer, but Uncle Danny, who didn't have any children yet, said that was ridiculous and wimpy. And my father, the pragmatic chef, said they were all turning soft and silly.

At the time he told me the story, he still wasn't sure why he had said this: He hadn't wanted to kill the lamb, either.

But then they were all saying things they didn't really want to say as they converged on the knock-kneed lamb. Hal held the lamb on one side, Jack held the other. Danny held the legs. Bud held the head. Frankie unsheathed the big, sharpened knife and held it up with trembling hands. Bud had owned this knife a long time and cut many things with it, but never before a living thing. In that moment, he had no memory of ever having killed a living thing. Was it true? Had they done the slaughtering back in Jordan, or had it been done for them? He started to ask, but then his brother's eyes bulged, the knife rose, Bud turned away, and Frankie slashed. He made a terrible, ineffective cut, deep enough to make the lamb scream and buck, for blood to course freely, but not deep enough to kill it.

The lamb was wild. Its head rolled back, and its neck gaped like a bloody smile. The brothers panicked and lost their grip. The lamb kicked in a frenzy; its back hoof cut right through the fabric of Uncle Danny's pants and gashed his knee. Hal grabbed the knife from Frankie and tried to make a better cut, but he missed and made another shallow cut in its face. The animal bawled and writhed. Jack picked up a rock, wildly attempting to knock it unconscious, but it again lurched out of their grip. Finally, Bud gripped the knife with both fists and, as the lamb stumbled to one side, plunged it straight into its neck.

Then everything went still. They could hear a bird trill three fragile notes from a nearby tree. The barn walls were covered with blood; the floor was covered with blood; their faces were covered with blood; their arms were covered with blood. And then my father realized that what he'd thought was a bird was the sound of weeping. For a dreadful, unreal moment, he thought it was the lamb. Then he heard Cousin Sami's voice rise from the hayloft: "I want to go home!"

Telling the story twenty or so years after the fact, Bud looked a bit gray, his face filmed with distantly recalled panic. He closed his eyes, remembering the way the lamb's neck strained, its soft, wide-open mouth, its babylike cry. The meat was spoiled, shot through with blood and adrenaline. But Uncle Hal insisted on salvaging a few pieces and ground it up to make stuffing for the squashes. None of them touched any of it.

"We thought we could still do it," Bud said. "But we couldn't."

Making shish kabob always reminds the brothers of who they used to be—the heat, the spices, the preparation for cooking, and the rituals for eating were all the same as when they were children, eating at their parents' big table. But trying to kill the lamb showed them: They were no longer who they thought they were.

PEACEFUL VEGETARIAN LENTIL SOUP

1 cup lentils (if using dried
   lentils, soak overnight,
   then drain)
1 medium onion, chopped
¼ cup olive oil
4 cups water
1 stalk celery, sliced

1 carrot, sliced
3 cloves garlic, crushed
1 teaspoon ground cumin
Juice from 1 lemon
Salt and freshly ground
   pepper

Wash the lentils thoroughly, picking out any debris. In a large saucepan, sauté the onion in the olive oil until translucent. Add the remaining ingredients and cook over medium heat for 30 minutes, or until the vegetables are tender.

SERVES 6.

TWO

Hot Lunch

During the week, my father comes home from work late at night with a Cosmo's pizza box, a big, floury cheese-and-oil pizza sliding inside, and he eats standing at the kitchen counter, folding each slice in half. He is so late returning from two, three, four jobs—mopping floors, cooking eggs, selling carpets, guarding stores—that to me he's just a sliding bar of light behind the door, looking in as I'm sleeping; the murmur of voices and the TV in the other room. He is tired, but he's full of the immigrant's hopefulness and determination, ready to take any job.

Bud misses the old country so much, it's like an ache in his blood. On his days off, he cooks and croons in Arabic to the frying liver and onions songs about missing the one you love. I ask him whom he misses, and he ponders this and says, "I don't know, I just do." Then he gazes fondly at the frying liver as if it is singing sweetly back to him. But I don't understand this yet. I was born into this snowy Syracuse world. I have no inkling of what other worlds are like.

NOSTALGIC CHICKEN LIVERS

¼ cup butter
1 clove garlic, minced
4 medium onions, sliced thin

1 pound chicken livers
⅓ cup lemon juice
Salt and freshly ground pepper

Melt the butter in a frying pan and sauté the garlic and onions until they are golden. Add the chicken livers and cook for 10 minutes. Bud recommends that you sing softly to the livers as they're cooking, so you don't rush. Stir in the lemon juice and simmer for 10 minutes. Season with salt and pepper to taste. Serve with a nice loaf of warm pita bread.

SERVES 6.

One day Bud takes me through the streets to a place where little girls in uniforms are lined up in rows. I'm also wearing a uniform—a green plaid woollen jumper, a badge sewn over the heart with the school's initials. I have a pencil and a notebook. I can't get over myself. My father puts me in a line that may or may not be the right line and says he has to leave me now, and I turn and wave to him, panicked but trying to look dignified. Though I don't say anything, my wave is desperate: Oh, my God, don't leave me here, what are you, crazy, don't go! Bud gets back into his VW Bug and watches me from the curb while I stare back at him—the only parent still there.

Then the nuns take over the world. There are nuns and nuns. They stream from the school building. So many of them: lipless, eyebrowless, boiled skinless, and swathed in acres of black veils with white bibs. They come with rulers. They herd our raggedy lines into sharp military formations. These women mean business. I have never seen anything like it. It seems that they live in the church, another problem place for me, where you are supposed to wear your hat or kerchief. Right away I start forgetting my hat or kerchief and have to wear a Kleenex bobby-pinned to my head. I have trouble getting up to go to school, so sometimes I go to bed with my uniform on over my PJs to try to save time. But I'm so sleepy in the morning, I forget and go to school still wearing my pajama bottoms under my jumper.

Gram, my mother's mother, is Catholic, and she says I will get a better education at Saint Mary's school than out among "the hoi polloi." So my parents have decided to send me to this place, in hopes that I can be transformed into one of the charming, docile girls in my classroom who sit quietly with their shining smooth hair and scabless knees and socks that stay up. This is my first indication that my parents don't know much about me.

Fortunately, I am in Sister Paul's class. Sister Paul is a strapping young woman with a long, oval face beneath her wimple and a special patience for untied shoes or gum in the hair. And unlike Sister Martha, Sister Matthew, or Sister John, she never raises her voice or swats her ruler against her thigh in an ominous way.

The school cafeteria is in the basement with its network of exposed pipes that runs hissing along the ceiling. It's a clammy, drafty place where the metal folding chairs are chilled to a jolting tang each morning. The girls try to buffer this by sitting on their hands. But between the straight skirts and kneesocks, there's always a vulnerable couple of inches of skin, and the shock of sitting in the nuns' cafeteria is one of our punishments for the sin of being born female. The cafeteria is also my first exposure to truly awful food: Its rotting, industrial stink permeates the room, and I come to think of this smell every time I hear the nuns speak of penance. I see for the first time foods dropped on molded plastic trays, items with names like tapioca, tuna casserole, and rice pudding. These trays all hold a congealed, mealy gray mass that gazes sadly up at the ceiling. Every noon I recoil at the first whiff of the cafeteria. I bring a bagged lunch that my mother writes my name on. It contains plastic bags filled with garlicky chicken kabobs, crunchy falafel, or fresh spinach pies. My stomach tilts in sympathy for the children who must eat the cafeteria food. These so-called hot-lunch children seem like another breed—a lost, forlorn tribe.

In the shadow of the cold war, the nuns enjoy staging air-raid drills, which break up the monotony of the day. They hustle the children into the cafeteria under the metallic hammering of the alarms. We sit at the long white tables while Sister John stands at the front of the room with a handheld microphone. There, she leads us through an interminable recitation of the rosary. I close my eyes and the words blur together. Then one day I notice the residual aromas of tapioca and Spam casserole ripening into this mental haze. "HailMaryfull-ofgracethelordis . . ." My stomach clenches, my mouth floods with saliva. "Thelordiswiththeeblessed . . ." I try to calm myself, try to block the smell by lowering my head, squeezing my eyes; nothing helps. I put my pen—a tool we've recently begun using in first grade— in my mouth. Like my pencil, the pen is corrugated with teeth marks. At that moment, an errant note of tuna surprise wafts from the clattering kitchen, where the cafeteria ladies are ignoring our air raid. My stomach lurches; I bite down. The pen explodes. My mouth is full of bitter blue ink, my hands and white blouse are covered, it's in my hair, it streams down my jaw.

I jump up from my seat and cry out, "Uh-oh!"

My classmates gape, openmouthed, and one tiny girl named Elvira Mickopoulos starts to cry. I for one am astounded by the newly discovered treachery of pens.

Sister Paul hurries over, takes a good long look at me, then says in a papery voice, "Diana Abu-Jaber," not needing to add, "all my suspicions have been confirmed." But then she also charitably congratulates me for speaking right up, and I feel pretty darn satisfied with myself.

They send me off to the washroom with a girl from third grade to keep a close eye on me. As I leave the room dripping, I hear Sister Anne broadcast to the students: "You see? *This* is why we have air-raid drills!"

My hair springs in frizz and coils all over my head: It won't lie down like the other children's bright caps. My grandmother has a name for it, which apparently means something like "Crazy Hair" in German. I am a hapless kid. My shirts are covered in food. I lose myself in searching for four-leaf clovers and get left behind when recess ends. I look up from my hunting to find myself sprawled alone in a clover field, a sunny sky full of white, sailing clouds. I get lost on the way to school. I get lost on the way to the washroom. I get lost on the way home from school. I bring home children from other classes and tell my mother that they'll be living with us now. But in the plus category, I have a friend named Francis, a soft-voiced boy with telescopic glasses, whom I boss around the school yard. I used to have a girl baby doll named Frances, so it never occurred to me that a boy could be named Francis. It seems there's something wrong and beautiful about it. I enjoy giving him orders. We play a scary game that Francis invented called Mom's Home! that can take up all afternoon. It consists of me yelling, "I'm home!" and then chasing Francis around the playground, snapping my jump rope at his heels.

One day I'm once again playing the role of Mom during recess, out in the play yard, which is simply the street in front of the school blocked off from traffic, when I'm stopped by Sister John. She is not my teacher; she is in charge of another classroom of children in the same grade. Sister John is concentrated and diminutive. There's a line of black hair sprinkled over her upper lip and converging on her jaw-line that makes her vaguely menacing. She wants me to escort Jessica Michaels, another first grader, into the empty classroom, find the girl's "fainting medicine" in the sister's desk drawer, and bring it out to the sister.

We go in and get the medicine, but Jessica wants to take her pills there. She's adamant. "I know how much to take," she says with a lofty ennui. "I faint all the time."

That strikes me as reasonable, so she goes ahead and swallows her pills. But when we come back out without the medicine, Sister John flies into a fit. "No!" she cries at me. "Nononononono! What if she'd taken too much medicine by accident?" she demands. She screams herself purple—how *dangerous, silly, thoughtless* I am. She howls, "*What if she dies?*"

I am dumbstruck. I gaze after Jessica, who's already abandoned me and is off jumping rope, making her death seem all the more brutal and senseless. I realize that I'm what my uncle Hal calls a "fancy idiot." Why did I ever think I could play Mom! My body seizes into a terrified semi-crouch. Perhaps it is the look on my face, or perhaps her passion has simply spent itself, but abruptly Sister John softens. She asks my name, age, height, and address, she asks about my sisters, parents, my cousins, and my grandparents. When I tell her my father is from Jordan, her eyes narrow and I see myself come into focus.

"The *Holy Land*," she breathes. "The *river Jordan*." She holds her cross in both hands.

I don't say anything, but I'm pretty sure she must have a different place in mind. Bud never mentioned anything about a Holy Land. Despite this, it turns out we are now best friends. She hooks one sharp arm around my shoulders, and since she is tiny and I am already getting tall, there isn't much difference in our height. We traipse around the play yard linked like this, going nowhere in particular but doing it fast, because, as I discover, Sister John does everything fast. It's a little off tempo, like a three-legged race, as I rush to keep up with her, but she never lets go of me. This becomes the new game during recess. Francis gazes after me wistfully in the play yard, but I barely have time for a backward glance as we rush past.

Sister John has me moved to her classroom that day. She rhapsodizes to the class about how my father is from the *Holy Land*. He's just like the *baby Jesus*, she tells them. Can you imagine? she asks them, and points to me. "Diana's father!" Puzzled, I think of the ceramic baby Jesus in my grandmother's crèche with his creamy, rosy porcelain face and swirls of blond hair. I'm the teacher's pet. This is widely acknowledged in class. It means that I can get away with memorizing only half the prayer, that I get to sit at the front of the classroom with Sister John and listen to the other children stumble their way through poorly recalled prayers. "You're so lucky," my classmates say to me. Yes, they're right, I think. For the school's spring pageant, I am mysteriously elected to be the one to carry the crown of daisies down the aisle and set it upon the pale Virgin Mary statue in the chapel. I glow with privilege and responsibility, holding the fresh white flowers on the tips of my fingers like a sacred relic, walking alone through the center of the church. The other children watch in silence.

But sometimes I reflect on the days when I could play Mom's Home! with Francis—when I wasn't locked in this perpetual three-legged race—and I feel an absence, as if I'd lost track of something important.

. . .

During the spring the air swells up, huge and hot and humid, glowing. There's often a storm coming in. The late afternoon swirls in the house with shadows, and in the kitchen it smells like onions frying in butter. There have been some changes at home since I've started school. For one thing, there's a new baby in the crib, grumbling, a big, loud complainer. One-year-old Monica has a special way of rocking her crib so it chugs through the room on its wheels like a train engine. And the other baby, my sister Suzy, has been displaced. She's nearly three, barely able to amble around, but she frequently points to the second baby and says, "Get that kid outta here!" One day she actually pushes the wheeled crib to the head of the tall stairs and is about to give it a good hearty shove—I look up at this, chortling—before our mother sprints out of the bathroom and intervenes.

Since I've acquired my newly elevated status at school, I've lost interest in family disputes. I've got new concerns. For instance, a small corner of our refrigerator is now reserved for food for Sister John. I have noticed Sister John sitting with the other nuns in the cafeteria, hunched over, picking silently at her horrible food tray. I cull bits of stuffed grape leaves and diamonds of baklava from family meals to bring to her. Sister John unwraps these various offerings in class and proclaims, "Food from the Holy Land!" She has the students pass the morsels around our classroom to examine, then she reclaims the food and eats it all in front of us while making voluptuous little sounds of appreciation, her lips bright with oil.

When I brag to my parents about Sister John's new dining habits, they glance at each other. They decide to invite the sister over and have a good look at her. My father roasts some stuffed eggplant with garlic and rice. She sits with us at the formally dressed-out dining room table, poking her face at everything in the room.

"So," Mom says tentatively. Sister John faces her with those rivet eyes. "Diana says you and she have become great friends."

"Diana"—she fans the air—"is an *angel from heaven.*"

I have the uncanny sense of having left the room. Mom examines her with one eye a little tight, as if to say *Are we talking about the same person?* But Bud nods approvingly. "Oh ho ho ho," he says, and heaps Sister John's plate with slices of dripping garlicky eggplant. He plays Santa Claus at the local hospital each Christmas, and he sometimes slips back into character.

First Sister John cuts all the food on her plate into a thousand tiny pieces; then she begins eating with her eyes closed. She makes deep, fluttering sounds that seem to emanate from the center of her chest. Her hand floats to her sternum. I have never heard her make these particular sounds before and stare at her openly. She relaxes her mouth mid-chew and releases a sighing exhale. I am enthralled. This is the most openly sensual display I've ever seen from an adult, and my mother taps at my fingers to make me look away.

"So," Mom says, breaking into Sister John's reverie, "Diana tells us you're interested in Jordan."

Sister John's face pinches into a smile as she chews. She bats her eyes and cranes her pleated neck at my father. "Well, my goodness, who wouldn't be?" she asks in a new voice, as if this were a private joke between her and Bud.

"Oh ho ho," Bud says, scooping up more rice for Sister John. "That's a good point!"

Sister John ducks her head and titters. Mom gazes off in the distance, her face drawn up as if she were pleading with invisible entities.

"It's where anyone who's holy goes," Bud expounds. "It's true— Jesus, Moses, Muhammad. All of them guys, they're somewhere around. They're hanging all over the place."

"Oh, *you*," Sister John says, as if they've been best friends for just ages. She spoons up great mounds of Bud's special rice for company—steamed, then drizzled with cinnamon and pepper and pine nuts toasted in butter.

Bud and Sister John linger at the table forever, Sister John eating and asking my father question after question about the Holy Land, my father in turn making up answers, waving his spoon, and weaving his theories-in-progress about "the beginning of the world" and "what it all means" and "the difference between men and women" and so forth.

Eventually my mother gets up, clears the table, and does the dishes—muttering darkly under her breath the whole time. She puts a half-thawed pound cake and some forks on the table and goes upstairs to bed. Suzy and I hang over the back of the couch, watching everything we can on TV while Monica chugs and fusses in her crib in the nursery. When Sister John finally stands, after what seems like the end of time, her whiskery, paper-bag face is lit up. She totes a sack full of leftovers. She wrings Bud's hand and says, "Oh, how can I thank you? Tonight has meant everything—everything—to me!"

Bud laughs and shakes his head and says, "Well then come back here for dinner again tomorrow!"

And her face flashes as if this is the most brilliant idea. "Oh, Gus," she croons, curling one veiny hand against her chest. "I'd be honored!"

The next day, Mom stands at the kitchen counter and writes a long note for me to give to the Mother Superior. She comments—not exactly to me—as she seals the note, "Once again, *someone* will have to draw the line *somewhere*."

Later at school, I stand fidgeting before her desk while the elderly, lipless woman reads it, whispering faintly, then turns it over and back, then reads it again. She closes her eyes. She says something to her secretary, then asks me to go to the outer office. I sit there, swinging my legs and sucking on a lock of hair. After a few silent, solitary minutes, I hear the too-quick footsteps in the hall. Sister John enters. She walks past me with her hot eyes burning through the floor, and I know not to say anything. Mother Superior closes the door to her office, and for a while all I hear are the dreamy, pillowy sounds of voices through the glass. Then Sister John comes out, her eyes burning another trail up the floor as she goes. Mother Superior comes out and looks at me. "Miss Abu-Jaber," she says, "why are you crying?"

I snuffle, I rub the back of my hand against my nose. Tears! My head is an absolute blank. "I don't know," I say.

That morning, I am back at my old scarred wooden desk, back in Sister Paul's room. Someone named Dolly carved her name into this desk with a black ballpoint pen. There are no more three-legged races at recess for me and no more lunchtime rendezvous. I realize that I am relieved. I start avoiding the rooms that I think Sister John may be in: I imagine her hiding, waiting for me behind doorways like a ghost. Whenever I play Mom's Home! with Francis, I imagine her watching me, observing the way I pretend to be Mom.

Only on rare occasions do I glance up and catch her looking at me from across the cafeteria, silent among the group of other nuns, her tray of food untouched, her eyes burning as if with some sweet but dimly recalled memory.

BUD'S SPECIAL RICE FOR SPECIAL COMPANY

4 cups water	½ cup pine nuts
1 teaspoon salt	1 teaspoon ground
2 cups long-grain rice	cinnamon
4 to 6 tablespoons butter	Freshly ground pepper

In a medium saucepan, bring the water and salt to a boil, add the rice, and boil for 2 minutes. Turn down the flame, cover the saucepan, and simmer for 20 minutes; the water will be absorbed. Turn off the heat and let stand for 10 minutes.

Melt the butter in a frying pan. Sauté the pine nuts until they are golden.

Place the rice in a serving dish, sprinkle with the toasted pine nuts and butter, and dust with the cinnamon and pepper to taste.

SERVES 4 TO 6.

THREE

Native Foods

Mom and I float alone in the darkened living room, watching TV. The dangerous jagged music of the nightly news with Huntley and Brinkley and the mournful, escalating music of *Perry Mason* both fill me with anxiety and a lonely ache. There are serious things on TV, reporters running through jungles and children starving and American Indians weeping. Mom leans forward, brushes aside the hair that is always in my eyes, and tells me that Bud has gone to Jordan looking for a job and a place for us to live. "Don't we live in America?" I ask. I try to read her expression, but Mom's soft, pretty face is calm as pond water. Her eyes are tinged with the faintest anxiety—possibly caused by her marriage to Bud—an eternal sort of anticipation that gives her an air of tragic beauty. In photographs, Bud makes monkey faces, flexes his biceps, makes horns with his fingers behind someone's head. Mom holds one of his arms and looks at the camera as if to say *I'm sorry*.

My mother's quiet presence is subtle yet familiar to me as a texture of air, like the fullness that lifts a room when the windows open after a long winter. Her eyes are like mine in the way we both have the dark rings around the irises and the lighter insides, and it is hard to truly see what color our eyes are because they are so flecked with other colors and odd bits of dimensions. But her eyes are blue, and mine are a murkier green: A person would either have to be very rude or somewhat in love in order to study them long and closely enough.

Where Bud is hot and worked up, she is clear and cool and waiting. Where Bud is talking all the time, she listens. Where Bud knows exactly where he is from, starting a thousand thousand years ago in the same place, Mom shrugs and says, Irish, German, maybe Swiss? Or Dutch? And she is taller than everyone in the room, with high, level shoulders. Her hair is short and quick and sleek as a bird's wing. She grew up in a shared bedroom with her own mother in an old New Jersey house full of extended Irish-German-Catholic family, so there is a deep, private center to her. She didn't expect to marry this antic, atomic character, and I think she has vowed never to let anything else surprise her again—only she is married to Bud, once and for all, so it's difficult.

But she is not serious or gloomy or hard—her voice is young, her face will remain smooth and unlined. She can enter a room without anyone seeing, entering consciousness pale and quiet as sea foam, the lacy edge of a dream. She does not struggle and grapple with the world; unlike Bud, she is at ease.

She brings me books from her school all the time, and I will proudly tell anyone, whether they ask me or not, "My mother is a reading teacher!"

During the time that Bud is away, Mom cooks: grilled Velveeta sandwiches on Wonder bread; triangles of date-nut bread and cream cheese; meatball sandwiches. Gram, Mom's mother, considered cooking a form of specialized imprisonment—like ironing—and encouraged Mom to rely on instant, just-add-water ingredients. Without Bud, we are living according to Mom's rules. In the evenings, I get to stay up late, and we watch more somber, sepia-toned television shows together on my parents' big bed. Monica and Suzy are unusually cooperative and go to bed peaceably. Bud is somewhere, I don't know where. Everything is suffused with an air of uncertainty.

COMFORTING GRILLED VELVEETA SANDWICHES

2 tablespoons butter	2 thick slabs of Velveeta
4 slices Wonder bread	(this doesn't work as
(or other soft white	nicely with cheddar,
bread)	trust me)

Melt the butter in frying pan. Place the cheese sandwiches in the hot butter. Cover and fry until golden on one side, then turn and fry on the other side. The cheese should be oozing and hot. Cut the sandwiches on the diagonal.

SERVES 2.

After several weeks or more of this suspended animation, Mom says it's time. Then there are huge smelly suitcases, and hold-your-sisters'-hands, and some important and constantly missing items called pats-sports. There's an airplane ride full of milky, walkable, stirrable clouds, a ride that takes all day and all night. I am incapable of sitting still for much longer than five minutes. I stand in the aisle and push up from the backs of the airplane seats and swing my legs until everyone in a four-aisle radius is openly glaring and clenching their jaws.

We emerge from the plane onto a steaming hot tarmac, wave at all kinds of soldiers holding big guns, pass through long, echoing glassy corridors, and there is Bud—who's grown a mustache! Then we climb into a funny, old-fashioned car shaped like a cracker box and discover that the streets and buildings here have all turned to white stone and dust. The sidewalks are not like the orderly, straight-line sidewalks of our old neighborhood. Here, they wind around and roam this way and that, as if they've decided to go where they pleased.

Our new house is actually a ground-floor flat inside a larger building. There are veined marble floors, cool underfoot in the summer heat, and a deep, moody living room crisscrossed with shadows and draped with silk curtains as long as bridal trains. All the rooms are low ceilinged and rectangular, and it seems to take a long time to get from one end of the room to the other. My sisters and I share one big, echoey room across the hallway from my parents. Directly above us are four more identical flats, stacked up like layers on a cake. Across a little walkway is a matching building; the twin buildings are encircled by a courtyard, and running along the inner courtyard is a garden thick with big, nodding sunflowers, and marigolds, and mint plants, and now it's my duty to go pick the leaves to steep in the teapot. I'm practically eight, and I know how to do this; my sisters, on the other hand, are two and four and utterly hopeless. There are also furious-looking cats that moan and skulk all over the garden. The night comes at a new time, and the moon looks sideways like a silver cup. There's so much to look at that for a while I feel that all I can do is stand in one place and stare. One morning, after we've been there a few days or weeks, a gang of grinning, dirty-kneed kids pounds on our front door. They cheer when they see me, as if they've been searching for me for a long time, and they pull me outside. The gang expands and diminishes like a flock of starlings. We run everywhere and into everything, up stairs and down alleys. I don't understand anything that they're saying, but this doesn't matter because I know how to run.

In a matter of days, I am familiar with the labyrinthine windings of our ancient neighborhood. There are buildings so rickety and narrow that they look as if they're built on stilts; there are staircases leading into murky darkness that I gape at but refuse to ascend; there are apartments—many apartments—that smell powerfully of babies and dinner all the time. One day my gang of friends takes me to the roof of our building and I discover yet another world of children running around, women gossiping, clotheslines brightly draped and flapping gaily as sails. I lean over the precariously low railing, five stories from the ground, and someone gives me a play shove from behind that swipes the breath from my lungs and makes stars pop in my head. I swing around and lay eyes on Hisham for the very first time. I can tell right away that he is the one I like best of all: He is about my age, small and thin and dark with close-cropped hair, soft, myopic eyes, and full, round, almost feminine lips. Of all the children, his sweet, soft face is the most appealing to me.

My new best friend, Hisham, Hisham's seven or so younger brothers and sisters, and a varying number of neighborhood children play in the courtyard of my building. No matter what time of day or night I step into the street, one or, more likely, all of them will be out there singing, skipping, throwing things, running. Hisham and I hang on the balustrades of the swinging iron gate of the courtyard railing and ride it shut, the rusted hinges shrieking as it goes. Then we get off, open it, and ride it shut again. Then we play our talking game. Sometimes I go first, sometimes he does, but frequently we go at the same time.

I say, "Idon'tknowwhatyou'resayingbutIwishIknewwhatyouwere sayingIwishsomuchthatyouknewwhatIwassayingreallytrulyIreallydo becauseit'ssoweirdit'sreallycrazybutyoudon't . . ."

And he is saying, "*Yabaainteesadeekatibessintimajnoonashway moomkinbazunbessanamishakeedleeanoabensamabafimtwaintee matfimtkamaamoolaishhathamabafimtculshi . . .*"

It seems we spend whole afternoons in this way, talking and swimming through our private thoughts. In the distance, the calls to prayers from the eight neighboring mosques rise and overlap, quavering through the streets and alleyways. We silently spy on Hamouda the gardener as he washes his hands, face, feet, and neck with the garden hose behind the house. He lays out a few sheets of newspaper and uses that as his rug to pray upon, bowing solemnly in the direction of holy Mecca.

Eventually our talking game starts to change, slowly at first, with meaning creeping in around the edges of what Hisham is saying to me, like a slow burn eating at the edges of a page. And one day, after weeks of running around in the streets, I am speaking Bud's language. It's the language we spoke in tiny specks and pieces back home, a confetti language that Bud saved for his brothers or for getting angry or for driving in traffic. Suddenly, all of it is there in my head. (The first complete sentence I learn in Arabic is *Atini nosher beyda*, "Gimme a dozen eggs," which the shopkeeper puts loose into a brown paper bag. Then I dutifully run home and deliver up a bag of squashed egg mess.) My mother is the first to notice—she interrupts as I'm chattering with the Bedouin woman who works for us. "Since when do you speak Arabic?" she says to me.

I look at her and I see there is something in her eyes when she says this that I feel in the center of my chest, just under the bone. Instantly, I don't want those words in my mouth anymore.

The neighbors are more than neighbors. Their apartments spill onto the same central courtyard, and their meals spill into ours. They sit together on low cushions in the courtyard and tease me about my pale skin, kiss my head and cheeks, and read my coffee grounds. They give me bread and baba ghanouj and *jameed*, balls of yogurt that have been cooked, dried, and hardened in the desert sun. Usually, people eat *jameed* only after it has been softened by weeks or months of marinating in olive oil and then smeared on bread. But I discover that it's challenging and absorbing to gnaw on the hard little unmarinated yogurt rocks. It will keep forever in this form, which is lucky because no one on our street, or anywhere in the neighborhood, seems to have a refrigerator.

But two weeks after we arrive, my mother acquires a refrigerator. It's a wonder. This was apparently one of her conditions for moving the family from New York. I don't know where they found it. It takes ten men to drag it from the truck into the kitchen. It is a refrigerator unlike any I've ever seen before—big, enameled, sometimes roaring like a jet engine, sometimes moaning like an elderly man. I have to hook both hands around its chrome handle and lean back with my full body weight to get it to open. In Jordan, even I start to marvel at the fact of a refrigerator—I, who used to hang on the fridge door back in New York, just browsing. Now I see it in all its glory.

The refrigerator is roaring. Munira the Bedouin stands beside it at the ironing board, moving her black anvil of an iron over the clean shirts. Every pass takes her whole back. I can see the muscles in her shoulders flexing through her thin white blouse as if she is swimming. Mom sits at the kitchen table, frowning at her needlepoint. I stand at the end of the ironing board, staring at Munira's intriguing face, bisected by more wrinkles than I could imagine in one place; her too-black eyes glisten as if she is permanently weeping. She talks and talks and talks. I lounge at the ironing board, my arm slung over an unused end, translating whatever she is saying: "Munira says that the food in Jordan is much, much better for us because it's real food. It sticks with you and doesn't just evaporate. She says eating American food is like eating dust! She says it's full of jinns and bad omens—she can tell just by looking at us. She says we've been eating nothing but air and bones and flying insects. She says we got here just in time! She says it's going to take a little while longer for us to recover from being Americans. . . ."

Abruptly Mom puts down her needlepoint, stretches her long arms and legs, and says, "I think I feel like pancakes today."

My mouth falls open; I'd forgotten about pancakes. In that instant I miss them unbearably and completely. It washes over me, all the foods I forgot I loved: pancakes, ice cream, hamburgers. (Bud takes us out for falafel and says these are Jordanian hamburgers. And even though I've eaten falafels back in the States and I know their smoky taste of cumin and sesame, I'm so hungry for the tastes of home that I'm willing to imagine that in Jordan they are transformed. But what a disappointment—they don't taste like hamburgers at all.) Our breakfasts here are much the same as our breakfasts in America— cheese, bread, hard-boiled eggs, olives, tea. But at the moment there is nothing better than pancakes.

Mom, my sisters, and I all go to the Big Market by ourselves. When we first arrived, Bud always went to the market with us. But lately he is busy, he says, with not finding work in this ridiculous excuse of a country. He drives off in the morning in a suit and tie, to see about another job that he predicts will be an "impossible aggravation." So it's just us today, which makes it more exciting than usual. And it is always exciting at the Big Market, much more invigorating than at the P&C back in Syracuse. Here, people are shouting and walking around and gossiping and haggling fiercely. Food and things are stacked in great towers; there is straw and dust all over the floor, canvas walls, empty boxes, burlap sacks, chicks scratching at the floor. You might find anything in the world here—big, swampy barrels of olives, roasted chickpeas that taste dark and musty in your mouth, bread so fresh that it has wilted its paper wrapper, crates full of candied almonds and midnight-rich foil-wrapped chocolates from Syria, hand-cut blocks of olive oil soap, big square sheets of pressed apricot leather wrapped in orange cellophane. The original scent of Jordan is here: sesame, olive, incense, rosewater, orange blossom water, dust, jasmine, thyme.

It takes us such a long time to find anything that the market starts to seem like a dream we are having—nothing looks like what you'd expect. Mom picks up mysterious items from the shelves, smells them, shakes them, looks at me. I stare back at her, concerned. The milk comes in boxes with pictures of comets and TV sets, the butter comes in green foil bricks, some of the loose eggs are streaked with what looks like blood. We gradually uncover the right ingredients: flour, baking powder, milk, eggs. There's no maple syrup, so, Mom says cheerfully, we will make do with honey. Honey! At this news, I scowl at a baby peeping at me over his mother's shoulder, and he rolls his eyes in terror.

Back in the States, we made pancakes from a mix in a box that asked for nothing more than water and stirring. So there's a loose, improvisational quality about today's project. We take it all home, and the neighbors come and stand in the kitchen and crowd the hallway to watch. There's a carnival spirit in the air. People are smoking and telling jokes. At twenty-seven, my mother is not yet a relaxed and natural cook like my father. But she's dedicated and determined; her neck is stiff, the muscles in her back pronounced. And I feel that at this moment we all want pancakes more passionately than we've ever wanted anything. Even if it means messing up every bowl and spoon in the kitchen to make them, which for some reason it does.

We mix and stir, enduring all sorts of unsolicited opinions from the neighborhood spectators—who all seem frankly dubious about today's undertaking. Munira sits in graven silence at the table, offering neither advice nor assistance yet still somehow emitting an air of wrathful judgment. Mom ignores her, dragging out the black iron pan that starts to smoke on the stove even before she pours in the batter. We watch the pancakes bubble, watch Mom try to pry them loose before they scorch. She piles them up, one curling cake on top of another.

They are strange, these pancakes, not the downy wonders I remember from the box back home. These are dense and chewy and smack of fried butter, wheat, olive oil, and scorched iron. They can't really taste right anyway without the sugary syrup that we used to squeeze from tall plastic bottles. But it doesn't matter too much because we call them pancakes and they look a bit like pancakes. I manage to finish half of one. Scowling, Munira watches me eat, her brow heavy over her intense eyes. I offer her a bite from my fork, but she's used to eating with her hands, so she holds the fork shovel style, eyes the whole apparatus skeptically, then pulls the bite of pancake off the tines with her teeth. All of which, I can tell, she considers a ridiculous waste of time. But as she chews, her brow lifts as if in question, speculation, exploration. I seem to see the flavors of the pancake and honey traveling through her mouth. She swallows loudly and nods and proclaims to the room in Arabic, "Okay, well, now that's something a Bedouin could eat. That's something that will stay in your stomach all day."

"What does she say?" my mother asks, hands on her hips, her arms flour-caked up to the elbows.

"She loves it!" I crow.

The neighbors gather around, wanting to try what they're calling "burnt American flat food," sniffing and tasting and asking, inexplicably, for the recipe. And they also bring good bread with sesame seeds and fresh hard-boiled eggs and tomatoes warm from the garden, fragrant mint and tubs of rich yogurt and salty white cheese and olives and pistachios. It's an excellent pancake breakfast.

Even the chewing gum tastes different. They sell it in knobby gray nuggets, a handful for one fil—about one penny—at the *dukana,* or corner shop. The gum is dry, tacky, and unsweetened and tastes like tree bark, but it's still gum. So we all stand on the corner, chewing till our jaws ache. Me and Rafat, Talal, Dalia, Rana, Hisham, Nadia, Hussein, Hind, Azzam, Nazri, and Belal. But sometimes a little pile of real bubble gum turns up in the *dukana*—hard, pink, sugary compressions, valuable as gold. I buy it with the fils Bud gives me, then we take turns chewing the one piece, passing it around until the last modicum of sweetness runs out and then chewing it till it turns tacky and stiff. I show them how to blow a bubble, only I don't know how to do it inside my mouth. I have to use my fingers to press and hold it pasted flat against the outside of my lips, and then I blow and a bubble comes. Almost instantly, as if by magic, Hisham understands how to blow a bubble starting from inside his mouth—the way some kids are born with a special aptitude for math or languages or knowing how to whistle with their fingers—and then there is no getting the gum away from him.

Hisham is barely ten, but he already looks as if he needs a shave. While the other children dart around like sparrows, hunch over, laugh into their hands, stand on one foot, stagger like madmen, there is a stillness and a wholeness about Hisham. The look in his eye suggests that, for him, being a child takes great concentration, self-possession, and presence of mind. He does not—as some American children are encouraged to do—confuse being a child with being an adult. He just takes it all very seriously, so the other children tend naturally to look at Hisham first whenever there is a decision to be made, a high wall to be climbed, or a very dark corridor to be looked into. When I first started tearing around with this gang, I noticed that Hisham watched me with a particular sweetness, a solicitousness, as if somehow it had been given to him to understand how strange and solitary it is to suddenly awaken one morning on the other side of the world. He has an older brother in the Jordanian army whose creased military photo he keeps in his back pocket. Hisham watches me with his heavy-lidded eyes and suggests that he and I might want to get engaged now because he can virtually guarantee that he will grow up to look like his brother. He brings me to their house for lunch, and his mother serves a luxurious buttermilk soup with translucent strips of onion floating in it. When I finish mine, Hisham gives me the rest of his. He and his mother watch dotingly as I gulp it all down.

I am not used to this style of friendship—one without any of the reserve of the American suburbs we just left. The children here know the moment we move in, and they demand my presence. These children don't own a thing beyond the clothes they are wearing. There is nothing between us but running and shouting. We're as affectionate with one another as maiden aunts; we walk together, ten or twelve abreast, our arms around one another's shoulders.

But then one day Bennett appears in the courtyard with his scooter and I forget all about Hisham and the chewing gum. My first months in Jordan are like that—I attach to and detach from various people, toys, and foods willy-nilly. For an entire week, I listen to the same Arabic record, *Music for Belly Dancers,* over and over until Mom says I am literally driving her out of her mind. It's as if I've lost my coordinates and until I can adjust to this new place, I have to take everything in small, intense fragments.

Bennett is a powerful distraction. He is from England, and he has moved into our building. I suppose he has parents, but I see no sign of them. They're like a legend; he speaks of them, but they never quite materialize. Nor does he seem to have any aunts, uncles, grandparents, or cousins telling him what to do or any troubling little sisters to watch over! His life is a paradise. Bennett has see-through skin and yellow hair that rises and falls like corn silk. Within three minutes of meeting him, I hold my hand over his head. He flinches, but his hair rises magically to tickle the inside of my palm. He wears impossible woolen shorts from God knows where and gray knee socks, and his pinkened knees knock together with every step he takes. It's very likely that he is the first person I meet in Jordan with eyes the same ocean color as my mother's. He also possesses an engine-red scooter with two wheels, a steering bar, and a platform to push from or to stand on once you get going. I already know about bicycles, ice skates, sleds, Big Wheels, and roller skates, but I've never seen a scooter before, and once I do, I know that it's just perfect.

Bennett refers to his invisible parents as "Mother and Father," which sounds as foreign to me as if he were calling them Mr. and Mrs. Bennett. He quotes all sorts of rules from this "Father" pertaining to what he calls "the natives," as in "Don't talk to the natives" and "Don't eat the native food." At first, Bennett refuses even to leave the courtyard, which he says his invisible parents have confined him to. That leaves us a meager twenty or so feet of marble walkway to roll around. I assure him that the courtyard rule must apply only to England. When he still purses his lips, I yawn in the manner of Munira, who yawns every time a shop owner offers her a special price.

"Oh well," I say, sighing indolently, "I guess I'll just go play with my other friends and their scooters." To my great pleasure, he turns a bright purplish, eggplant color; then he says, "Well, perhaps we could go outside the gates, for a bit."

For the next week or two, Bennett is my best friend. I forget all about my previous life. As if by some tacit agreement, perhaps in acknowledgment of the superiority of the scooter, Hisham and the others start playing with the rooftop children instead of down in the courtyard. At times I'll guiltily sense a shadow cast from high overhead. But when I look up, all I see are the carrier pigeons flapping from the cornices or the fluted edge of a drying bed sheet.

Bennett and I ride and ride in the street in front of the courtyard. Sometimes there are cars, sometimes not—we scarcely notice. We trade the scooter back and forth, then we ride together—I crowd in behind Bennett, balancing and hugging his waist for dear life, each of us pushing like crazy with one foot. We crash this way several times, and then after a while we can ride together without crashing, as if we are made to do this. I prefer riding to talking. When Bennett does speak, I feel embarrassed for him, for his withered voice, his lace-doily style of speaking, and the way he barely moves his cherry lips.

His father, he says, works as some sort of horrid diplomat, whatever that is. Bennett's father and mother give "dreadful, just frightful parties," he says, at which he is required to wear a suit and tie and to play piano. I learn that even though he says he's from England, Bennett has never actually been there, not even for a visit. His family has been moving around Jordan for over a year now, and he finds it "unbearable" but much prefers it to Singapore or Guyana. He doesn't like the weather in Jordan: "It burns," he says, rubbing his red-tipped ears, the skin ragged and peeling from his nose and cheeks. He doesn't like the food: It's dirty. "I only like clotted cream and crumpets or nothing," he says. And he doesn't like the Jordanians: "They're much too loud and hairy."

Early one morning, a sound wakes me and I discover a little basket filled with sugar-powdered *sambusik* cookies propped on the wide marble windowsill of my room. Underneath the cookies is a small scrap of paper with a heart and a tremulous letter *H* written in pencil—probably the first letter in English Hisham has ever written. I look upon these cookies with nostalgic tenderness, as if it has been years since I've seen Hisham. *Sambusik* cookies are among my favorites and a specialty of Hisham's mother—hers dissolve on the tongue in buttery flakes. I offer one to Bennett, who takes it, inspects it, then replaces it daintily, saying, "I never eat native food. Neither should you."

I look at him out of the corner of my eye. I'm having trouble with Bennett. No matter how much he swats at himself, there is always a fog of dust on his face and clothes. And he's forever drinking tall glasses of something he calls "nutritious Horlicks"—both words, every time. It seems to be milk mixed with something musty and leaves a white mustache on his upper lip, which I stare at pitilessly as if it is further proof of something terrible about him.

After three weeks of the scooter, he puts one hand on his hip and one hand on the steering bar and says to me, "So we're best friends, then?"

I scowl and don't answer, even as I recognize that this is very bad behavior. I eye the scooter, calculating how much longer I can stand being best friends with Bennett. I no longer want to be nice to him at all. Suddenly I have a question. "What does a crumpet taste like?" I ask in a surly, skeptical voice.

"Oh!" Bennett's eyes flutter. "They're lovely! Lovely, lovely things." Then he sniffs a little, presses the toe of his shoe in the ground, and adds, "Course, they're not available here."

"Why not?" I ask, even surlier now. "We can get pancakes here. I know for a fact."

"Pancakes are entirely different," Bennett says. Then, as if reciting an inscription on a stone tablet, he says: "One cannot get a proper crumpet in a land like Jordan. Father says. Not now and *not ever*."

I glare at the scooter, and it occurs to me for the first time that when Bennett talks about native foods, he is talking exactly about the sorts of food my father prepares. A sick, disloyal feeling floats in my center.

After four weeks of Bennett and the scooter, our across-the-courtyard neighbor Mrs. Haddadin stops me as I walk in the front gate. Mrs. Haddadin has a kindly voice and a grieving, ancient expression that makes her look decades older than her forty years. She is Palestinian, but she came to Jordan long ago, when, she says, she and her whole village were driven out by the Israelis.

Mrs. Haddadin says that she was meant to have a son—he would be eighteen by now, and his name would be Herve. He would be in the air force, not yet a captain. She knows this, she says, because she has dreamed it, very vividly, on several occasions. But her destiny was tampered with. The Israelis frightened her so badly that everyone could see the mark of that fear on her and no man would ever marry her. "They smell it on my skin," she says, pressing the tips of her knobby fingers together, as if she keeps the scent pressed between her fingertips. I inhale deeply but smell only the cardamom pods she arranges on her windowsill, the smudge of turmeric she sifts over her pastries, and the fresh peppermint in her tea. Every morning she brings out a pot and two cups and gives one to me, then she stares into the steam above her cup and sighs two great damp sighs. Later in the afternoon, she will patrol up and down behind our courtyard gate, on the lookout for the moment the Israeli army will come pouring into the streets of Amman. As a result, she sees absolutely everything that happens in the neighborhood.

On this day, she stoops to look in my eyes and says, "Why aren't you playing with your other friends anymore?"

I mull this over, desperate for a good reason. Finally I have to confess. "They don't have scooters," I mumble. She straightens up, her mouth a taut line, her eyes fogged over. I watch her expression, horrified. I ask her in a tiny voice, "Don't you like Bennett?"

She looks down at me, eyes glittering like dark gems. "That boy is a bitter melon."

One night after my sisters and I are in bed and the baby cats have ceased their long streaks of crying, my parents come to our room, whispering and nudging each other, their smiles sly and flickering, as if they share a private joke. They shake us out of sleep and say, "C'mon, we're going to do something!"

We yawn and slide out of the warm caves of our beds. Monica looks tousled and sleepy as a small animal, her cropped silky hair spun to a froth on her head. But Suzy is wide awake; she gives me a darting, uncertain look—what are these so-called parents of ours up to now? The unlit house is watery, and my limbs feel soft and weak, as if I've been running in my sleep. Our parents guide us out the front door, their laughter lowered and mesmerizing. Then we hurry across the stone courtyard, Suzy, Monica, and I barefoot in cotton pajamas, the stones cool and waxy beneath our feet. The neighbors and the street are all asleep, the buildings shut up, rose tinted under a brassy round moon. I have never seen a sleeping street before, never known what secret intimacy could rise from the pavement like steam. In one corner of the courtyard, tilted under the staircase to the upper floors, is the red scooter, its bold shine muted now. For a moment I think of my grandmother back in New Jersey, who wears a lipstick in the same fluid tones: red shot through with an undercurrent of blue. I look back at it as my parents open the car.

We drive through parts of the city I've never seen before, where the lights glow like melted butter and the girls on the sidewalks are wearing hats and high heels. Men smile and turn to watch our car passing, my hands pressed to the window. Everyone is awake! Then we race beyond the glowing streets, and the road ahead of us is long and dusty blue and smells like the woolly heat of a sheep's back. Bud snaps on the radio, its slim red line twirling through static, and then there are songs from an entirely different planet that have bounced around in the ocean for years and finally found their way to our radio: "Downtown"; "Chelsea Morning"; "To Sir, with Love"; "Georgie Girl."

When we finally get out of the car, there's a gravel lot, an expanse of folding chairs, patios, sparkly restaurants wedged in a long crescent along a glittering flat blackness. Bud holds his hand out toward the gleam. "And what did I promise you kids?" he asks, though I recollect no promises related to anything like this. "It's the Dead Sea!"

We've come, as usual, with no preparation, so my parents let us run into the water in our underpants like the Jordanian kids around us. The salt water is satiny, so soft and dense that it seems to bend beneath our arms. Bud, who is generally afraid of the water, comes out and shows us how this water is so rich with minerals that you can sit in it like a lawn chair. He lies back in it, and Suzy tows him around by his hair while he makes boat sounds.

One of the restaurants on the shore has a string of red lights that drop their reflection in the moonlit water like maraschino cherries. These make me think of the lonely red scooter. I straggle out of the water, yanking up my soggy underpants with their sprung elastic waistband. Mom is stretched out on a canvas chaise longue, holding a drink with a little parasol on the side. She wraps me shivering into a beach towel and makes room for me beside her on the chaise.

I blink out of my towel cave at this astounding new place around us, then touch my mother's ribs through her cotton shirt. "Mom, how long do you have to be best friends with someone if you're best friends?"

She flitters at my bangs; they're stiff with salt. "Well, honey, I don't think there're any rules about that. I guess you can be best friends your whole life if you're lucky."

"Are you and Dad best friends?"

It's hard to make out her expression under the cherry lights along the shore. She appears to be thinking about it, staring out to where Bud is still drifting around, piping and tooting like a tugboat.

"You have to do whatever your best friend says, right?"

Now I can see her face—a little amused and wary. "Why do you say that?"

"Dad said to come to Jordan, right?"

There is even less sound now than before, if that is possible, just a slight slip of waves on the shore, a sighing wash like the sound of someone saying "Hush, hush" or the papery rustle of the palm fronds arching over the sand. "Your father . . . needed us to come here, he needed to see—what it felt like."

Now we seem to be whispering.

"What does it feel like?" I ask quietly, not quite knowing what I'm asking, just following the path of the questions.

"I don't think—" She stops, glancing back. Bud is climbing out of the water. "I don't think it feels the way he remembers it."

I put my clammy hands on her waist—something that feels a little like a spark of alarm bounces through me. "Does he know that? That it doesn't feel the same?"

She looks over her shoulder, Bud's shadow falling toward us in a long, cool slip as he walks beneath the neon lights. "He's finding out."

The medicinal waters of the Dead Sea roll behind us, and the wild, heavy scent of honey, rocks, and thyme tempers the air. People come to dip themselves in these waters, to be cured of everything from skin ailments to spiritual wasting. The air here is active, undeniable. I breathe it in deeply and sense a sort of dawning sweetness—of loss and nostalgia. Mom must feel some of this as well, because she draws her hand around a ripple of sand beneath her beach chair and says dreamily, "It's lovely here. Just lovely."

I touch the liquid sand as well. It turns from beige to amber. It is that simple. Just lovely.

I know the story of their first meeting by heart. My father was working at a malt shop called Cosmo's in the student-busy section of town near Syracuse University. He wore a long white apron and swabbed a heavy string mop all over the tiled floor, trying to eavesdrop on the conversations in mysterious, hard-sounding English, the language striking in right angles all around his head.

Bud wasn't supposed to be there. He was supposed to be streaking through the bruised light over Jordan, a pilot in the king's air force—he and his friend Mohammed ("Mo") Kadeem, two impatient young men with a flair for scary, last-second decisions. But then Bud's cousin Soraya turned down Bud's marriage proposal, and his dignity was so injured that he did the most dramatic thing he could think of and moved to America. In a flash, he was here in this palace of ice cream, lightning-white tiles, and ice-smooth floors, mopping and mopping, wringing his bold youth into a bucket of suds.

Until he saw my mother, and there went the mercury of his heart again. "She was as tall as a goddess," he tells us in the story of the Day. "So smart, I could take one look at her"—he points to his eye—"and see it right on her face!"

My father slicked in between her and her date, the much-mourned Billy Murphy. ("*Such* a nice, nice, handsome boy," Gram says, very sad.) He eased her coat off so it seemed to float from her shoulders. She turned to stun him, once again, with her ocean blue eyes, a fringe of mahogany hair, and a slow, secretive smile.

Were they supposed to come together? I don't know. Bud didn't really speak English, and he wasn't actually a waiter. His Greek boss, Cosmo, watched, bemused, as Bud leaned over their table with a pen and pretended to write down their order. "I thought, What is that nut doing now?" Cosmo says. But Cosmo knew what it was like to be too young, skinny, and crazy in America and was always hiring "special cases."

Bud ran over to the grill while Cosmo stepped back, folded his arms, and watched Bud rush around with the spatula and bread.

"She want grill-chee-sanweesh—what is grill-chee-sanweesh?" my father lamented, running between ingredients. And even though he didn't know what white bread was, didn't know what margarine was, didn't know what American cheese was, he made her some sort of grilled cheese sandwich. He brought it out to her on a white plate with a sprig of parsley—the way he'd seen Cosmo do it for the daily specials. He didn't make anything for Billy Murphy.

When I ask Mom how the sandwich turned out, she smiles her drowsy blue-eyed smile, chin on her hand, and says, "I don't remember."

The morning after the Dead Sea, I wake with a wonderful hankering for gray gum. I feel as if I've been away on a month-long vacation to a cool, distant country and it's great to be home again. I run to the *dukana* and buy a piece. As I stand on the corner and start to chew, my friends begin to saunter over—Mai and Rafat, Belal and Hisham. They greet me as cordially as if I haven't been away at all. We spend the day on foot, running along the alleys in our old style. I am set free. At the end of the day, Hisham and I race to my house. I have flying hair, a skinned knee, and grubby nails—I look like every other child in the streets of this neighborhood. Hisham, as usual, gets there first, but then he pulls up short. Bennett is standing just inside the court-yard, still as stone.

Suddenly the door to a steep place that I didn't know was inside me has been thrown open. I know I've done something wrong, though I can't put a name to it. "Hi," I say, guilty and angry.

Hisham looks as shocked as if Bennett is a statue come to life. He takes a step back and bumps into me.

"Don't touch her!" Bennett snaps at him. He shakes a finger at Hisham. "Do you live here? I don't believe so! This is *our* courtyard—not *your* courtyard." Bennett's face is a streaked, liverish color, as if he's just been slapped. He shrieks at Hisham, his voice leaping into the highest registers, his body rigid and doll-like. "I think you'd better get out of here. I think you'd just better get out!"

Hisham's mouth opens and closes, as if he can barely get enough air. I grab Hisham's wrist and am about to suggest we go play in another courtyard, but Hisham turns to me and whispers in Arabic, "Something is wrong with this boy—I'll go get my mother!"

"No," I answer, though I'm frightened of the sharp, thin line of Bennett's mouth. "I'll stay here. I'll talk to him."

After Hisham has gone, for a long moment, Bennett doesn't speak and doesn't even give the impression of seeing me there. Then quickly he says, "You know, that isn't proper. It isn't proper, and it isn't done. It isn't done at all."

I take hold of the iron spikes of the courtyard railing; they feel cold and rough in my hands. I wish that Hisham hadn't gone away. "What isn't?"

The color starts to subside in his face, and I can see him collecting himself. He purses and unpurses his lips, he crosses his arms in a businesslike fashion. Finally he slits his eyes at me as if admitting to himself, at last, that I really don't know much of anything. "You don't belong with them! You *know* that. You know that. The sort you are belongs with the sort I am. Like belongs with like. Father says. No in-betweens. The world isn't meant for in-betweens, it isn't done. You know that."

He speaks as if this is a conversation we've had countless times and he's tired of going over it with me. I lean back and swing on the iron railing while he stands like a stake in the ground, glaring just past the top of my head. I've started attending a private school run by the French nuns, and what Bennett says reminds me of something the nuns say. We are forbidden to speak Arabic in school because, according to Sister Hélène-Thérèse, "Arabic is the language of animals." She taps the list of three languages on the blackboard, explaining that English "is the language of mortals" and French, she says with a satiny smile, "is the language of the angels."

"No in-betweens." My voice is a pale vapor.

"They belong with their own kind. You with me, they with them," Bennett sums up. "No in-betweens. It's not allowed."

I squint at Bennett; his face is blotted out by the sunset behind his back. I don't know what these in-betweens are exactly, but I feel sorry for them. They might look like the embroideries of the sad-eyed sheep—the solitary ones, apart from their flock, trapped inside the circle of Munira's embroidery hoop, stitched eternally apart. I imagine them walking the earth, friendless, lonely, and improper, *not allowed*, lost somewhere in the embroidered corners between the animals, the mortals, and the angels.

"How do you know it?" I press. "How do you know that I belong with you?"

He rolls his eyes. "Well, it's obvious, isn't it?" He thrusts out his arm. "Look at the color you are!"

He presses his arm to mine: His is a gleaming, nearly bone white, dotted with freckles and a faint sheen of burn. Mine is grimy and golden with a telltale greenish cast I'd never noticed before, not till I'd compared myself with someone like this. I'm not like Bennett, and he yanks his arm away as if I've just done something unexpectedly wrong. But in that moment I realize I'm not like Hisham, either. Not dark. I think about the way the relatives come to visit, standing in our bedroom doorway, appraising me and my sisters, the way their words trickle through the air, dividing us. "There's the dark one," they say. "And she—she's the light one. . . . That one is American, that one is Arab. . . ." I'd never before thought to wonder which of us was which.

Despite Bennett's decree, my interest in the red scooter has miraculously dried up and gone. I'm once again running up and down the steps with Hisham and my old group of friends. When Bennett approaches me in the courtyard, pushing the red scooter before him like a sacrifice, offering to let me ride it alone for the entire day, I walk past him without a word. Is it possible that I am this heartless? Bennett turns into a shadow and then disappears just as suddenly as he appeared. He slips completely out of my mind and imagination, as do his native foods, his nutritious Horlicks, and his in-betweens. I forget him so quickly that his memory now comes to me in grainy, half-dissolved strokes, like an image made of powder.

Weeks after forgetting him, I am swinging on the iron railing with

Hisham, negotiating the details of our engagement, when Mrs. Haddadin calls me over to her chair near the flowering mint plants. She swirls her cup of tea and informs me that "my little English friend" and his mythical parents have moved back to Singapore. It takes me a minute to understand whom she is talking about. Then she gestures toward the staircase and there it is, where it has been all along, ever since I abandoned him, yet somehow completely invisible: the red scooter. "He left that behind."

The breath goes out of me in a gust. It waits like an accusation.

She watches me and frowns. "Do you know why he did that?" she asks, very curious. "Why didn't he take his English toy?"

I shake my head, astounded. I don't know the answer, not inside my head. But I sense it somehow, the truth prickling, a thing that will take a long, long time for me to bring into words: So I won't forget him.

Mrs. Haddadin sits, gazing up at me, squinting into my eyes, taking my measure. Mrs. Haddadin, who remembers everything and everyone—even a son she has never had—cannot fathom how deeply, powerfully forgetful I have already become. Though I am only eight, I too have already had to leave behind entire countries and lifetimes. Her eyes are orange inflected and amber, too light for her dark cinnamon skin. She gazes up at me from her chair and I look down: I can almost see the thoughts moving within her lamplike eyes, dark and illuminated as jinns. Perhaps at this moment, now that he has gone, she has forgiven Bennett, just a little. Perhaps, instead, she is wondering about me now, as I sometimes wonder about myself: What sort of person am I? Where are my loyalties? And who will I remember when I grow up?

"FORGET ME NOT" *SAMBUSIK* COOKIES

1 cup clarified butter	4 cups flour
⅓ cup sugar	1 cup confectioner's sugar
¾ cup milk, room temperature	

FILLING

1½ cups ground walnuts	1 teaspoon rosewater
½ cup sugar	

Preheat the oven to 350 degrees. Stir together the butter and sugar. Stir in the milk. Add the flour in small batches and knead by hand until smooth. Roll out the dough to ¼ inch thick and cut with a 2-inch cookie cutter. Combine all the filling ingredients and place a good mounded teaspoon of the filling on each round, fold it over, and pinch the edges closed. It's traditional to then curve the cookie into a half-moon shape.

Bake at 350 degrees for 15 to 20 minutes, until the cookies are lightly browned. Remove the cookies from the oven, let cool, and then sprinkle liberally with confectioner's sugar.

MAKES ABOUT 35 COOKIES.

I have many favorite people in Jordan: Every morning I run to the boy selling *ka'k*—fluffy loaves of seeded bread rings—from a tray on top of his head. "*Atini ka'k, minfudluk,*" I say, and give him two fils. He gives me a hot crusty seed-dusted loaf the size of a Christmas wreath, then he goes back to bawling, "*Kaaaaaa'k!*" in the streets. There's the man whose donkey pulls a wheeled tub full of butter and bobbing roasted ears of corn, and another man who sells hard-boiled eggs and *zataar,* a spice mix made of thyme, sesame, and sumac. He gives me a free egg, then salutes as if I am a military commander. And then there's Munira the Bedouin, who dusts and tidies, does our laundry, and keeps her eye on the children. There is something glorious and half-wild about her, with her falcon eyes and gold teeth. Her hands and chin are tattooed with strings of curling designs, and she blackens her lids with so much kohl that they look as if they're smoking. Sometimes she talks and talks in a freestyle English-Arabic mixture, as if the words have been bottled up inside her from the moment of her birth. Other times she collapses into a sort of pure, solitary silence. I avail myself of these moments to station myself at her side and tell her all my own problems, which are legion.

Early on—before Bud's language is in my head—I complain bitterly about the confounding trouble I'm having making myself understood and understanding others. Munira calls me *habeebti*, which means "my dearest," and she assures me that I do indeed know "how to speak" but that I've willfully let myself forget and will just have to wait until it comes back to me. She counsels me that as soon as anyone says anything I don't understand, I should just keep responding with *aish*. *Aish* means "what," and this advice quickly gives me a reputation for being a hard-of-hearing, rather crotchety eight-year-old. Munira also teaches me how to divine the future by tossing some stones against the garden wall and reading the constellations they fall into. I don't know how we afford to employ Munira and Hamouda with Bud so often out of work. It's possible we don't give them anything more than room and board. When I ask where they came from, Bud says they came with the family, that their ancestors have been serving Abu-Jabers for generations, and that, in fact, he had been raised by Munira's mother, and his father had been raised by her grandmother. Munira tells me she learned to speak English as a little girl because Bud's mother read fairy tales to her while she helped with her own mother's embroidery work. Because of this, she knows words like "enchantment" and "mermen" and all about the strange Little Matchstick Girl, but not the English words for house or soap or spoon.

When I think how I initially met Hamouda, it seems to me that he was already in our house, sitting on his bare wooden chair in the storeroom off the kitchen, waiting for us when we arrived from America. He's slow moving and cheerful and doesn't understand our jokes: Munira has to tell him everything four times before something in his features catches and his face brightens. Hamouda fixes things around the house for us, prays, gardens, and does odd jobs. He has captivating hazel eyes in a cinder-dark face. Bud says he is Circassian, from the hills of the Caucasus Mountains; pious Muslims, he and his family have lived in Jordan since the reign of Stalin. He has a pronounced limp that he says he got when his horse fell on him for some reason. I love mentally replaying this tragic scene in a swoon of pity and terror: horse falling, Hamouda falling, crying out, leg splintering. Hamouda lets me and my sisters knock on his hard calf through his pants as if we are knocking on a door. Every time he calls out, "Who's there?" and then grins so we can see he's missing almost every other tooth in a splendid repeating pattern. Privately I hope that someday he will hike up the pant cuff so we can see this petrified leg, but he never does.

He is a sweet-natured, sensitive man who tells me that the entire world is contained in our courtyard garden and that I never need leave it, because if I remain in this exquisite place, inevitably all things will come to me. He's given to exclaiming, "*Alhumdullilah!*" ("Thanks be to God!") as if everything good—from a clear day to a scrap of bread—has fallen down to him straight from heaven. He has the mystical power to whisper soothing things to my baby sister, Monica, that make her simmer down and stop driving her crib around the room. And he is the one who escorts us out to the big traffic circle for ice cream every afternoon, holding our hands tightly as we dart across the busy streets.

I adore both Munira and Hamouda, and I worry about their well-being. Hamouda in particular seems so tiny and fragile to me, I'm forever worrying that he will stumble or be injured by some new peril, another crashing horse, perhaps. It comes to my attention that his and Munira's daily meals consist almost entirely of our family's leftovers, and every day I fret over whether or not enough food will be left for them. I make sure to always leave half of my dinner on the plate. On one particularly warm day, Hamouda comes in from gardening blotting his temples with a rag, his skin blotchy and uneven. He looks peaked and his limp is more pronounced than usual. While he is taking his daily nap in the storage room, I decide that we will save him the trouble of escorting us to get ice cream. I know where Bud leaves the ice cream money and the extra house key, so I gather up my little sisters and we take ourselves out.

It's an easy walk through the lime white streets. After months of running all over the neighborhood with my friends, I already think of these streets as mine. My sisters toddle and bump along, uncomplaining. Even at their tender ages—two and four—they realize it's more interesting to go for ice cream like this than in the predictable grip of Hamouda's leathery hand. I have a new little brass bell that Bud bought for me, the kind they drape on goats. I like to wear it around my neck on a piece of string and swing my head back and forth like Frankenstein so I ring with each step and notify the neighborhood of our movements.

We get to the circle where the ice cream vendor is. As with so many things—fruit, pancakes, eggs—the ice cream here, which looks the same and feels the same as American ice cream, tastes nothing like it. It comes only in a striped Neapolitan, which Hamouda refers to as "Napoleon": The chocolate is thin and flat, the strawberry is berryless, and the vanilla you generally save for last, until there's just no avoiding it, its resinous, perfumed flavor tasting faintly of rose petals and soap.

But it's ice cream! So we approach the man at his stand, and he stares over our heads, looking for our usual guardian. He gives us a long, dismayed look and says to me in Arabic, "Where is your keeper?" but I simply stare back, afraid that he will send us away. I hold the coins out flat on my palm, and the transaction takes place. He hands us the soft yellow cones with their cylinders of brownwhitepink ice cream. Then my sisters and I huddle together in the busy center, the ice cream sliding all over our hands and faces; and I'm disappointed all over again with Neapolitan and wish for the hundredth time for chocolate marshmallow.

Inside the big traffic circle, there's a great deal of commerce and activity. A woman with thick black eyeliner ties up cut flowers in raffia, a man dips falafel balls into vats of spitting oil, another man carves through stacked layers of *shawerma* meat, piling the grilled tips into pita sandwiches. Children—tough, rakish little boys with narrow faces and quick, narrow eyes—stare at us and our abundance of ice cream, and some big girls hold hands and talk, affectionately tilting their heads on each other's shoulders. I look straight ahead and notice that somehow we crossed an enormously busy street to get inside the circle—cars and taxis careen around us, horns blaring.

It dawns on me that I'm not entirely clear about how we did this or how we will undo this. The cars whir by, blurring the air. A haze of smoke and dust hangs in a ring around us, and a quivering sense of anxiety runs up my arms and down my spine. The tough boys seem to be moving in closer, and the ice cream man is shutting up his stand as if disavowing all responsibility. I see that my youngest sister has lost her ice cream in a gluey mass down the front of her shirt, and though I've finished mine, I still taste the awful vanilla in the back of my throat—medicinal, wrong. I reach for my sisters' sticky hands. Everything is wrong: I hear English-Arabic, French-Arabic—someone is leaning in too close to talk to me, and the makeup around her eyes turns to smoke. The flower lady. Her words come to me as if from far away: "What is your name, little girl?" she asks in English. Then she tries French: "Where do you live?"

I say, "My name is Diana, and we live on the other side of the traffic circle!" But for some reason this comes out in Arabic.

She looks so startled that for a few seconds she doesn't speak. Eventually she exclaims in Arabic, "You're Jordanian! How could it be?"

Then, from off in the distance, I hear a familiar voice, and this sound cuts through my imminent panic like a bell in the fog. I look over the bank of cars through the haze to the opposite street, and there is Hamouda. His limp is distinctly more pronounced as he hurries, nearly running toward us, his face contorted and working.

I'm faint with relief and squeeze my sisters' hands so my middle sister, Suzy, complains. But when Hamouda gets closer, I realize that he's crying. I've seen children cry and I've seen a few women cry, but never before a man. I didn't think that men actually could cry, and even through my panic and shock and relief, I can't stop staring. He runs directly into the swirl of traffic, and as Jordanian drivers are masters of sudden shocks, their cars part seamlessly as he hobbles across, dodging, swerving, and jumping, patting and pushing hoods as if he is wading through a herd of wild goats. He runs his lopsided run the last steps of the way, and when he reaches us, he calls out, again and again, "*Alhumdullilah!*"

I run to him, inhaling the musty tobacco scent of his shirt, shut my eyes and memorize the feel of his hands on my shoulders, the sense of pure, ineluctable rescue. I gaze at him, drink in the sight of his eerie pale eyes in that dark country of a face and the transparent lines of tears. He woke and we were gone, he tells me. He wondered for a second if he had dreamed us. He looked for us everywhere, and finally Mrs. Haddadin told him where we went.

"*Alhumdullilah*," I echo like an old Bedouin or an old Circassian. It is exactly the thing to say at a time like this, like letting out a breath. And he stares at me a moment. Then the tiny man bends over, takes the three of us in his arms, and hoists us like an offering. His arms are tough and wiry as cables. "*Alhumdullilah*," he says again, very seriously and purposefully. He hugs us wildly. I laugh and look up, and the sky over his head is as blue and sleek as a piece of slate.

AMAZING ARABIC ICE CREAM
Done right, this is incredible.

1 teaspoon powdered *sahlab** or 1 tablespoon cornstarch	¼ teaspoon mastic,* crushed to powder
4 cups milk	1 tablespoon orange blossom water*
1 cup heavy cream	Chopped pistachios for decoration
1¼ cups sugar	

Dissolve the *sahlab* in 1 tablespoon of the cold milk. Put the rest of the milk in a saucepan with the cream and sugar and bring to a boil. Sprinkle in the milk-and-*sahlab* mixture, stirring. Stir the mastic into the milk, lower the heat, and simmer for 15 minutes, stirring occasionally.

Add the orange blossom water, remove the saucepan from the heat, and stir well. Pour the mixture into a freezer tray and place in the freezer. Once frozen, remove from the tray and beat well. Freeze again until ready to serve. Serve in small silver bowls, if you have any, and sprinkle the pistachios over the top.

SERVES 6 TO 8.

*Sold in specialty stores.

SAHLAB is a white powdery starch made from the ground tuber of an orchid.

MASTIC is a natural resin produced in the Mediterranean from an ever-green shrub of the pistachio tree family; it also happens to be excellent for stomach ailments.

ORANGE BLOSSOM WATER, a uniquely fragrant flavored water, is also used to make "white coffee," a popular Middle Eastern drink made by adding orange blossom water to boiling water and sugar.

It's as if there's only a certain amount of space in my brain, and the more space Jordan takes up, the less room there is left for America. Sometimes I lose track of what language I'm in and gibber between the two of them, substituting English words for Arabic and vice versa. My favorite breakfast is no longer pancakes, but bread doused with oil and *zataar*. Just once in a while, something reminds me of my former life: a woman who laughs like my grandmother or a Jordanian cousin who smokes his cigarette the way an American cousin does.

When these reminders occur, I stop and think: Am I still an American? And it confuses me, because it seems like a kind of unbecoming or rebecoming—to turn into this other Diana—pronounced Dee-ahna, a Jordanian girl who has forgotten the taste of fluffernutter sandwiches or Hershey's bars. But sometimes there are hints of other places. For example, there is a swanky hotel in the middle of town where we go to buy the American newspapers. In their carpeted lobby with the wrought-iron tables and chairs, they serve tea in china cups, alongside blue-and-white plates filled with hard cookies that taste of a million miles away. These "biscuits" disintegrate between my teeth, falling into basic component flavors—jam, sugar, flour. They aren't very good, and the tea is a weird mystery of crushed leaves and condensed milk—none of it is especially American, British, Jordanian, or anything else. But I crave this tea service because alongside the frilly plates and pots of this and that, they also serve a small kettle of piping hot chocolate for the children. Like the ice cream, it tastes nothing like my memories of powdered cocoa mix, but unlike the ice cream, it's much better than the original. It tastes faintly of cherry and cream, and deep inside this,

I believe I taste echoes of the sharp, sweet Hershey's bars of the corner store just down the street from our house in America.

SENTIMENTAL HOT CHOCOLATE

2 cups whole milk
2½ ounces good semisweet chocolate
¼ teaspoon ground nutmeg
½ teaspoon ground cinnamon
¼ teaspoon salt
½ cup heavy cream, whipped to soft peaks (optional but recommended!)

Stir all the ingredients except the heavy cream together in a saucepan over low heat until the chocolate melts. Increase the heat and cook until the hot chocolate comes to a low simmer but is not boiling. Pour into mugs and top with the whipped cream, if using.

SERVES 2.

Jordan, it seems, reveals itself slowly. There are layers of mysteries like scarves in a scarf dance. There is the mystery of the traffic circles all over town that have no clear rhyme or reason. There is the mystery of the Jordanian drivers, who drive partially by steering and partially by hanging out the windows and yelling at one another. There is the mystery of the woolly white dust that travels through the air and deposits like silt along curbs and store windows, which we dust from our shelves and tables every morning, only to find it redeposited by afternoon. There is also the mystery of the particular wind that brings the dust, a storm the Jordanians call the *khumiseen,* meaning "fifty," as in fifty days and nights of blowing dust storms. Munira tells me to never open my mouth when this particular wind is blowing. It's the sort of wind, she says, that carries bad omens, random or misplaced spells. It is a wind filled with unanswered questions, unfinished conversations, and lost personal items of great sentimental value. Munira warns that if this wind gets inside you, it will blow through your organs, dry your throat, howl in your ears, and stand your hair on end.

One day, after we've been in Amman for nearly a year, Bud says we're going to visit the source of the winds, at the center of the valley. This is where our family started, Bud tells us, within this tribe, this territory; and some of my father's oldest relatives, including his grand-uncle, the sheikh, still live there. According to family lore, my Bedouin grandfather could barely stand to sleep with a roof over his head. Bud's father wanted to raise his children in the country among the Bedu. But their city-raised Palestinian mother had other ideas. She bought a house in town close to the school and taught her children to sleep in beds and eat from plates. Then in the summers she turned them over to her husband, who let them sleep outside with the animals and, as my grandmother put it, "run around like savages."

Eventually all the brothers but one left the Bedouins to move permanently to the city or immigrate to America and pursue their sophisticated lives. The last, Bud's youngest living brother, Uncle Ramzi, went to live in a mud cave all by himself in the desert. People said that Ramzi was somewhat peculiar, a little "original." The uncles called him "the Last Bedouin." The one time we went to visit him, Bud had us children wait in the car while he and Uncle Hal crouched outside a hole in the side of a hill and shouted his name. Uncle Ramzi crawled out of the hole, his face and long hair streaked with gray mud. I watched him laugh, throw his arms around Bud, and lift my big, strong father right up off the ground. Then he crouched down and waved at us through the car windows, and we waved back at his great, weathered, extraordinary face—the sort of face a tree or hillside might have—all of us crying, "Hello, Uncle Ramzi!"

Today Bud is wound up; he sings Arabic love songs about nightingales and broken hearts and the seashore, and he drums lightly on the steering wheel. This is the most upbeat we've seen him in the past several months, as he's come home increasingly dejected from this or that "donkey animal" of a boss, this or that "blistering nightmare" of a job. It seems that something inside of Bud isn't suited to certain indignities of work: His ambition is tremendous, but he chafes under petty managers and has no patience for formal education. His father intended him to be the family warrior—pilot, fighter, fencer; a gentleman soldier. But he left that life behind when he immigrated to America. Now, back in Jordan, nothing quite adds up for Bud, not in the way it does for some of his brothers. He is going to meet with his granduncle, Sheikh Ali Alimunah, the head of the Bedouin tribe, because he says he is seeking answers; he has big questions he has to ask the sheikh.

"What's your question, Dad?" we plead and whine, hanging on the backs of our parents' seats, kicking at the bases, and crawling over Munira's hard, narrow lap. But he only grins and shakes his head. And part of me is glad he won't tell. I have the feeling that perhaps even he isn't sure of what the question is yet.

The wind gets stronger as we drive the serpentine back road into the valley. The soil is parched yellow here, and dust hangs like cobwebs in the briars and weeds. The sky reels back, falling away in a white canopy. We turn the car onto the broad valley floor and it's ferociously sunlit; birds pass like chips of glass through the hot air, sand swirls into question marks. I'm practically drunk with my sense of the moment, jittering with my own questions. I've never met anyone who's lived in this kind of heat before.

Eventually, the whiteness of the sky separates itself from the pale earth and there is another whiteness at the center of it all, moving like many hands lifting, the sides of a hundred tents. Each of them ripples as if about to take flight, billowing and floating with wind. Crammed in the backseat between me and my sisters, Munira sits forward, her expression intent: It seems everything in her has sharpened with the smell and heat of this air, the sight of these tents. "Now we are returning to the center of life," she says in Arabic, and squeezes my wrist. I want to tell her that I couldn't be returning—I've never been here before. But the glowing wind rushes through the half-open windows, and the words are rinsed out of my head.

Baby goats and blatting lambs mill around as the car turns into an open clearing by the tents. It takes me a moment to realize there are people here. They blend into the swirling air with their robes. I've seen plenty of Bedu in the city: Their weirdly ancient style of robes and loads of heavy silver jewelry, their sun-cured, nearly blackened skin, tough feet, and frightening teeth all make them seem like an ornate variety of street people. But we've never gone so far into the countryside before, and in this wide, wasting light, this white rinse of land, they seem transformed and so appropriate—as if it is the city and its soft, pale people that shouldn't exist. Here, there is no such thing as time, there are only curling robes, high winds, undulant camels. I also notice a mud-blasted Range Rover kept in the stables and a transistor radio propped on a cushion in the men's circle like a talkative guest.

We park beside a donkey, and the Bedouins clap and ululate and stroke the car. Then they lift their hands and Munira seems to levitate from the backseat right into their arms. I go with her because I can't quite release the crease of her robe I have clenched in one hand. Suddenly I'm in a press of women, their hands streaming over my head and arms, bangles, necklaces, anklets ringing, rich perfumes as dark and heady as blood running together in the atmosphere. Their shining voices fill the air as well. I can understand only snatches of what they're saying—running commentary on my unimaginable hair, skin, eyes, lips, fingers, toes.

"Look at this, where did this come from?" one woman seems to be asking about me.

"She's mine!" Munira answers, slinging one arm across my chest and pressing herself into my back. "She belongs to me."

It seems likely that the curious women will strip me naked right then and there and carry me off, but my equally impressive mother—taller than both the men and the women—wades into the crowd, calling for me and creating more of an uproar. My little sisters, I discover, are already bedecked in silver bracelets, their eyes being painted with kohl by some of the other women.

After the shock of their greeting wears off, however, I begin to understand that spending a day with the Bedouins is not so different from spending a day with my father's family in town. The men and women drift into their separate activities; Munira takes me by the hand and leads me to a large, fire-heated rock outside one of the tents. Here a crone with a black-seared face sits flat on the ground, one leg to either side of the wide flat stone. Another woman mixes flour and water, another pats the dough into shape, and the crone tosses this onto the hot stone, where it browns and puffs up. Another woman plucks the hot bread from the rock, and yet another places it in a stack of loaves.

They laugh and chatter, and their bodies relax into the murmurous air—it reminds me of the *debkeh* dance—the ring of interlaced participants, arms around shoulders, the movement dissolving into sound like sugar into milk. I sit among the women, my body filled with the charged scent of the bread, the lilt of their voices. I am understanding more and more of what they are saying, and it finally dawns on me that they're speaking Arabic—a stiff, bookish sort of Arabic, the kind in our school texts—classical Arabic—from hundreds of years ago, the verbs and pronouns more timeworn than "thee" and "thou."

One of the women points her tattooed chin at me. "What does she eat?" she asks Munira.

"I like *jameed*," I pipe up. "And *ka'k* and *zataar*. And also chewing gum and hot chocolate at the big hotel."

The women all stop what they're doing and stare at me. The crone hoots. "She speaks!" she says in her crackling voice.

Munira smiles a modest little smile. "A bit," she says.

"But why does she speak like that?" the first woman says. "Like a cat eating a bone."

Munira shrugs. "They all talk like that in the city."

"Come on, child," the crone urges me. "Say more!" They swivel back toward me.

Unfortunately, I wasn't born with the ability to think on the spot. I open my mouth, take a deep breath, and blurt out, "Bread! Table! Mouse!"

The women bleat with laughter and the crone doubles over, almost toppling onto the heated rock. I glow with this unexpected triumph. "Milk, moon, tree! Feet, water, lizard! Bus, neighbor, napkin!" I gesticulate a little for emphasis.

They echo my words in confirmation, one of them crying, "God is great!"

The crone reaches over and pats Munira's knee. "What a bizarre child," she says, and wipes her eyes. "Truly God is great."

At the main open tent, the men are seated like the women, but on cushions. Their ring is large and wide open so every man is included and equal—no one sits behind or in front of anyone—unlike the women's crowded, unruly circles. The men's ring is more intense, charged with debate and dramatic storytelling requiring hands to be flashed through the air, voices to leap. Bud leans into the conversation. He is more than happy—he looks bigger, wilder, louder, truer— as if some vital piece of him that I never knew existed has been returned to him.

Seated next to my father at the top of the circle is my great-grand-uncle, the sheikh, a tall, graceful man with a white waterfall of a beard that covers the front of his immaculate white robe. His old, noble nose is big, round, and important, and while he doesn't say much, his eyes pull at you with all sorts of magical powers. It's immediately clear to me why Bud would bring his questions to this man. When we arrived the sheikh kissed my father four times on each cheek, rumpled his hair, and asked if Mom was one of Bud's daughters. The women bring the sheikh his tea first, and a young boy stands at his right side, languorously waving a fan.

I gaze over the ring of women's heads as I watch my father talking. Then I notice my mother loitering at the edge of the women's ring, holding my sisters' hands. Her expression is hard to read through the hot, watering air, but her head is lowered, moody and wary. I catch, in that glimpse, what profoundly different planets my parents are from, how improbable it is that they are joined together. And I sense a deep weirdness about my own existence in the world. How could these two people have ever found each other? How could I have ever come to be?

A baby goat is killed discreetly and somehow silently, behind a tent. Mom stupefies me by grabbing the back of my shirt and saying that this is something I don't need to watch. A few hours later, it takes three strong, stringy men to upend the immense cooking pot onto a serving platter big enough to hold Monica. People gather around to watch the great pouring of the *mensaf*. The meat, rice, bread, and sauce mingle, satiny as a risotto. Its aroma streams through the air, thick and liquid; the air sparkles with it. The silver tray nearly covers the table, and we stand in a circle, pressing against the edge. The men and the women eat separately, but because we are special guests, they invite us to eat with the men. It's so crowded that we must stand sideways, with one hand—the right—turned toward the food. The tent is a goat-hair canvas staked to long poles covering our heads but open on the sides so the wind pours through and works the canvas like a bellows. The moment feels charged and fabulous, like the opening seconds of a play, and everyone presses close. The old sheikh nods and says, "*Sahtain, sahtain, alhumdullilah.*" ("To your health, thanks be to God.") And so we start.

Mensaf is to be eaten hot-hot, as soon as it emerges from the heat. The whole first month we lived in Jordan, my mouth and tongue stung and I was constantly sucking air through my teeth, until I finally understood that I had to let the food cool off a little. *Mensaf* is also to be eaten with the hands—as the Bedu eat everything: You dip your fingers into the mixture, and the rice is hot and wet on your skin. You scoop up a bit of food in the palm of your hand, palm it gingerly so it is round and soft, an impromptu dumpling, then push it into your mouth with your thumb and forefinger. This is all done quickly, cheerfully; everyone eats from their own private section of the tray, yet there is a good deal of rearranging of the meat so the choicest pieces are arrayed in front of the guests. There is an intricate blend of aromas in the air: I smell onions and nutty rice, as well as the rich field-and-dust scent of the cotton robe on the man standing in front of me, and mingled with all of this is a teasing thread of spices—ginger, nutmeg, pepper.

The goat melts into the rice melts into the sauce, and I cannot separate the eating from the food itself. The steam from the food dampens my face. The Bedouin men all take turns carefully feeding the little foreign girls, our skin pale and shiny as soap, our eyes round as coins. Monica compliantly accepts everything offered—which will turn out to be too much, later on. But for now, she lolls on a woman's lap while a man squats before her, tenderly offering her morsels as if she were a baby bird. There is so much food that it seems limitless: No one will ever go hungry.

After the dinner come platters of fruit—oranges, lemons, figs, pomelos, grapes, bananas, dates, *eskidinias*—or loquats. The men unsheathe short, pointed daggers from their sashes—stashed beside their longer curling swords—and peel the fruit so its sweet incense fills the air. The food has released them from their need to debate great topics. Now they are in the mood to recite poetry and sing. The men and women seem to recall the pleasures of each other's company, and they intermingle, the men offering the women peeled fruit. Two men sing dreamily about longing and the impossible necessity of love beside a fragrant wood fire, while a woman draws a bow over the stark single string of her *rebab*. The crone nestles her long bony body against the sheikh's long bony body, and he gazes at her and runs his fingertips along the side of her lined cheek.

Munira sits beside me on the ground, picking out the intricate pomegranate seeds to feed to me. And I wait, content and expectant, as if I'd been born to have someone sit beside me and painstakingly feed me. I love the crunch and sweet, winy squirt of the little seeds and resolve to eat many more pomegranates in my life.

Munira strokes my hair back behind my ears and says, now in the city Arabic, "Wouldn't you like to stay here with me forever?"

I feel as if I'm drifting backward into the ground, as if my drowsiness is drifting up from the earth. "Yes," I say. "I'd love that."

"You could be my little girl. I would feed and dress you beautifully." Her hand sweeps over my head. I'm lying down, gazing into the sky—it's still light out, but I can already see the moon. "Your mother has the other little girls, and she can have even more. But I have none and I don't have a man to give me any!"

"Why don't you get a man?"

"I'm much too old now, it's too late." Her voice is hazy and far away.

"How old are you?"

"Almost thirty, I think."

I consider this. "I would be your little girl," I murmur.

"Besides, this is where you belong." She draws one finger along my face. "You're a wind baby."

"Am I a Bedouin?"

"The Bedu were here first," she says as if she doesn't hear me. She looks up at the emerging stars, and I admire her angular profile, her skin tanned as old leather. "We were here before any of this city non-sense, before any of these crazies from Europe or anybody."

I nod dreamily, imagining the Bedouins at the beginning of time.

"We know things that no one else does." She puts her hand over my wrist, and the matter is settled. "I'll teach you everything, just wait."

I nod again, surrendering to the hand.

I doze a bit, the scents of the day ribboning through my sleep. When I wake, there's a soft woven blanket wrapped around me. The sun has set and the moon is pointed and stark in the cold new air. I roll over to one side and see a group of men strolling together toward the open desert. I hear the sheikh and my father's voices. I think, Bud must be asking his question.

Then they're laughing; they're holding something up over their heads, and there are vivid cracks of light. They're shooting off their guns. Is this an answer?

Munira is asleep beside me: The firelight is soft on her face—I've never seen her sleep before—the map of wrinkles is blurred, and her face is younger and smoother, as if in a fairy tale. One of her hands rests on the edge of my shirt. I sit up and watch her sleep for a while before, somewhat regretfully, I get up and go in search of my mother and sisters. I find them sitting in the crook of a log before another fire, my sisters asleep, my mother gazing sternly into the flames. "You ready to go?" she asks, her voice crisp. Her face is painted with the golden light; she is as beautiful as the sun behind the mountains. "I think it's time."

A broad-winged bird flies low over our heads under the moon. Its call is spicy and low. If I had stayed by Munira's fire for one more moment, I might never have left at all.

The car is full of sleep: Bud is the only one awake, driving. But the reflected starlight slips over my eyelids and into my dreams. Finally I sit up inside our dark, shared chamber. My mother's head tilts as she dozes, her hand resting lightly on my father's leg. There's a white Bedouin scarf loose on his shoulders, and he smells like sumac, thyme, and fields.

"Dad, Dad," I whisper to him, "did you ask your question?"

He doesn't respond right away. Then he seems to nod faintly. He sighs and says, "Did you know . . ." His voice trails off as if he is distracted by his own thoughts, then picks up again. "Did you know that your grandfather's eyesight was so good he could see the eye of a bird flying by? And that your great-granduncle can smell the water hidden underground? And your uncle Ramzi—they say he can hear an earthquake before it starts shaking."

Aha, Bud is in one of those moods. I've seen it before—where he sits up in the dark and gazes out the window at whatever it is he sees. It's something I puzzle over until the night I catch myself doing the same thing.

"I've already forgotten everything," he says, his fingers slipping over the notches in the steering wheel as if over a string of prayer beads. "I forgot how good the food tastes under a tent. And the wind smell in the valley."

I think of the big blowing tent and the hot *mensaf* and how purely good everything tasted after a day in the open air. Then for some reason I imagine Uncle Ramzi, this man alone in his cave, murmuring with the earth, its deep voice telling him all sorts of things about the stars and moon. Something snags in my chest, the tiniest barb, as if I am catching Bud's mood. I can see the city lights just beginning to glow on the horizon, their diffuse rosy haze. I wonder if we will ever spend time among the Bedouins again. Deeper down, from beneath that question, emerges a larger, more formless question, something about whether people have to decide exactly who they are and where exactly their home is. Do we have to know who we are once and for all? How many lives are we allowed? But it's too strange and somehow a little frightening to ask anything like this.

Easier instead to slide back down on the seat, into the gentle scent of Munira's clothing, close my eyes, and pretend to fall fast asleep.

BEDOUIN *MENSAF LEBEN*
Lamb is substituted for goat here, in deference to what is stocked in American grocery stores.

2 pounds lamb shanks
1 egg, lightly whisked
1 quart buttermilk
Salt and freshly ground pepper
1 cup rice
1 large onion, chopped

¼ to ½ pound butter
3 loaves of *shrak** or pita bread, torn into pieces
¼ cup pine nuts or slivered almonds

Place the lamb in a large pot, cover with water, and bring to a boil. Turn down the heat and simmer for 20 minutes. Skim off any fat that drifts to the surface, leaving behind a lamb broth.

In another large pot, stir the egg into the buttermilk and bring to a boil over medium heat, *stirring constantly;* otherwise the buttermilk will curdle. Reduce the heat to a simmer and continue stirring, for about 20 minutes.

Transfer the lamb to the buttermilk mixture and reserve the broth. Add 1 cup of the lamb broth to the buttermilk mixture and stir thoroughly. Simmer for about 1 hour, stirring occasionally. Add salt and pepper to taste.

In the meantime, cook the rice in 2 cups of the lamb broth. Add salt to taste.

Sauté the onions in 1 tablespoon of the butter until lightly browned. Add the onions to the buttermilk mixture toward the end of the cooking.

Layer the bread on the bottom of a large serving platter or wide, shallow cooking tray. Pour enough of the buttermilk mixture to soak the bread. Spread the rice over the bread in a low dome. Place the lamb over the rice. Pour the buttermilk over the meat (but not so much that it becomes soupy. Reserve any extra buttermilk sauce and serve it on the side for those who'd like more).

In a small pan, sauté the pine nuts or almonds in 2 tablespoons of the butter until the nuts are lightly browned. Sprinkle over the meat.

Dot the whole dish with slices of the remaining butter before serving.

SERVES 6.

Shrak is a very fine, thin bread available in some specialty food stores.

FOUR

A House and a Yard

America is a cold breeze that snaps us awake. We've been gone for a year, but once we're back, I keep recognizing types of trees, stores, buildings, and blurting out, "Oh yeah!" We've left Jordan, with its lush winds, dust, and sun-stained air. When I wake in a hotel bed on the first morning back in America, I'm dazed by a blankness around me: the sleekly painted walls, the air slack without the scents of mint, olive, and jasmine, and an immobilizing silence. I close my eyes and conjure the songbirds Mrs. Haddadin kept in a gold cage hanging from a tree branch; the wobble of Munira's singing as she dashed a broom through the courtyard. It is almost too much to imagine I will never hear them again, so I lie in bed for as long as Mom will let me, listening.

We've returned to Syracuse, to a split-level house that does not have another family living in the upstairs apartment or a communal courtyard or thick hedges of mint. But this house does have a generous backyard for tearing around in. All around us are trees and confined, suburban fields.

There is something mothlike about the houses in this new neighborhood—in the morning they look half-dissolved. They are sided in tentative shades of beige, dove gray, avocado, cream, and colonial ivory that shimmer in the cold New York morning fog. There are picture windows, two-car garages, foyers, family rooms, and big basements. The neighbors seem hesitant to emerge from their glimmering homes, and we almost never see anyone outside. But we quickly find out about Mrs. Manarelli next door. She lives in a house nearly identical to ours, with her grumpy husband, Johnny, and her son, Marco, who's my age and notable for having what could be the world's largest collection of Monkees 45s. Mrs. Manarelli has powdered white down all over her face, two rouged spots high on her cheeks, and a low, peaked hairline. But she also has a gaze that feels soft as kisses on both your cheeks and a way of looking at you that makes you want to lean into her. Her parents were both from Italy, and since she was born in Brooklyn she says that makes her an immigrant, too.

Mrs. Manarelli travels around the neighborhood with covered bundles that at first I think are babies. Then she comes to our house and I find out that it's food: pasta slippery with fresh pesto, or a plate of grilled sausages, or a whole roasted chicken. She cooks and then she looks for people to feed, because Johnny is always on a diet and Marco is delicate and sensitive and allergic to everything. When she and Bud meet, it's as if they've found each other at last. She raps on the glass of the kitchen door as Bud fries some lentils and tomatoes and onions. "Hey, you!" she calls. "Whatcha doing in there? What is that in the pan?"

Bud lets her in and she waves at us on her way to the stove. "You put butter or what in there?"

And so their conversation begins.

She hovers around my father while he cooks, asking accusatory questions about his technique and attempting to doctor the spices. He laughs and tries to hold her back with one arm.

"What you doing it like that for?" she demands, her newly set hair in a stiff wave around her head. Then she bawls through the kitchen door at my mother (who's reading, stretched out easy, long legged, on the couch in the next room), "Pat! He's about to put *something yellow* in this beautiful rice!"

"Sumac wakes it up," says Bud the poet. "You don't know yet. Just wait."

"I don't want my rice awake or sleeping," says Mrs. Manarelli. "Can't I just have it in a bowl?"

But once she tries it, spooning it right out of the pan, she nods with her spoon in the air and says, "Okay, yeah, I see your point."

. . .

My favorite neighbors are my new best friend, Sally Holmes, and her parents. Bud says that they are "real Americans." Sally has a pert turned-up nose and pink freckles and ringlets of ribbon red hair. Her mother wears her hair in a glorious upright pillar called a bouffant. Every year, Sally's parents put up a ceiling-high, rotating, carol-piping, aluminum-silver Christmas tree in their family room. When I first behold this tree, my heart speeds up and little jittery bursts pulse under my skin: I feel shame over our own three-foot, stationary, non-snow-sprayed tabletop version. Sally and I sprawl stomach down on the floor of her darkened living room and play Ouija board by the red, green, and white strobe lights of her tree. We ask, "Who does Harry Meyer like?" and, "Will I ever in my life have a boyfriend?" The planchette flies over the board, spelling out hostile maniac answers like "You wish you, HA HA HA" and "Never you you never now."

Mrs. Holmes comes out of the kitchen with a silver tray of instant chocolate pudding in single-serving aluminum tubs and says, "Cocktail hour, ladies!" It tastes like burnt plastic, but I study the way Sally and Mrs. Holmes scrape their tubs and lick the spoons. Later she pours us crystal cups of gummy eggnog from a carton. I jiggle my glass, fascinated with the way its surface quivers in place.

This is American food, I tell myself. I don't like it, I think, because I've somehow forgotten it. I must remember.

The days grow crisp and sharp. People raise their eyebrows, look at the clouds, and say things like "Yup, it's coming all right."

On the news, the reporters recount stories about how many people were buried alive in cars under snowdrifts in previous years and how many more they anticipate going under this year. Then I look up one day from a book I'm reading in English class to see that the windows of the classroom are filled with whirling, white chaos.

There is no day, no night, just snow and our huddled weak light inside.

Three days after Christmas, Sally's father, Max, unravels the garden hose and floods their backyard; by the next morning the yard has frozen into a skin-smooth skating rink. Sally loans me her old skates and she wears her new Christmas pair, the leather a gleaming bone color. At first my ankles feel loose and untrustworthy and I sway from side to side, but the feeling gradually starts to come back to me, from years of skating at the public rink with my grandmother. As I remember, I begin to relax, to lower my wobbling, windmill hands. Sally and I spend hours that day skating in circles. Mrs. Holmes brings us hot chocolate with tiny crunchy marshmallows floating in it. We sip and warm our fingers, but we stay out on the ice. The sun goes down early and my toes start to tingle and then hurt, but I can't stop.

Finally Mrs. Holmes stands in their back door. The light glows through her apron ruffle and makes a halo of her shellacked hair. It's time for Sally to go in for dinner. "Diana, honey," Mrs. Holmes says, "your mom just called, she's looking for you."

I wave to Sally, who clomps up the back steps in her skates. I'm about to leave as well, but I stay for just one more turn around the rink. Then I think I will take one more. And then one more and one more. Now that I remember skating, I can't quite bring myself to stop. I keep gliding through the expanding dark. After a while, I notice to my surprise that my toes have stopped hurting. How can I stop now? A heavy snow starts to fall, and I hear the warm family murmur and the clink of dinner through the wall of Sally's house, and this gives me a delicious sense of sadness that I press into. I imagine that I am a poor, familyless orphan condemned to skate forever while the rest of the world eats its cozy dinner. For some reason, this makes me think about Jordan, my friends there and the balmy air of the courtyard. I haven't thought of them in months, and the unexpected memory makes my throat tighten, and then my lashes freeze together and my scarf freezes to the breath on my lips.

Eventually, I hear footsteps crunching along the side of the house through the glazed snow and my mother's navy blue sigh through the frozen air. She allows me to walk home in Sally's ice skates. The streets and houses sparkle with cold, and the night looks mauve in the wells and footprints of earlier pedestrians. We pass two cars freshly stranded in snowdrifts and another spinning its wheels on the ice.

"People should just skate everywhere," I remark as I teeter along. "That would solve all kinds of things." I laugh when Mom inquires about my extremities. My toes feel dumb and blocky as chunks of wood. "But they don't even hurt, Mom! Not even a little!" I boast.

"Well, that's nice, dear," Mom says, squinting toward our house.

At home, I sit on the foyer bench, tug off the borrowed skates, and release my toes, which still feel lifeless and blunt. For a moment I flash on Hamouda's wooden leg and wonder if something about this isn't quite normal. Mom peels off my socks, and my feet are an astonishing beet red except for my toes, which are grayish green. "Ooh," says my sister Suzy, touching them. "Lookit."

"Wow," I say, bent over them. "Whooie. They don't even hurt."

Suzy taps one. "It feels like Super Balls."

"Hey . . ." I laugh. "I don't even feel that! Try this one." We work our way down my toes, plonking each one in turn like plates on a xylophone: nothing, nothing, nothing!

Eventually I look up and notice that Mom's eyes are burning. She is staring at my feet and clutching her mouth with her hand. I gulp air as adrenaline charges through me. "Mom, Mom, Mom!" I bleat. *Am I dying?*

Bud appears, eyes wide. "What did you do with your feet?" he bellows, as if I'd given them away.

Mom says, "Should we call a doctor?"

Then something weirder happens: My mouth falls open and I'm shrieking, "No, no, no, nooooo! I don't wanna gooooo!" Tears burst from my eyes. My panic shocks even me—I'm vividly reliving my last doctor's visit, when we were given six inoculations at once for our trip to Jordan and my arm swelled up as if it'd been pounded with a crowbar. I cling to Mom's leg, fall over my useless feet to my knees. "Please don't make me, please, I'll be gooooood!" I howl, my voice husky with terror. Monica starts crying upstairs in her crib. Suzy starts crying, too; she clings to my arm.

"Okay, okay, okay!" Mom shouts, covering her ears with the flat of her hands.

Besides, there's no easy way to take me anywhere. The snow has started up again, shaking and fierce in the windows, and cars are winding sideways through the unplowed neighborhood streets. While Mom rubs my feet, Bud calls his sister in Jordan, the famous Auntie Aya, who can cure anything.

The sounds of Arabic wash through the room. There is a flash, a soothing memory of my aunt's stone house. I breathe; I begin to edge back down to earth. After he tells her the problem, the first few minutes of their conversation are about Bud apologizing for being such a fancy idiot and moving us all to this dangerous land. This never would have happened in Jordan: "Yes, yes, of course you're right, I know, I know. . . ." Then he is getting instructions. He thanks her, hangs up. There is the sound of water bursting into a pot, then the pot banging onto the stove. A scrambling of cabinets opening, jars clinking.

"Hon?" Mom calls out, her voice taut. "What are you doing in there? What did Aya say?"

"She said make soup!" he cries.

I stare at Mom's face, afraid to look away. "What's going to happen, Mom?" I ask. "What's going to happen?" I can't look at my toes anymore. Now the dead color frightens me. I'm no longer sure they're attached to me or that the ghoulish whiteness won't begin to creep up my ankles. I can't remember exactly how many times I ask what's going to happen, I only know that she doesn't answer.

Finally, Bud brings out his soup, steaming and fragrant in the pot. It smells less like soup than perfume, like oranges and flowers. He gives me a mug of it, and the mist in my face makes me tranquil and drowsy. He's poured the rest into a big pan, added some tapwater to cool it to a middling warmth, put it on the floor, and told me to place my feet in it. "In the soup?" I look at Mom and she looks at Bud, who doesn't look entirely certain. But five-year-old Suzy claps and says, "Feet in the soup!" So I plunk them in.

For a while not much happens. We all stare at the mysterious soup. Now my feet seem even more alien, like some kind of pink fish asleep in a puddle. I sip at my mug of soup, the bits of herbs bright and appealing, mingled with chewy morsels of orange peel. It is too dark and earthy, to my child's palate, to taste delicious, but something inside of me is called away by it. I start to forget about my sleeping fish feet. Suzy gets bored and goes to bed. Then, as I am starting to nod off, something does happen. I feel it starting like a sliver, deep inside the bones of my toes. A warmth and then a heat that grows and grows and then flashes like a struck match. I shriek and yank my feet out, crying, "The soup is burning me!" And Mom and Bud both grab me as if I might fly away. Mom holds me tightly, and Bud says, "Don't be afraid." And Mom says, "It's not the soup burning, honey, it's your toes."

They hold my feet down in the soup while I shake and my skin turns to silver and my toes bloom red as roses in snow.

Our sprawling neighborhood is filled, in its family rooms and rec rooms and extra bedrooms, with a nation of children. There's Karen, Carl, Lilah, Raymond, Lisa, Donna, Sally, Jamie, the Malcolm twins, and many more all within the first three blocks of the school bus route. Jamie Faraday used to be best friends with Sally Holmes until I appeared in the lunchroom with my bags full of cold roasted chicken kabobs slathered in hummus and wrapped in pita bread. Sally dragged back the seat beside me, plumped her chin onto the heel of her palm, and said, "What you eating?" Down the length of the long linoleum table, I see Jamie abandoned. She lifts her head and I see myself come into focus; her forehead rises with a look almost like recognition. Now Jamie eyes me warily every time she gets on the bus, takes note of Sally seated beside me, and waves with an enraged little flip of the hand. Then she clatters down the aisle far from our seat into exile.

I notice all this but don't completely take it in: I'm trying to get my bearings. Throughout our first year back in the States, I seem to see everything through a glittering mist. I hear the expression *American dream* and I think that, somehow, this quality of mistiness must be what it refers to. The children in the neighborhood are so soft and babyish that they barely seem to have outlines. In other ways they are deliberate, remorseless, and exacting. The politics of the school bus and the rumor mill of the classroom are fierce, filled with intrigue and menace. It all feels so different from the good-times kids I knew in Jordan, with their shared gum, their sharp, brown shins and broken-toothed grins. In America, I learn there is a certain way to dress (hip-huggers, flared jeans), a certain way to wear your hair (gleaming, Prince Valiant bobs), a certain lunchbox to carry (Barbie for girls, G.I. Joe for boys—I am nearly cast out of fourth grade when I show up with a Flintstones box). And there are, it turns out, many things that—under any circumstances—you do not do.

For example, the neighbors don't barbecue in their front yards. That is apparently what the backyard is for. The backyards here are fenced off and guarded—spaces as private as other people's dreams. But our front yard has the better view and has easier access to the front door, which is closer to the kitchen and hence a very practical place for grilling. Also, the front yard will allow us to share food, cross our legs on the plastic lawn chairs, and gossip with the neighbors, as we did in Jordan. We have survived a long, howling, isolated Syracuse winter that hardened into filthy icebergs of decaying snow. By April, Bud is ready to pronounce it spring and set up his hibachi. On the first warmish sunny day, we drag out the picnic table, digging mud furrows through the half-frozen yard. Bud has chicken marinated in olive oil, vinegar, rosemary, and a whole head of garlic. Its butter yellow skin hisses and crackles over the coals, and the aroma fills my head. The beautiful charred smell of the grill circulates through the spring air and bare tree branches, still shocked with cold.

"DISTRACT THE NEIGHBORS" GRILLED CHICKEN
*This is a delightful, simple dish that will
fill the neighborhood with a gorgeous scent.*

4 tablespoons olive oil
3 cloves garlic, crushed
Juice from 1 lemon
3 teaspoons brown sugar
3 sprigs rosemary, chopped
¼ teaspoon ground cumin

Salt and freshly ground
  pepper
½ teaspoon cayenne pepper
2 pounds skinless chicken
  pieces

In a large bowl, mix the oil, garlic, lemon juice, brown sugar and spices. Add the chicken pieces (you may cut the chicken into cubes, if you prefer), stirring to coat the chicken with the marinade. Cover and refrigerate for 3 hours or longer, turning occasionally.

Place the chicken parts on the grill (if cut in cubes, the chicken can be threaded onto skewers). Grill over hot charcoal for 10 to 15 minutes, turning frequently and basting with the marinade. This is very nice with bread and salad.

SERVES 4.

We set the table, bring out bowls of elegant baba ghanouj and sprightly tabbouleh salad full of bulgur and fresh parsley, a basket of hot bread, and skewers heavy with onion and tomato wedges to be roasted. We sit, marveling over our good fortune—to live in these rolling green lawns, these creamy houses, and the bold vaulted sky of our new neighborhood. The chicken is crusty and redolent with garlic and rosemary. We eat well, shivering just a bit in our jackets. I have a sense—as I often do when I contemplate this blue moon-stone sky—of the future. It is a broad, euphoric feeling. Does the rest of the family feel this way? I don't know for sure, though I imagine they do. Whenever we all drive home together, Mom asks as we pull in the driveway, "Who do you suppose lives in this little house?"

We are lost in the food, in the smell of grilling, and in the spring when there is a powdery sort of sensation sprinkling down the back of my neck and suddenly I realize a man and a woman are standing at the edge of the street, just a few feet away, staring at us.

I put down my chicken leg, which has rolled juices and smoke between my fingers. "Hi!" I call brightly. New neighbors! They look hungry. The woman starts and blushes, as if she didn't imagine that we could see them. Her eyes are a pale linen blue, of such crisp clarity that she looks as if she could X-ray with them.

Bud stands, maître d' of the front lawn. "Welcome. I'm Gus, this is my wife, Pat—"

The two strangers pull back and lightly bump into each other. I dimly register the sense that they didn't think Bud could talk.

"We just moved here in November." Bud gestures at the house as if they might assume we were picnicking on someone else's lawn. "I hope you're hungry! We've got all this crazy food—shish kabob, baba gha—"

The woman's kerchief white hand flutters up to her throat. There's a pause, and Bud bends back a little and asks me quietly, "*Haddol nawal?*" ("Are they Gypsies?") They look marooned and stateless, standing there mute in the street. But I remember seeing a family of Gypsies once in the old market in Jordan, with their fringed scarves and spangled earrings and high-voltage expressions. These mild, normal people don't look anything like that—the man in belted beige slacks and tasseled loafers and the woman in a milky, synthetic blouse and culottes. Finally the man clears his throat and says, "Oh no, no, thank you—we . . . we just, um, ate. Um." He blinks. "We, uh . . . we uh . . . we live over there, on Cumberland Drive? We uh . . . well, our neighbors—you know the Tinerkes on Roanoke Circle?"

Bud frowns, trying to process the name. I picture rabbity little Timmy and chinless Bitsy Tinerke sitting in the third seat from the front of the school bus.

"Anyway. Well, see, they live really close by here, too." The man and the woman glance at each other. He puts his hands on his slender snaky hips. "Well, they saw you-all out here eating or burning things or something and then called us to say there might be some kind of— I don't know, exactly—maybe some kind of trouble going on out here? And so we just came on over to check into it—you know, we all like to keep an eye on things—this is a nice neighborhood— and so . . ." His voice trails off; his face is slowly turning an alarming, bruised color.

Bud is still standing there, still frowning, as if this man is speaking in tongues. Then my mother stands and the couple look startled once again. She is nearly six feet tall, with good level shoulders and a long neck and unwavering Cassandra eyes. She also puts her hands on her hips, almost casual. "There's no trouble here," she says in her smooth, leaf-blown voice.

They put up their hands and back away as if she is waving a pistol at them. "No, no, no trouble at all—sorry for the—the—misunder- standing. . . . Welcome to the neighborhood!" Then they are gone.

And that's about when I get the feeling that starts somewhere at the center of my chest, as heavy as an iron ingot, a bit like fear or sad- ness or anger, but none of these exactly; it is simply there, suspended between my ribs. I look up at the neighborhood and the mist has cleared. All the mean, cheaply framed windows are gaping at us, the sky empty as a gasp.

The next day on the school bus, Jamie climbs on, gives me her hard smile, hesitates, then flounces down on the seat next to me. She tilts her head and parts her lips. I look up in alarm. "Just to let you know," she says in a sweet, burning way.

"Let me know what?"

She crosses one bare leg over the other, and her brilliant white socks bounce with the rocking of the bus. "Well, you know, of course. My parents saw you out there the other night. I heard them talking with the neighbors. They said it was an 'unholy disgrace.' See, okay, the thing is, you better know that in this country nobody eats in the front yard. Really. Nobody." She looks at me solemnly and sadly, her bangs a perfect cylinder above her brows. "If your family doesn't know how to behave, my parents will have to find out about getting you out of this neighborhood."

She squints, pinches her lips together in a narrow, bitten-down way. I can see every pointed pale lash, the pink ridges above her lower lids.

I feel the iron inside of me. It drives through every bit of my body. It vibrates like a bell clapper. I turn away from her and tip my forehead against the frigid pane of glass. There's an echo in my head saying: *She's right.* Shame fills me: I see it in the rain stroking the windows, so bright that it burns holes in the backs of my eyes. When Jamie finally slides out of the seat, I don't even hear her go.

I mope, barely speaking, for a solid week, appetiteless, rejecting Bud's lunches of stuffed squash, *shawerma*, kibbeh. Even Mom's peanut butter and Fluff on white bread brings tears to my eyes, and I stuff it in the garbage barrel at the cafeteria.

Mrs. Manarelli asks me what's wrong.

But I have no way of explaining to her that I have awakened from the mist and now our neighborhood looks hard and squat and drudgy. I have no way to explain Jamie Faraday's pink-rimmed eyes and long bulb of a nose. Instead I just mope and shrug and sigh wordless blue shadows. So she slants her head to one side, then swats at my behind and tells me I don't have no sign of a butt at all. And I get indignant and say I do so have signs of a butt. And she says fine, well, okay then, come on inside, I need your help in the kitchen.

The entrance to Mrs. Manarelli's house smells like roasting tomatoes and garlic. She doesn't go in much for opening the window curtains, which she says fades everything, so the whole downstairs is doused in shadow and all the furniture crackles under clear plastic covers. Directly over the couch in the living room is a spotlit, giltframed painting of the Last Supper, and here the notes of tomato sauce are so pronounced that you could imagine this is what the apostles are eating. Her husband, Johnny, sits on the couch, ankles crossed on the coffee table, always glaring at what seems to be the same word in the newspaper. The family room smells of red wine, fruit, and chocolate, and I know the bedrooms upstairs smell either of bread when she's baking or of the fresh cedar, lavender, and pine hillsides of another country. Once, in the upstairs bathroom, I was so transported by the scent of rosewater that Mrs. Manarelli found me there a half hour later sitting on the edge of the tub, combing my hair and singing.

We go into the kitchen and there is something shimmering in a gelatin mold on the counter. She instructs me to soak a kitchen towel under the warm-water tap and wipe this along the mold. Then she turns it out onto a pastry board dusted with confectioner's sugar; a puff of sugar blooms in the air. It is so brilliantly white that it reminds me of the nuns speaking of food that removes all sin. Mrs. Manarelli wipes a knife with the hot towel, cuts into the whiteness, and brings me a slice of *panna cotta* gleaming and dewy on a Melmac plate.

She sits beside me at the speckled linoleum table just like our own and says speculatively, "Only men in my life—husband, son . . . why do you suppose that is?"

I blink. I want to dwell on my own problems, but this is a novel idea to me, in our house of mostly girls. I reach for my grandmother's favorite explanation: "Maybe it's because Jesus says so."

"Jesus!" she snorts. Then she sighs and fans herself and looks off at the place where the ceiling meets the wall. "Eat your dessert," she says. "*Jesus.*"

The first spoonful of *panna cotta* is so startling, I want to laugh or sing or confess my sins. It tastes of sweetness and cream and even of the tiny early flowers the cows have eaten to make the cream.

I take another bite of *panna cotta* and another. Before long, without even realizing it, I'm talking, telling all, secrets dissolving like *panna cotta* in the mouth. Mrs. Manarelli scrapes her chair in closer, puts her chin on her hand, and watches me talk about grilled chicken and the Gypsy people in loafers and the school bus and how Sally now likes me better than Jamie and how that is my fault and Jamie's cinched smile and how I don't have the right lunchbox or the right pants or shoes or socks and how things are different from Jordan and how I can never remember my sins in confession so I make up new ones and isn't that a sin of a sin and does that mean I am going right to hell, are they going to kick us out of the neighborhood, and can we move back to our apartment in the courtyard with my boyfriend Hisham?

When I have exhausted myself and have scraped up every bit of *panna cotta* on my plate, Mrs. Manarelli goes and stands at the stove as if she is cooking something, but the little red light on her stove isn't on. She is muttering things in different languages, and her voice sounds serrated: I hear angry odds and ends of words. Finally she turns around and says, "There's nobody going to hell around here except for the ones think they aren't gonna go. That's if you ask me. And they damn better not ask or they'll find out a thing or five they don't want to know!"

This comment raises more questions for me than it answers. While I'm mulling this over, she grabs the phone receiver and shakes it like a mace. "What're their names?" she demands. "I got a few choice words for them."

"Who?"

"The Gypsies! The Gypsies and their loafers!"

"Maria Elena Theresa, do not call the neighbors." Her grouchy husband's voice erupts from the living room where he is rattling the newspaper. "We are no longer in Brooklyn, we are in civilization up here now. People don't do that kind of stuff up here."

"Don't tell me what people do!" she shouts back. "The Italians invented civilization!"

"I was Italian five years before you was born," he retorts. "I got a PhD in civilization."

She shakes the receiver a few more times at the wall behind Johnny's head, jaw set at an indignant angle, as if she is still arguing with him. But she seems to concede the argument because she slams the phone back down and turns to the counter. Now Mrs. Manarelli is busying herself with a new plan of attack. She wraps up the *panna cotta* in waxed paper, then cloth napkins, like swaddling a big baby. She puts it in a basket with some cold sliced roast beef, some soft white cheese in a jar, some tender roasted red peppers in oil, tiny black olives, and a crusty round loaf of bread. "We're going out!" she shouts at her husband. Then she says to me, "C'mon, kid."

We walk next door to my house and Mrs. Manarelli knocks loudly, then comes halfway in, yelling up the stairs to my mother. Mom comes down the stairs, patting at her new bouffant hairdo, tall and firm and shiny. Mrs. Manarelli holds up her basket, tells her that she's brought a picnic and doesn't want to eat it at the round, speckled table in the kitchen, she wants to eat it outside. Mom starts laughing. "But it's fifty degrees out—and I just got my hair done!" I admire her long neck and towering hair, all of her descending the foyer stairs like a goddess on a trophy.

"Hoity-toity, Pat," Mrs. Manarelli says, and nudges me. "Now, there's a woman."

Mom stares at us a moment as we stand grinning and wind whipped in the doorway, gives a last, regretful pat to her hairdo, and goes in to put on her parka and collect my sisters. Mrs. Manarelli also looks magnificent. Usually she's plump and hunched up, her hair trapped in a net like a dark fish. But once we go back outdoors, she comes unfurled: Her short brown hair bobs in the wind, her lips are round and scarlet against the whiteness of her skin. She stands straighter, and under her wool church coat the hem of her cotton print dress flails around her knees. It's the end of April and we had the last snowfall four weeks ago, our ill-fated barbecue three weeks ago. The neighborhood windows and doorknobs still stay rimmed with frost an hour after the sun comes out.

The hibachi is stowed away in the garage, but the picnic table floats abandoned on the thawing grass out front, and this, of course, is where Mrs. Manarelli wants to eat. She spreads out a checkered tablecloth, and when we can't get the cloth to stop blowing off the table, we sit on top of it. Mom brings out plates and wineglasses and Kool-Aid for me and my sisters, and there is a look on her face as though we've just told one another a good joke. Her cheeks gleam with the cold, and her high hair unravels in the wind like a ball of yarn. It's so cold that I'm having trouble tasting anything, and Monica says she wants to go back inside and see the rest of her soap opera. (She's only four, but she's already addicted to the high drama of *General Hospital*.) But then Mrs. Manarelli unveils the baby *panna cotta*: It shivers and gleams white as a star. We eat it directly from the waxed paper with plastic spoons.

The neighborhood cars pass, some quickly, some slowly, and we wave at them all with the wave we've seen at Macy's Thanksgiving Day parade, a feathery tilt at the wrist, forearm upright. No one can tell us anything. We are five queens drifting over the suburbs on our own private float.

MRS. MANARELLI'S CIVILIZED *PANNA COTTA*

2 cups heavy cream, minus
   2 tablespoons to dissolve
   gelatin
¼ cup sugar

1½ teaspoons gelatin (½ packet)
4 to 8 tablespoons fruit
   purée, sweetened fruit,
   or chocolate sauce

Heat 2 cups of the cream with the sugar in a heavy saucepan and simmer for 15 minutes. In a small bowl, sprinkle the gelatin over the remaining 2 tablespoons of cream. Remove the simmered cream from heat and add the gelatin mixture, stirring to dissolve. Pour ½ cup of this new mixture into 4 lightly oiled metal molds and refrigerate for 4 to 6 hours. Dip the mold in hot water and run a knife around the edge; unmold the *panna cotta* onto individual serving dishes. Serve each with 1 to 2 tablespoons sauce, either fruit purée, sweetened fruit, or chocolate sauce.

SERVES 4.

FIVE

Madama Butterfly

For as long as I've known her, Gram has wanted revenge. There are many things she wants it for:

A bossy, domineering German father.

A wavy-haired husband who emptied their bank account, ran off with one of her students' mothers, and abandoned her with a young child.

The Great Depression (brought about by men).

A soft-eyed, wavy-haired foreigner who married, and thus stole, her only child.

So, in other words: *Men.*

Gram has had it with *men;* she's had it up to here with them. The topic makes her eyes steely and her lips tighten. "Don't get me started," she says.

Luckily, she has some granddaughters to work with.

Gram and I open her big, flour-breathing Betty Crocker cookbook, and Gram leans forward on the counter. I'm staying with her for the weekend, on a vacation from my family. Gram lives in New Jersey, and sometimes, when I feel inspired, I take a five-hour bus ride down, present myself at her door, and say, "Here I am!" We're pals. When I was a baby, I'm told, I loved to hold her tissue-soft face between my palms and meditate on her bluebonnet eyes. It looks as if everything about her is soft, from her permed blond hair to the cute short pants she calls pedal pushers, but her white forearms on the counter are like crossed swords. "Men are trouble," she says intensely. "Listen to me—I know."

I roll my eyes: I'm ten, and believe me, I've heard it all before. She tells me every chance she gets: shopping for shoes—men have nasty feet; watering a garden—men trample everything; watching a game show—men are all cheaters.

Gram likes life to be orderly and refined, clear and comprehensible. Each and every Sunday, Gram and her old-lady friends in their woolen coats and stiff, tail-biting mink stoles all ride to church together in Mrs. Harvey's son's big, big car. Mrs. Harvey lives one floor below Gram—she is the reason my sisters and I are not to run like "a herd of wild buffalo" through Gram's apartment.

But Gram also has a powerful, undeniable inner nature. Storms of emotion roll through her, spreading a deep red geranium bloom from her chest up. She indulges her grandchildren like a maniac, takes us to the supermarket and allows us to fill the shopping cart with every candy that catches our eye, from the classics to the esoteric—malted milk balls, Good & Plenty, red licorice whips, saltwater taffy, Red Hot Dollars, jawbreakers, chocolate papooses. Two years earlier, I slept over at her apartment on the night before our first trip to Jordan. She shared the bed with me, smearing away tears and holding me tightly, making me swear not to tell my parents about her crying. And on the day we returned to America, she squeezed the air out of my lungs and whispered into my hair that she'd never let us move away again, never.

Now we pore over Betty Crocker, the reasonable, neutral recipes for pot roast and macaroni and cheese. Gram prefers the ordered cosmos of the cookbook world; she loves the optimism, clarity, and direction of recipes. But she frowns as she reads, chews plum lipstick off her lower lip: The recipes never turn out the way she wants them to. Or perhaps they turn out as she expects them to—the pork chops curling, the Swedish meatballs crumbling, the baked chicken limp and bland. She cooks like someone who never wanted to spend time over an iron or a broom or an oven, like someone who never wanted to clean up after anyone else again.

Naturally, Gram and Bud are always at odds, like mythical adversaries. Their competition—over race, culture, values—is primordial and monumental. Gram was appalled when my young, long-legged, coltish mom, before she was Mom, told her mother that she was going to marry this—this—foreigner with the black eyes and the black mustache and the black hair all curly and glistening with Brylcreem and powerful doses of Old Spice and lemon perfume. Gram asked Mom for a photo of Bud to display to the parish priest, to prove, Gram said, that he wasn't black. (I never got around to asking what happened if he was black.) So Mom sent the photo and Gram proved it. But somehow, in the long run, since he wasn't precisely white, either, it didn't solve anything. The two of them struggle endlessly. Sometimes the fight is still and quiet and sometimes loud and operatic, but it's always there.

According to family lore, when Mom first brought Bud home to meet her mother, Gram covered the table with dishes, the biggest one containing a glistening, clove-studded ham—not realizing that Muslims don't eat pork, or perhaps realizing it very well. Bud shows us the expression that was on his face when the pink pig appeared on the table: eyeballs bugging out, mouth agape. On the second meeting, she served shrimp, not realizing that Bud—who had never seen such things before—would think they were giant insects. Bud's expression this time: eyes slits, mouth yanked back at the corners. "I think for sure she is trying to kill me," he confides to us years later. Both times he left the table hungry and slipped out for White Castle burgers. But he still married my mother.

The problem seems obvious to me: Gram is a baker, Bud's a cook. Cooks are dashing, improvisational, wayward, intuitive; bakers are measured, careful, rational, precise. Gram can follow a recipe, but the drama for spice isn't in her bones. "Oh, rosemary," she says to me dismissively as we discuss a chicken recipe. "Rosemary is for show-offs." On our Easter visits she makes an honest roast beef that browns and caramelizes for hours in her oven, accompanied by a velvety mushroom gravy. But if there's more to her repertoire, I don't know about it.

Mostly it seems that Gram contrives not to cook at all—dinners are BLTs, noodles and butter, or tuna salad sandwiches. Even as a child, I am obsessed with cookbooks, and I lose myself for hours wandering through the food section at bookstores; but Gram more or less restricts herself to Betty Crocker and her much-treasured

I Hate to Cook Book by Peg Bracken. All her dealings with the male animal, she says, have given her more than enough surprises for one lifetime. She likes to know exactly what her food is going to do. Beside the books in the kitchen are her two life guides: a stack of *Good Housekeeping* magazines bookmarked at "Hints from Heloise" and—the bane of my existence—a little pink book of etiquette that has rules on what color purse may be carried after Labor Day and the correct folding of hankies. Today, after she's spent a few minutes poring desolately over the same five grease-dotted recipes for tomorrow's dinner, her fingertips drift off the page and she taps the table absently. "Maybe . . . ," she says, then stops and looks in my direction, but her gaze trickles out a foot before it reaches me.

"Maybe what?" I ask. She watches me tear another strip of *gamardine* from its cellophane wrapping and stuff the shred in my mouth. *Gamardine* is a Middle Eastern precursor of fruit leather. The pressed apricot comes wrapped in big golden rectangles, slick on one side, corrugated on the other, a lush, yellowy-sweet melting flavor. Since I've returned from Jordan, it's displaced malted milk balls as my favorite food. Gram scowls at the *gamardine*, her features pulled together like a purse drawstring. She sniffs and turns away when I offer her some and says that it's full of insect wings. Then she turns back and smiles in the way that tells me I don't yet know all there is to know about my grandmother and says, "Have you ever eaten Oriental food?"

I jerk my head up from a recipe for "Easy Cheezy Macaroni" and study her face. Tiny sparks run over my skin, raising every hair. "No, never," I say, a low thrill blooming in my voice.

"Neither have I," she says. She opens her eyes wide; they are cornflower blue, magnified behind cat's-eye glasses. She closes the recipe book slowly on one hand, as if keeping her place, then slides out the hand. "But I think it's high time."

I can't sleep that night, thinking about the Oriental food. What might it be? The next day, just around the crack of dawn, I slide out of bed and call Bud, waking him. I tell him about the Oriental food plan. "This is a kind of food? From where?" he asks, yawning.

I ponder. "Well. Yeah. I don't know."

"Is there a sauce?" (Yawn.) "Is there bread or rice?"

I twine the phone cord around my finger. "It's *Oriental,* Dad, there must be a sauce."

"When I first come to this country, I met a man on the boat from As-seeni. When we get to New York, he made a soup with seaweed and jellyfish. It was excellent."

I frown and curl up my tongue. I have a special aversion to jelly-fish, which sometimes speckle the Jersey shore. I ponder this and come up with a satisfactory resolution. "Well, that was different. That was *As-seeni.* This is from . . . Orientals." Because, of course, As-seeni is Arabic for Chinese.

He whistles, marveling, laughing. "Well, Ibn Battuta," he says, referring to his favorite ancient Islamic explorer, "you'll have to tell me what Orientals eat for dinner. I'm going back to bed."

Gram decides we will make what she calls an "Oriental event" out of the day. She opens the special hall closet where everything is covered in the smell of mothballs and the crackle of dry-cleaning paper. She pulls out two fur coats—the first is an ankle-length, fluffy imitation raccoon duffel. I gasp and immediately want to wear that one, but Gram says, "Let's just try this first," and slides my stick arms into the satin lining of a sheared seal imitation with a trapeze shape. The three-quarter sleeves come to my wrists and the body of the coat bells out below my knees, but the fur collar nuzzles my jaw and magically draws out planes I'd never noticed in my face before. I look in the full-length wall mirror and see something shift in my features, sug-gesting the face that I will grow into.

"I wore that to my high school grand pavilion dance," she says, stroking the sleeve fondly.

"Who did you go with?" I ask, very curious.

"Oh, I don't remember," she says, carefully adjusting the collar. "Some nincompoop."

I turn this way and that in the mirror, stunned with admiration for myself. From over my shoulder, Gram nods at my reflection. "It might be faux, but it's still very, very classy."

Gram wears the big raccoon coat, and we two very classy ladies wait on the curb in front of her building for the bus. Since she doesn't drive, this is our usual transportation to Manhattan, and these excursions are always marked by the smell of diesel smoke. Later, after I'm grown, the smell of buses will always make me feel keen and expectant. There's a wet snow tumbling from the sky, so Gram gives me one of her immense supply of plastic rain hats—tiny squares that unfold into a sort of Saran Wrap babushka with ties that knot under your chin. I find these just as intriguing and marvelous as the fur coats, and I wear my hat until we've boarded and Gram suggests that it's safe to remove it.

We sit in my favorite seats—the ones positioned at a right angle to the rest of the seats, directly behind the driver—and I swing my legs, eyeballing the passengers behind us. Two stops later, a distinguished older gentleman with swirling white hair, a powder blue suit, and a maroon ascot climbs on and sits next to me.

I sense Gram straightening her back, a telegraphed message to behave. I try, with limited success, to stop swinging my legs—number seven on a list of "Ten Unladylike Behaviors" enumerated in the little pink book.

The older gentleman nods to Gram over my head, and she says, "Oh, hellew," in her cultivated voice.

The older gentleman says, "And where are you two ladies off to today?" He smiles and reveals a gigantic set of ivory teeth.

"We're going to eat Oriental food!" I gasp at the man.

"But first we're going to see *Madama Butterfly* at the Metro-politan," Gram says, enunciating syllables and tugging at her ivory-smooth gloves. The pair I'm wearing have little plackets at the wrists held together with polished-bone buttons, and they smell like lavender sachet. I curl the fingers under my nose and inhale.

Gram takes me to these places—Carnegie Hall, the Russian Tea Room, the Guggenheim—stuffing me with culture every chance she gets. Gram attended normal school as a young woman, and she has been a teacher for nearly all her life. I'm her special education project. Nothing intimidates or unsettles Gram. At a Museum of Modern Art exhibit of Robert Mapplethorpe's photos—all burnished, naked men—she crossed her arms and said, "Well, that's interesting. Maybe someone will explain it to me sometime." Later, when I'm in high school and I ask her how she managed to read all of *Finnegans Wake,* she says, "One word at a time, dear."

"Well, that's all delightful," says the older gentleman, then turns to me and pats my sleeve. "And well, well, aren't you something? Look at this wonderful ensemble. Is that real seal you're wearing?"

"Sure!" I say. "It's faux."

Gradually, a conversation about the finer things evolves between Gram and the older gentleman, their voices light and bright as pins. All the while, I sense this man's attention flaring beneath his words, his eyes sharp and avid when he glances in my direction. But this is so unbelievable—that such a very distinguished, very old person would pay any real attention to me—that I simply don't take it in. Not even when the man comments on the length and delicacy of my neck and the particular shade of green in my eyes, speaking as directly and appraisingly to Gram as if he is judging a vase or a painting.

Eager to bring the conversation back around to my own new, cherished topic, I blurt out, "Have *you* ever eaten any Oriental food?"

He looks taken aback, then says, "Many times," in the voice of a condemned man. He dabs a scented hankie at his mouth, clears his throat, and adjusts his ascot. "The Oriental people have an unwholesome obsession with the flesh of the young pig."

They do? I am struck dumb, ruminating on the possible connection between this moment and the time that Gram served Bud the ham. The distinguished gentleman makes eating pig sound like a mortal sin, and even though Mom regularly serves my sisters and me ham-and-Swiss sandwiches with mustard, for a moment I'm worried that I won't even like Oriental food. What then?

"Well, what else do they eat?" I ask impatiently. "Besides young pig flesh?"

He sprinkles his fingers through the air, as if this is all too much.

"Please, that was another lifetime ago." His fluty voice trembles. "I've put all that infernal eating out of my mind. Now I consume only green and orange plants and crackers. If it were up to me, I would take all my nutrition in through the sun and the air."

"Like a little fern," Gram says.

"I've always had an abhorrence to the entire operation of chewing. So finally, I took matters into my own hands—"

Suddenly, there's a wet suction sound and the man's whole mouth seems to jump forward. He curls back his lips, and I can see that his rich pink gums and massive white teeth have separated from a paler, wizened pair of gums still in his head. I gape and move forward on the seat to get a better look, but he shifts his jaw and clacks the teeth back into place. I feel I've glimpsed something miraculous, like a unicorn.

"I told my dentist, 'I'm done! Remove these offending items!' And he pulled every last tooth. Now I wear my prosthetic only when I'm among the public and might need to make polite conversation. Otherwise I leave my gums at liberty. It's the most free and wonderful feeling!"

"I'm sure it is," Gram says.

"Like running around naked," I offer.

"Do you like to do that?" he asks with a chuckle.

I suck the breath back into my chest and stare.

Throughout our exchange, Gram has been studying the man. He gives off an air of prosperity and sophistication, yet even I realize that he's taking a bus. Gram clears her throat daintily and touches her sternum and finally asks in her most high-class way why a man such as himself would trouble with public transportation. He sits back and declares with a wide gesture, "I love the bus. The bus is the world! Well, of course I'm quite wealthy and I could take a limousine anywhere I liked, but I meet the world's most interesting people this way. Why, imagine if I had taken my chauffeur today, what I would have missed!" He lifts my hand on the edge of his fingers, lowering his head as if he will kiss it, then hesitates and simply passes the wedge of my knuckles under his nose, nostrils flaring.

Gram smiles coyly and bends her head to one side. She slinks one arm around my shoulders and pulls me in close so my hand slips out of his. I'm filled with relief.

He blinks at this gesture and then quickly states that he owns "several lucrative and high-class enterprises," adding that a man in his position is frequently lonely and in search of a friend, someone to coddle and spoil and heap with riches. Then he invites us to come visit him at his main place of business and painstakingly prints instructions on how to take the bus there on the back of a Howard Johnson Motel postcard. Finally he gives Gram a scalloped, gilt-edged business card with his name and the words *Pre-Owned Cars* and, under this, *Associate.*

"I do hope you'll honor me with a visit soon," he says at the end of the ride, and looks at me once more with such a raw longing that I withdraw a few inches, tucking in my chin and leaning against Gram's shoulder.

Gram assures him that we most certainly will consider this generous offer. Then, as soon as we walk into Port Authority and lose sight of him, she flips the card in the garbage and says, "There goes another one, walking around all loose and fancy free. Typical!"

"Typical what?"

She looks at me as if it's scrawled all over the tiled walls of the station. "Typical man!"

THE TENDEREST ANGEL FOOD CAKE
For those who don't like to chew very much.

1½ cups large egg whites (about 12 to 15 egg whites)
1 tablespoon warm water
1 cup sifted cake flour
1¼ cups superfine granulated sugar
2 teaspoons vanilla
1 teaspoon cream of tartar
½ teaspoon salt

Preheat the oven to 375 degrees.

Put the egg whites and water in a clean large metal bowl. Sift together the flour and ¼ cup of the sugar into a medium bowl.

Using a standing electric mixer, beat the egg whites on medium speed until frothy. Add the vanilla, cream of tartar, and salt. Increase mixing speed to medium-high and beat just until soft peaks begin to form. Gradually beat in the remaining cup of sugar, 2 tablespoons at a time, occasionally scraping down the sides of the bowl. Increase the speed to high and beat until stiff, glossy peaks form. Sift a third of the flour mixture over the whites. Beat on low speed just until blended. Sift and beat in the remaining flour in two more batches.

Gently pour the batter into an ungreased tube pan and smooth the top. Run a rubber spatula or long knife through the batter to eliminate any large air bubbles.

Bake the cake in the lower third of the oven until the top is golden and a tester comes out clean, about 40 minutes. Remove the cake from the oven and immediately invert the pan over the neck of a bottle. Cool the cake completely, upside down. Turn the pan right side up. Run a long, thin knife around the outer edge of the pan. Remove the outer rim of the pan and run the knife under the bottom of the cake to release. Invert to release the cake from the tube, then invert again onto a serving plate.

All I remember of *Madama Butterfly* are the ornate chandeliers suspended from the ceiling of the opera house, arranged to resemble twinkling constellations in the cobalt black sky. They remain faintly illuminated throughout the performance and hold me enthralled while I speculate on the nature of Oriental food.

After the show, Gram is misty, transported, humming lines of music that I'm sure I've never heard before. "Wasn't it just lovely?" she asks over and over. "Those Orientals are so dainty and refined," she muses. "Like little porcelain dolls with their little shoes and parasols."

I fervently agree to everything. I have no idea what she's talking about. I'm nearly in a panic to get to the Oriental food.

"Did you see?" she asks. "Did you watch what that awful captain did to poor Madame Butterfly? Left her stranded!"

"Yes, Gram."

"Isn't that just typical?"

"Yes, Gram."

"That's what a man will do."

Just a few blocks from Lincoln Center, the Imperial Palace is a massive edifice flanked by twin stone dragons on scrolls, glaring at incoming customers. A man in a red satin jacket opens one of the carved, ten-foot-high doors. He says, "Welcome, Imperial Palace," like someone who has said this a thousand times a day, every day of his life.

We enter and I feel my heart rock against the side of my chest. My hands fall open and the breath catches in my throat. It's a Disney ride of a restaurant, with a soaring ceiling, banners of fabric in fiery colors, hostesses and wait staff crisply turned out in short skirts and tailored jackets with mandarin collars, hair spun into ivory combs. There are cages full of songbirds and a real little waterfall bubbling down from the far wall to run into a circular pool in the floor. I feel light-headed, and a white buzz fills my ears. The air smells gorgeous, like marrow, roasting garlic, and grilled meat. I'd be happy just to stand there drinking in the aroma, openmouthed in the entryway, but one of the angrily efficient hostesses snaps up two menus. "You come now!" she commands, and plunges us into the roaring restaurant.

We're offered seats at a table in the center of the room, which I think is an ideal viewing location. But Gram grumbles about being placed at what she calls a "dames only" table. We're handed padded menus bound in crimson velvet and heavy as blocks of wood. I flip through the many pages, and even though there appear to be no Asian customers in the restaurant, all the meals are listed in both English and Chinese. The menu is a treasure map that takes me on its dotted line over snowy mountains, through hushed trees, past jade lakes. I read about bird's-nest soup, thousand-year-old eggs, fried blowfish tails, jellied pigs' knuckles, batter-fried eels, braised shark fins, dishes named for generals and princes, forgotten cities, and sinewy rivers.

I'm desperate to order the flying monkey soup and house-fried birds' feet, but Gram decides that for our first exposure we should stick with the dishes listed on the first page under the heading "Chef Recommends." She selects wonton soup and egg foo yong for us to share.

Our waiter is a remote, stately man with graying temples who looks out of place among the brisk hostesses and dapper young waiters, their hair sleek as chips of onyx. He bows very slightly, smiles a vacated smile, and recites the specials in a faint voice. His name tag, a bit of jade green plastic surrounded by a scroll, says "Chen"—the only Chen in the sea of Marys and Johns and Roberts walking around here. Gram gives Chen our order, then presses one confidential hand to his jacket forearm.

"We just went to see a won-der-ful performance, all about your people!" Her voice is full and voluptuous, as if she's congratulating him personally on the performance. I look away, my mouth wavy with embarrassment. You never know who Gram is going to talk to or what she's going to say to them. "It was a wonderful show—at the opera house!" she goes on. "Such a spectacle—the little Oriental girl was so dainty and refined."

I study the marble columns in the back of the room, imagining that Chen is now rolling his eyes. There's a pause; then I hear Chen say, "You see Chinese opera?" I'm astonished to hear an electric wire of excitement in his voice. I turn back. All his brusque efficiency has fallen away. He is staring at Gram.

"Yes! You would have loved it," she gushes as if they are old chums. "It was just glorious. The singing, the costumes, the set. Ohhh . . ."

"Yes, Chinese opera very important, very ancient art form. Center of cultural life."

"Oh, I know, I know! It was spec-ta-cu-lar." Gram draws out every syllable. "So sad and meaningful. It was ex-tra-va-gant."

Chen looks as if he will pull a chair right up to the table. He stands but is nearly bent double to speak as closely as he can with Gram. "Where you hear it? Where you hear Chinese opera?"

"Why, it's right down the street," Gram says. "Right at Lincoln Center!"

His eyes follow Gram's gesture as if he could gaze through the walls. "This is venerable art form, this opera. In the Cultural Revolution, opera is the only kind of art we are allowed. Chairman Mao says it is not bourgeois. But I don't care about this, I don't think about politics. Always as a boy, I loved the opera," he says, his voice suddenly so sweetly yearning that it seems too intimate of a confidence.

Gram's cheeks bloom; she looks as if she will rest her head against his chest. She places the flat of her palm at the center of her sternum. "Oh, Chen," she says, "I understand completely, I really truly do. I too have always been a lover of the arts, but when I was married my husband would never have gone to the opera."

I bite my lips, and my neck stiffens with embarrassment. I want to bark at her, *Gram, get a grip!* But she's not paying any attention.

"I think maybe only most sensitive people understand the opera," Chen says. Gram nods mournfully. He and Gram stare at the same point on the floor. I look back and forth between the two of them: *What about the egg foo yong?*

"Only the sorts of people who've really known suffering really appreciate the opera."

"From suffering come the greatest art," Chen says.

"Oh, what a true, true, tragic thought."

I jitter in my seat, swing my legs, yawn like to unhinge my jaw.

Finally, after a moment of charged silence, Chen seems to come to. He abruptly bows and withdraws from our table.

While we wait for our food, Gram leans over and begins chatting with a family of five flaxen-haired boys and their mother. They're hard to avoid since there's barely a hand's width of space between our tables. The mother tells Gram they are visiting from Kentucky, at which point Gram turns, covers her mouth, and murmurs to me that Kentucky was "neutral" in the Civil War. She swivels back and, flapping her hand, goes on to tell them all about our afternoon at what she is now referring to as the "Chinese opera." When she reveals that the opera was *Madama Butterfly,* the family matron, a gentle-eyed woman with tightly permed steel wool hair and wearing a Ma Kettle dress, says to Gram, "Why, darlin', I thought that was a Japanese type of music opera? Maybe even written by an Eyetalian?"

And Gram laughs gaily and says, "Well, yes, I suppose she was supposed to be a sort of Japanese girl. But here in the North, we don't really like to make those sorts of distinctions. We feel it's more polite to call them Or-i-en-tals," she enunciates.

"Oh my, well, y'all don't say!" remarks the flushed matron, fanning at herself a little. Then she redirects the conversation, complaining that she doesn't know how to take all these spices.

The youngest of the five big, round-shouldered sons at the table is hunkered down, holding his plate and using his chopsticks like a snowplow blade to shovel chicken with cashews into his mouth. He gazes at me steadily without slowing his food intake.

"There's a little boyfriend for you," Gram says, elbowing me.

This type of observation from Gram increasingly has the power to make me crazy. "I thought you hated men!" I roar back at her.

She tut-tuts, rolls her eyes, and says, "Oh, for the love of Pete, that's not a man."

Our exchange is preempted by a cool-eyed waiter with military posture and an impassive face holding up a tray crowded with steaming dishes of meats, vegetables, and rice. I scan them wildly, searching for the young pig flesh. Behind him, serene and dashing, is Chen. He stands beside the young waiter and orchestrates the exact placement of each dish on the table, then dismisses him. While the Kentucky family looks on, he crouches between me and Gram and murmurs, "Egg foo yong too plain! Chinese opera lovers need real Chinese food!" He has taken the liberty of switching the egg foo yong for crispy shrimp with almonds and adding a plate of shredded beef in hoisin sauce.

I swell up, proud of my sophisticated tastes, and glance over at the other tables, hoping that some ignoramus has ordered egg foo yong.

Chen shows me how to fit the chopsticks to my fumbling fingers. After a few trembling attempts, I manage to get a small piece of beef to my mouth. I close my eyes and my senses swim in my head. The flavors are so complex and capacious, I don't know how to make sense of them. It's enthralling, the way the dark, sweet sauce clings to a salty bit of meat, the twenty-five shades of flavor secreted in the grilled crust of a shrimp. Who would have thought to bring these ingredients, these ways of thinking about food, together in such startling ways? It's so good that it seems nearly intimate, an impossibility that this unknown chef, a total stranger, would know how to touch all the hidden places in my mouth.

"Yes, yes, yes. . . ." Chen's voice enters my reverie, coaxing and seductive. I open my eyes and he is looking at me. His own eyes are dark glimmerings. "It's good, isn't it," he says. "You taste it, don't you? I see that you taste."

I fumble with the chopsticks, feeling anointed and embarrassed. It is at once too much praise and no praise at all—who doesn't know how to taste food?

But Chen's gaze goes distant again. "The chef here, a very fine, sensitive man—he was one of the cooks for the Chinese emperor." He lowers his eyes. "No more. Now he must cook for people who have no tongues and no noses!"

I concentrate on arranging my chopsticks, wanting to please this displeased man. Something about him—perhaps the failure to find the identical charms and graces of his first culture in this new one; the failure to recognize the new promises of his new country—reminds me of Bud. He's also just as obscure as Bud. Who are these people with "no tongues and no noses"? I mull over the deepening mysteries of the Imperial Palace restaurant.

"Well, all I can say is I wish her big chief father were here," Gram confides to Chen, tipping her chin at me. "That man, he thinks he's the alpha and the omega when it comes to dinner. Fuss, fuss, fuss, nothing's good enough, nothing's right."

"Many men I know this way."

"Only the little onions, the itty-bitty cucumbers, only the meat from *his* butcher," Gram minces. "Only this and that sort of rice. Oh, for the love of Pete, the rice! Only a certain kind of rice, washed, dried, oiled, sprinkled with ground lamb and fancy pine nuts. He spends more time on his rice than women spend on their hair."

Chen glances at me again when Gram mentions the rice. "So you come from cooking," he says. "I thought this when I see you eat."

I lower my chopsticks in confusion, worried that I've broken another rule from Gram's little pink book.

Chen apologizes profusely for the fact that he has a job and bows several times as he backs away, promising to return promptly. But I want only to return to my fumbling chopsticks, to retreat inside the smoky, sensuous dimensions of the food. I close my eyes as I chew. Slowly, I begin to remember something I saw in my parents' encyclopedia set. I love browsing through these books and rely on them for the bulk of my school reports. I start to recall the entry for Japan, reading about some sort of dreadful, protracted trouble . . . with China. I don't recall exactly what, though I dimly recollect something about invasions and atrocities. It occurs to me quite suddenly as I'm sitting there chewing that the Chinese and the Japanese don't think of themselves as the same people at all.

The chunk of tofu and scallions in my mouth begins to turn cold. I swallow with difficulty and eye the generous abundance covering our table. Gram is offering bites to the Kentucky matron, who looks at everything fish-eyed and says, "Now good heavens, what is that?" before she waves it away.

The pleasure begins to leach out of everything. I try to keep eating, but my fog of gratification is dissipating. I'm ashamed, terrified of what the waiter will think if he finds out that we didn't see a Chinese opera at all, but one about their sworn enemies. Anyplace with a thing like an emperor, I think, is a serious place. An emperor is even more than a king—it's like a king and a president mixed together and seated on a mountaintop. I imagine the sad, refined chef who has lost his emperor, imprisoned in his strange new kitchen, hoping that some unknown diner out there will taste his food and the diner's soul will be touched and will vibrate with the tender soul of the chef. This is the food for the emperor, I think, finally putting down my chopsticks.

Gram, however, is still blithely prattling away. She cuts through the food with a fork and knife, sprinkling it with what she is calling "salty sauce." "Oriental men are so dear and lovely," she says, scooping up some beef in its intense hoisin base. "They're really not like men at all."

"That's not a good thing!"

"Oh," she says smugly, "you don't know the half of it, missy."

"What?" I can't stand being told that there's something I need to know. "The half of what?"

"Oh, no, no . . . you're too young for that."

"Tch!" I cross my arms.

She eyes me and then finally says, "You see, there's all sorts of trouble in bed, dear. That whole business is overrated. No, the best sorts of men cook for their women."

My face burns and I am aggravated to be caught off guard by one of Gram's risqué assertions. "So . . . what kind of cooking?" I rest my forearms on the table

She frowns and I remove my elbows: unladylike violation number five. "Any kind—that isn't really the point."

I look at her slyly, surprised at the color in her cheeks and how clear her eyes are. "Chinese food?"

She smiles like a conspirator. "It could be."

"Rice with ground lamb and pine nuts?"

Her smile evaporates. "Oh, for the love of Pete," she says.

When Chen next appears Grams asks for a doggie bag. I cringe with embarrassment, but Chen beams, saying, "Little appetite for little women. And no waste food—that is very good, very good. Americans like to waste food!"

This is, in fact, one of the themes dearest to Gram's heart: the non-wasting of food. Her refrigerator is booby-trapped with a hundred slivers of leftovers, each shrouded in its own piece of plastic wrap and enshrined on the shelves. Gram becomes agitated when anyone rummages in her refrigerator, which she says is her "system." Now she and Chen are glowing at each other. "That's exactly right, Chen," she says primly. "Waste not, want not."

"Oh!" he exclaims. "This is one of the themes of the Chinese opera!"

Gram settles her chin on the heel of her palm meditatively. "Yes, I suppose I can see that . . . in a roundabout way."

"During the war," he says, "there was much starvation. We learn— every grain of rice is precious."

"Exactly," she says, tapping his arm. "Just like during the Great Depression in this country."

I'm annoyed with Gram's claim to understand. I imagine Chen being held prisoner by a Japanese soldier who offers him one grain of rice at a time, balanced on the tip of his flashing sword. I want to signal to Chen that it is I who senses his terrible pain, but instead I just watch mutely, wondering when he will realize that we didn't go to a Chinese opera at all. Gram tips her head back, her features curled up with laughter, and my throat tightens with renewed anxiety. I anticipate our uncovering at any moment. My palms are slick and I can hear my own pulse in my ears, drowning out the sounds of Gram's and Chen's voices as they banter like old friends.

Chen stacks the takeout boxes into an oversize white shopping bag embossed in gold with the Imperial Palace's twin dragons. It is too generous, his expression too full—conveying a kind of heartsickness and solitude that is hard for me to look at directly. Our small connection seems to mean too much to Chen. We simply cannot disappoint him. And this is too much responsibility; I can't imagine getting away with it.

We stand to go, first shaking hands with the Kentucky family, who all stand as if we are visiting dignitaries. The mother smooths her hair and murmurs something about going to see some Oriental opera soon. The round-shouldered son swipes at his mouth, which gleams with chicken fat, and says, "Not me, not either." Gram peaks her eyebrows and says to me, "There, you see that?" as if he's just proved her point.

As Chen escorts us through the churning dining room, one courtly hand barely grazes Gram's elbow as the other fends off the onrushing wait staff. Gram brandishes her white bag before her. I've seen her clear entire tabletops after restaurant meals, sweeping into her shopping bag not only the leftovers but foil-wrapped pats of butter, little tubs of cream, and packets of sugar; she has a special drawer at home crowded with packets of salt. I just want to get out of here before our opera treachery is discovered. As we approach the main entrance and I see streetlights twinkling through the heavy glass doors, my shoulders begin to melt back down and my breathing levels out. It looks as if we may get away with it after all.

My hand is pressed to the good, cold glass of the front door when I feel Gram hanging back, tugging on my arm. I turn to see Chen offering up a woven straw basket filled with fortune cookies. Gram scans them closely, her fingers dangling over first this and then that cookie. I want to cry with frustration: I no longer care about Chinese food or chopsticks or dragons balanced on scrolls. I just want to escape while Chen still believes we are good people.

Gram enthusiastically breaks her cookie into a thousand pieces. "Oh, what does this say? Darling, I left my reading glasses at home." She holds the little paper up to me in a girlish, helpless way.

I turn my full incredulous scowl upon her, an expression I've been perfecting with the encroachment of adolescence. "I can't read it," I say, my voice a dark smear. "It's too small."

Chen gallantly volunteers. He removes a pair of half-glasses from his vest pocket and bends his head toward the tiny slip. His tapering fingers handle the paper so precisely, I imagine that it was a man with just this type of fingers who invented such cookies. Then it occurs to me that this is the kind of thing Gram would think, and I bite the inside of my lip, angry at myself.

Chen reads: "You will travel far and meet mysterious strangers."

Gram dissolves into giggles and swipes a cat paw at his jacket lapel. "Oh, Chen, that must be you!"

"Yes, and for me must be you!" Chen rejoins.

Consigning them to their private little world, I crack open a cookie and read my own fortune. Beside a line of Chinese characters, it says, "No blame."

"Oh, now what does that mean?" I burst out bitterly.

Another staff person looks up. He is roughly the same age as Chen, but his uniform is bright red and covered with shining buttons like a military commander's. It's the man who held the door open for us when we first arrived. Chen notices the other man and gestures. "Old Lee, come here," he says. "Old Lee from my village back home," he confides to Gram.

All my hopes for escape wither inside me. I stare miserably at the door—just an arm's length away. It might as well be on the moon.

Chen says something to Old Lee, and the man regards us skeptically. It won't be as easy to dupe Old Lee as it is to fool Chen. Chen turns back to us. "Old Lee in this country thirty-five years. But when he got old, he forget all his English!"

This sounds exactly like the sort of thing Bud would do. Chen tells him something in Chinese that makes Old Lee's eyes open and his forehead lift, and I know that Chen has made his big revelation about us and the Chinese opera. Then Old Lee says something and Chen turns back to us with the question that I've been waiting to hear all night, the most obvious question in the world: "Old Lee want to know, which opera?"

I spear my eyes at Gram and try harder than I've ever tried before in my life to communicate telepathically: *Tell him you can't remember! Tell him it was the "old favorite"! Tell him it's our little secret!*

Gram, of course, just smiles and says, "Well, it was *Madama Butterfly.*"

I glare at my shoes and wonder why I have the great misfortune to be standing here, in this place, at this time, having this conversation. I envy everyone who is not me, including those stone-headed dragons on the steps outside. I wait for Old Lee to begin roaring with indignation, brace myself for the looked of crushed betrayal in Chen's eyes. Instead, both of them smile blankly. "*Madam-u-Butter-fry-u,*" he says to Old Lee, who echoes the same words. "Never hear of that one."

I laugh a tiny, crazy laugh.

Chen smiles at me as if we are in on the joke together. He points at his friend. "Old Lee know all the operas, all the theater and arts. When Old Lee was young he teach ancient rituals back in China. He teach tea ceremony—Chinese and Japanese styles. But Chairman Mao gang say he's intelligentsia and throw him in prison. For twenty years, more, he practices the ceremony in prison every day, though he has only water and rice and broken plates."

Old Lee bows and says something. Chen nods. "Old Lee says Japanese tea style more refined, but no matter. Young people today know nothing about anything."

At which point Old Lee bows to me as if he's just paid me a huge compliment. Then he takes the fortune cookie slips and reads the Chinese aloud. He laughs and says something to Chen, who also laughs.

"What's so funny?" I ask irritably.

Chen recovers and says, "Old Lee say this mean everything taste good if you hungry enough."

I frown, confused, and crunch on a piece of fortune cookie. I wonder if a second fortune will cancel out the first one.

"Also it mean there is the right man for every woman." I look up and see that Chen is looking at Gram. His expression is subtle, sideways, and beckoning. Gram lowers her eyelashes and smiles.

"How could it mean two different things?" I protest.

"Does not matter," Chen says. "Still true."

I blink at the two of them, and a dizzy warmth spreads over me. My knees tremble, my ankles go weak, and a winged thrumming fills the air. If we don't leave now, I think, I may never get out of here. I clutch the front of my seal coat tightly, as if it will keep me upright. Old Lee murmurs something to Chen, who looks at me quizzically, then turns to Gram and says, "We think little girl doesn't feel well."

Gram looks at me, startled, "Oh, you're flushed, darling! Well, we really better go—it's past your bedtime." She flashes Chen a sweet, rueful smile. "We will come back and visit again soon."

He bows deeply, then straightens, his eyes glistening, his lips pressed together. I hold the door open for Gram. Just as I'm about to follow her out, Chen touches my fur coat so gently that it is nearly imperceptible: I think he is admiring it. "The rice," he says, "is of highest importance."

On the bus ride back, I sink into the warm nest of our coats and the sound of Gram humming the unfamiliar music of *Madama Butterfly*. As I drift off, I hear Gram saying, "Isn't Oriental food wonderful?"

For years after that, Gram will ask if I want to go to dinner at the Imperial Palace. I always refuse, saying that place is for tourists, their food is too salty, too bland, overcooked. "It's typical fake Chinese," I say, "I only like the real thing." And we never visit the Imperial Palace again.

GRAM'S EASY ROAST BEEF
When you want something good to eat
but don't want to spend very much time preparing it.

4- to 6-pound round   Salt and freshly ground
  roast   pepper

Preheat the oven to 350 degrees.

Put the roast, fat side up, on a metal rack in a roasting pan and sprinkle with salt and pepper.

Add about ¼ inch water to the bottom of the pan and place it in the middle of the oven. Roast the meat for about 1 hour. Meat thermometers come in handy for checking doneness.

Let the roast stand for 10 minutes before slicing. Serve with a nice button mushroom gravy and buttered parsley potatoes.

SERVES 6 TO 8.

SIX

Mixed Grill in the Snow

Thanksgiving belongs to our house, Christmas to Uncle Hal and Auntie Rachel's, which leaves the annual mystery of where to go on New Year's Eve. The children are indifferent to this grown-up holiday. It's elusive. When I'm ten, Mom and Bud give me, Suzy, and Monica paper cups with sloshes of champagne and ginger ale. I solemnly take the fizzing cup and sense that I am entering into an adult region. Then I taste the cocktail and recoil. It is a mockery of perfectly good ginger ale. That is all that the holiday amounts to that year. The following year, for certain ineffable reasons, my parents decide we should do something. We'll be going back to Uncle Hal's house in Oswego, where my sisters and I, along with my cousins, will be allowed to stay up all night long. When I hear this announcement, I run around the house three times without stopping, electrified with excitement.

After the adrenaline subsides, I ask my mother to explain for the hundredth time what New Year's is supposed to be about. It doesn't have any of the colorful characters, like Santa Claus or the Easter Bunny, to let you in on how it all works. Mom talks about the world's birthday and the passage of years.

"Does it matter?" I ask nervously.

"Does what matter?"

"Does it matter that the world is getting so old?" Lately I've been preoccupied with the elderly people I see on city buses. It's not entirely clear to me how people get this way, but I suspect that we must all somehow choose what we are: Some people choose to be children, others choose to be old. But why would anyone make such a choice?

Mom compresses her lips. I am frequently a bafflement to her. "Hon, the world isn't really getting old, not in that sense of the word."

"But you just said!"

She rubs her temples. Bud says, "Never mind about that. New Year's is what happens when the famous explorer Ibn Battuta makes his journey around the earth again and everyone celebrates by having a picnic in the winter."

A picnic in the winter! This is an enigma that preoccupies me for days, overshadowing even Christmas. I lie awake at night, jittery with anticipation, and in the morning I wake from dreams of long picnic tables set with plates full of snow and sunlight, my jaw moving and my tongue curled up with pleasure.

Uncle Hal's house is thirty miles northwest of us, beside Lake Ontario. On this particular New Year's Eve, we have to drive through a dense, ghostly blizzard that has started early in the day and just keeps going. We wait to see if it will settle down, and around four in the afternoon there seems to be a lull, the wind falling. But by the time we get three miles down the highway, it turns to pure night and the wind returns, driving snow sideways over the road, then whipping it into solid tunnels, the flakes blurring up over the car's windshield so there is nothing to see but this spinning-open of whiteness. We roll down the windows and try to look out, but the whole world is perfectly draped in white. We hear on the radio that they've closed the highway behind us. The wind nudges at our car's front end and we drive slower and slower.

For a child in the close captivity of her parents' car, there is nothing to do in a nighttime lake-effect storm in upstate New York but let go. Let the snow take you into its breathing body, feel the subtle, fish-soft slips and slides of the car in motion, sense the wobbling moments before all that machinery threatens to skid and fly away.

In the backseat, Monica, Suzy, and I hold tight to an oversize silver tray as if it is another steering wheel. It's a glorious, ceremonial thing, decorated with scrolls and flourishes and outfitted with four little flat feet, purchased in Jordan and transported to America in its own slender suitcase. It is the finest, most auspicious setting for my aunt Rachel's fabulous *knaffea* pastry. Its weight and heft holds me down and reassures me. It feels like the true center of gravity of the universe.

Eventually the snow trance breaks like a fever and the long, glowing highway tapers into plowed roads at the edge of the town. Uncle Hal and his family live in a rural area that piles plowed heaps of snow ten feet high on either side of the street. We pull up to his house, jelly legged and faint of heart, the iced-over driveway creaking beneath our feet. My sisters and I lug the tray out of the car. Uncle Hal stands in the driveway to greet us. He waves tongs in one hand. Uncle Hal has set up his big kettledrum grill outside, under the icicle eaves of the house. The grill sends a stream of smoke up into the cold-bitten sky. This may well be the greatest meal of all time—ground *kofta* kabobs, shish kabob, beef ribs, and vegetables—all grilled outdoors during a snowstorm.

My parents shake the snow out of their hair and laugh. "What is the point of this?" Bud asks. With a sweep of arms, he's indicating not only the grill, but the snow, the cold, celebrating New Year's Eve, the alien lunar landscape.

"I don't know, brother," Uncle Hal says. "I do not know."

"Look at us! What are we doing?" Bud's black hair is now white and feathery with snow. "What is this, the North Pole? We're crazy to live here. This place isn't made for people to live."

"Ours is not to reason why," Uncle Hal says, turning pieces of chicken and squirting the coals with extra lighter fluid for good measure. He holds up a leg with his tongs and admires it. "You see this chicken leg? This chicken leg contains the wonders of the world and the seven heavens. Someday I will write a poem about this chicken leg."

The charred, winy aroma mingles with the sparkling flecks in the air. Uncle Hal grills a row of sheeshes, then stacks them on platters, and the children carry their own plates to the kitchen table. The adults sit away from the children in the dining room, which frees us to eat as wantonly and barbarically as possible. Ed illustrates how he can fill his entire mouth with roasted zucchini. The juices stain our lips, and we slump and make loud caveman groans as we chew. We use pieces of bread to push the meat and fire-scorched vegetables from the skewers onto a big communal platter—or right into our mouths.

The world seems exciting and strange tonight, the well-deep blackness in the window full of tracery, translucent clouds swimming over the moon. After we finish eating, I lean forward and mutter, "Well, I sure hope you appreciate that we're here tonight."

My cousins stare at me, waiting for the joke.

"Yeah, well, you know what? We were all nearly slaughtered to-night driving around out there."

Monica and Suzy exchange bright, startled glances.

"Oh yeah?" Cousin Jess grins broadly. "So what happened?"

I shrug lazily and eat a morsel of lamb *kofta*. "Oh, there's some sort of psycho killer who just escaped from prison, and he's out there driving around in the storm in an old beat-up black car, running people off the road and cutting them into little pieces." I hold up another chunk of lamb *kofta* between my thumb and forefinger. "About this big, I think. They say his teeth are pure gold. We heard about it on the radio. That's the real reason they closed the roads. Since we're staying up all night, of course, we're probably going to run into him at some point, and then God only knows!"

At this point, five-year-old Monica runs wailing to our mother in the other room. I grab my forehead. I have no idea where that story came from or what moved me to tell it, and now I realize it might have been better if I hadn't. Gram says that I'm a hostage of my imagina-tion. I have trouble teasing apart the worlds of dreams and reality. When I was eight some neighborhood kids told me that their mother wouldn't allow them to talk to me until I stopped fibbing. I'd been terrorizing them with a daily serialized tale about my work as an undercover agent combating a race of half sheep–half men from Venus. Then they'd be up half the night, howling at every creak in the house.

A familiar voice flares in the kitchen doorway, saying, "You are such a big noodlehead, Diana." It's our cousin Hanna, her American mother, Jean, and Hanna's tiny, mummified father, Abdelhafiz; they live down the street from Uncle Hal and specialize in dinnertime visits. Hanna and Jean are both heaped up with masses of flesh the color and sheen of cottage cheese. The corners of their mouths slant sharply downward, and their hair falls in glossy black ringlets around their faces so they resemble angry Kewpie dolls. Their every glance emanates an air of disapproval. Hanna drags my tearstained sister back into the kitchen, holding her by the wrist. "What sort of idiot tells her little baby sister that there's a psycho killer on the loose?"

"I don't know," I say sullenly.

Aunt Jean says, "Tch," and waves her hand at us as if to make us all evaporate. She goes off with her husband to join the adults, and Hanna plunks down at our table and pulls the platter of meat under her chin. "What're you morons eating?" She stuffs some *kofta* in her mouth and grunts. "Ugh, overcooked!"

Hanna is only fifteen, just two years older than Jess, but she refers to us as "the kids" and is forever lecturing us on how none of us will ever amount to anything. Hanna frequently informs people that she plans to attend Swarthmore, the college that her mother's second cousin attended, which she holds up as the pinnacle of education. She also likes to tell us that in all likelihood none of us juvenile delinquents will ever make it to college at all at the rate we're going. Even Monica looks annoyed with her. Our hour of eating barbarically is over. It's practically midnight.

BARBARIC LAMB *KOFTA*

This is at its most wonderful when barbecued over an outdoor grill.
Not necessarily at the stroke of midnight,
but it adds a certain something.

1 pound ground lamb
1 egg, lightly beaten
1 onion, finely chopped

2 tablespoons chopped
  flat-leaf parsley
½ teaspoon ground cinnamon

1 teaspoon ground cumin	½ teaspoon ground allspice
1 teaspoon chili powder	Salt and freshly ground
2 teaspoons turmeric	pepper

Mix together all the ingredients with your hands until evenly blended. Shape ¼ cup of the lamb mixture around a skewer in an elongated (3- to 4-inch) sausage shape along the length of a skewer. Repeat with the remaining mixture.

Grill the *kofta* over hot coals, turning, for about 5 minutes on each side.

Serve with yogurt blended with 1 teaspoon lemon juice and 1 crushed garlic clove.

SERVES 4.

After dinner, we watch Dick Clark and the ball about to drop in New York City. The moment feels laden with mystery and tension, as if for one second the world has agreed to pay attention to time itself. All the ghostly faces and Victorian figures in the old oil paints that line my uncle's walls stare at the big, boxy TV. All the books and Persian carpets and even the old piano hold their breath. Finally, absurdly slowly, the big ball slides down its pole. My birthday is close to New Year's Eve, and I was born on the cusp of a new decade, so when the year turns, I feel that I have aged along with the earth. I am newly eleven, but I am ancient. The lingering scent and smoke of the grill fixes the moment inside of me.

My parents, aunts and uncles, and Hanna all hug and kiss one another, and the children squirm away. My father and uncles exchange a look: another year that they've lost to their new country. Then the men groan and bend and collapse backward on the couch. From there they launch into one of their favorite pastimes—complaining.

My father, looking older than usual, drapes one wilted arm over the edge of the couch. Is there gray at his temples? He sighs, squinting at the TV, and holds up one tragic hand. "Who is this man, this Dick Clark?"

"I don't know," Uncle Hal says in an equally hollow voice. "I just don't know."

"Too many times I think we'll never get home again," Great-Uncle Abdelhafiz says. "It's like we've gone *poof*." He looks around the room unblinking, as if he isn't sure he's really there. Tiny Uncle Abdelhafiz has skin the color and grain of petrified wood and liquid, glimmering eyes. His mother was one of my great-grandfather's two simultaneous African wives, and I often have the sense when looking at him that he wishes he could somehow escape from these two bossy women in charge of him and go back to Senegal.

"So many people disappear," Bud comments dolefully.

"What about Danny Thomas?" Uncle Hal asks. "What happened to him?"

"Dead," Uncle Abdelhafiz says. "Nice Lebanese boy."

"Never mind about Danny Thomas, look what happened to your whole family! Look at young cousin Farouq, Great-Uncle Ziad, Auntie Seena, and Jimmy's son Jalal," Aunt Jean cuts in disapprovingly.

"Dead, dead, dead, and in jail," Uncle Hal says, dusting off his hands. "The police wanted me to come bail Jimmy's kid out last week, for the third time this year. I said, 'You guys take him for a while.'"

"He'll never amount to anything," Hanna puts in, easing her head back on her round neck in a bored, luxurious way. "No future, no nothing." She rotates her head to view the children. "Most of these Abu-Jabers can't survive this country. It's too much for them. They've got to have discipline, they've got to be watched every second. You should ship them all back!" she says with a regal fling of her hand.

Uncle Abdelhafiz stares at his wife and daughter for a few moments as if he cannot, for the life of him, recollect who they are. "*I want to go home*," he says in a voice like an echo.

Uncle Hal clicks his head back, chin up. "What home? Show it to me. You're planning to go home? Just listen to this poem I wrote yesterday on this very subject." He squares his shoulders and intones:

"Lo, the days of yore / When life was full / The sun was hot / And things were not / Such a bore. . . ."

Bud sits with his arms crossed and his eyes closed, nodding in solemn agreement. He opens his eyes to see the children bunched up on the couch across from them. "Americans," he mutters. "We're surrounded by Americans."

Their drowsy, hypnotic complaints go on and on. My mod green plastic wristwatch reports it's a disappointing one a.m.

Mom flees the room of complaints in order to prepare the dessert. She and Aunt Rachel turn the oven up to full blast—*knaffea* should be served piping hot. Then they try to clear a bigger space on the kitchen table for the immense silver tray. This is challenging because for the past twenty or thirty years, Aunt Rachel has been writing something called "the great American novel." It towers in great foot-high stacks of manuscript pages all over the table and the floor around the table, so if you eat there, you've got to put your plate on a pile of pages. Mom says that Rachel won't let anyone read it until she's done, so it has assumed an air of mystery. When you look closer, though, it turns out that the pages are mostly typed correspondence she sends to various newspaper editors sharing her insights, opinions, and idle ruminations on the issues of the day. There is a letter on top of one stack concerning the sorry state of the geopolitics of Southeast Asia.

Hanna and Jean walk around the stacks of pages with their faces tight and their hands drawn in. "I see you're still working on that book of yours, Rachel," Aunt Jean says. "Still the same one, right?"

This comment is bothersome and nasty, like a hairy sweater. Auntie Rachel barely seems to hear it, though; her mind is on higher things. She is wonderful to discuss life and literature with. She tells me that Samuel Beckett was a gangster and Joyce a pervert and that no one can really enjoy Henry James until they're forty-five. She says that Flannery O'Connor is a mad genius, Hemingway is much better than you'd think, and two years of college is almost enough to civilize most people. She's against suicide but has observed that, in contrast, murder makes sense. She says that dinner is a moral imperative and dessert is its own reward.

One time she shows me a novel by a popular writer and tells me that he's a big, bald-faced liar.

"But—I thought that he wrote fiction," I say, confused by the literary distinctions.

"The difference between fiction and lying," she says irritably, "is the difference between imagination and laziness."

She tells me all sorts of things and never seems to notice that she's talking to an eleven-year-old. I am passionately devoted to her.

Aunt Rachel removes the *knaffea* from the oven and places it on its sumptuous tray; the shredded phyllo dough is crisp and brown, crackling with hot, rose-scented syrup. Nestled within, like a naughty secret, is the melting layer of sweet cheese. The pastry is freshly hot, the only way to eat it, really, with its miraculous study in contrasts— the running cheese hidden within crisp, crackling layers of baked phyllo and the distinctive, brocaded complexities of flavors. It's so hot that it steams in your mouth, and at first you eat it with just the tips of your teeth. Then the layers of crisp and sweet and soft intermingle, a series of surprises. It is so rich and dense that you can eat only a little bit, and then it is over and the *knaffea* is just a pleasant memory—like a lovely dream that you forget a few seconds after you wake. But for a few seconds, you knew you were eating *knaffea.*

Aunt Rachel, an American like my mother, learned to make *knaffea* as a young bride during her correspondence with her husband's Palestinian mother, Anissa. My grandmother was said to have been intellectual and bookish, as well as an expert maker of *knaffea* and other pastries. When Anissa was made to leave her home in Jerusalem and went to live with my Jordanian-Bedouin grandfather in his remote desert place, she dreamed up a new home for herself in her books. My father, who never took to formal education himself, looked upon his mother's library as a pilgrim might have looked upon the icons in a cathedral. He knew this was something to revere. And years later, Aunt Rachel, who never really took to cooking, looked upon Anissa's recipes in much the same way.

My grandmother was only forty-eight when she died, not long before my mother married Bud. She had borne innumerable children—some say seventeen, some say only nine. She died while most of her sons were far away in America, before they had a chance to see her once more. Now the *knaffea* calms Bud and Uncle Hal down. It makes them remember their mother, and they forget again about being surrounded by Americans.

Uncle Hal goes back to the living room, gets out his one-stringed *rebab* and bow, and sits on the couch beside Bud, drawing forth the *rebab*'s rickety, stirring music. Together, they sing "Ridi Ha" in their soulful voices. The brothers lean against each other, gaze at the ceiling, and sing as if the song has been written just for them, a song for the time between late night and early morning, when life is filled with uncertainties and boundaries have gone blurry.

In the kitchen, Hanna and Jean ignore the music; they are holding their plates and forks in midair. They look disoriented and out of sorts. Hanna, who has just taken a bite, bleats at her mother, "But your *knaffea* isn't this good!" as if she has duped her.

Jean's features seem to elongate; she stares at her fork. Finally she sniffs, "I think it's too sweet." I look away, embarrassed for her—we all know that's a lie. Then she adds, "I suppose this is why you'll never finish your book, Rachel. You spend your time fooling around in the kitchen."

And then the room is holding its breath. The night expands and the kitchen ceiling lifts and the taste of the *knaffea* lingers in memory like a musical phrase. Like the wounded look in my auntie's eyes. The moment passes quickly, so almost no one sees what has occurred, neither the suspended moment of time nor the hurtful exchange at the kitchen table. There is a nearly imperceptible quickening in the atmosphere. But then my mother stands beside Rachel protectively, gathering dishes with a deliberate rattle; a cool efficiency settles over us like a compress.

MAD GENIUS *KNAFFEA*

1 pound *knaffea kadayif* dough,* thawed

2 cups butter, melted and clarified

1 pound *alawi*,† finely chopped

4 cups sugar

2 cups water

2 teaspoons lemon juice or 1 teaspoon rosewater or orange blossom water (see page 58)

Preheat the oven to 400 degrees. In a mixing bowl, cut and fluff ½ pound of the *knaffea* dough with your hands. Add half of the melted butter and mix until the dough strands are evenly coated. Spread evenly in lightly buttered 17 × 13-inch baking pan.

Spread *alawi* over the *kadayif* in the pan.

Cut and fluff the remaining ½ pound *knaffea* dough in the bowl. Add the remaining melted butter and mix with your hands until the strands are evenly coated. Spread the dough over the top of the cheese layer, pressing down firmly to form an even surface. Place on the lowest oven rack and bake until golden, about 30 minutes.

Meanwhile, prepare the syrup. Combine the sugar and water in a pan and boil for about 10 minutes. Take the pan off the heat and add the lemon juice, rosewater, or orange blossom water. Refrigerate while the *knaffea* is baking. As soon as the *knaffea* is removed from the oven, pour the cold syrup evenly over the pastry. Cut into squares to serve.

MAKES 24 TO 30 SERVINGS.

*Kadayif dough is a kind of shredded phyllo dough, similar in spirit to shredded wheat; it is available in specialty food stores.

†*Alawi* is a mild sweet cheese available in import food stores.

My eyeballs feel dry and tight, as if they are stuck in the wrong sockets. I turn to Jess. "I don't feel tired yet at all," I say, wired. "Do you?"

Her eyes look slotted. "Ha. I'm wide awake."

Monica is asleep with her head on the kitchen table. Suzy is sternly watching Aunt Jean as if she will be making out a report on her later.

Aunt Rachel's rooster clock on the wall above the stove holds its drumsticks up over its head. I stare out the window at the blue-smeared stars; I think, This is what two in the morning looks like on the North Pole.

The children who are still awake leave the grown-ups to their past. We retire to the library, sling skinny arms around each other's necks, and instigate several hundred more rounds of "Auld Lang Syne"—each of us with his or her own unique interpretation—until Hanna comes in and says we sound like a bunch of demented gorillas, then goes back out. We discuss this and decide that we'll sound better with musical accompaniment. Ignoring the prim upright piano backed against the wall, we rummage through the kitchen cupboards for pots and pans and large, club-size spoons. We pound the pots in time with our song and make such a fierce racket that the adults yell and grab their heads and suggest that it's time to take it outside. So we pull on our jackets and mittens and boots. We run past Hanna, who folds her arms over her chest and says, "Thank God! You were giving me a headache," just like someone's mother.

Outside, the night air is still filled with snow, though now it hangs above the earth in a sparkling curtain. Our breath curls in thick white rings from our mouths and we march in circles, banging on saucepans and hollering a hillbilly version of "Auld Lang Syne."

Besides us, there is no one and nothing outside. Just a few windows still gleam with light on the lonely country lane. The snow starts to thicken again; it turns the night a pale burgundy color. Our thin, chill-stripped voices rise and quaver together, throats raw from the cold and shouting, lost in the blanketing layers of air. The stars snap at us, and I can look and look until it feels as if I'm falling up and out into the whirling snow, dissolving into sky. Then I glance back at the house and see Hanna framed by the kitchen window. She stands close enough to the glass that her breath makes a circle of steam. Her palms float on the window like two pink starfish.

"What a grown-up," Jess hisses in my ear.

Two months from now, we will learn that Hanna is pregnant and has run away with her high school sweetheart, leaving behind a room full of rag dolls and drawings of horses and a single application to Swarthmore College, still in its original envelope. Aunt Jean will be bedridden with fury, her skin glowing and damp. She will shower Uncle Abdelhafiz with wild, inventive curses that impress both Bud and Uncle Hal and demand that he hunt them down and bring back the girl. Privately, Uncle Abdelhafiz will tell my father it is too too too late. "She left forever ago." And privately, Bud will muse that Abdelhafiz appears to be almost relieved about it all.

But on this night, plush with snow and a tropical darkness, we don't know anything.

Hanna waves, and I pretend not to see her.

It is so late, it has snowed us into a dream. A thin wind whistles through the fluff trim on my hood. I turn around and lift my arms to steady myself.

From out of the muffled, snow-packed blackness, a single ancient car comes grumbling toward us.

"What is that?" Jess asks in a puff of steam. "I thought the roads were closed."

We are all standing and blinking. No one says anything, but everyone glances at me.

"Maybe we should go in," Ed murmurs.

I gape at the encroaching black form. Did I summon this? A line of glacial sweat rises on the back of my neck. "No, wait—keep singing— don't look at him!" I murmur, thrilled and only a little bit frightened, half believing that I invented this, the unknown man who comes from the dark.

The car slows and then crawls beside us as we march along the side of the road. My clanging pot and straining voice are not enough to cover the thumping in my chest. The driver rolls down his window then, but he doesn't speak and I can't quite bring myself to look at him. All I see from the corner of my eye is a sharp form bent over a steering wheel. I think I can hear the tinny, canned sound of his car radio turned low, but this seems too sentimental a sound for a killer, so I ignore the radio and the astringent tang of alcohol wafting from his windows. We continue like this—singing and marching, the car rolling—for a few long minutes. Then the window goes up and he pulls away.

Jess whirls back. "Did you see that?" Her eyes are lit with exhilaration.

My breath lunges in and out of me as if I'd been running through the snowfields. We stand and watch in a pious silence as the car dissolves into the churning snow.

Suddenly we notice that the air has gotten too cold to breathe and our eyes are sugared over with frost. Ed proposes another round of marching, but Suzy starts to drift toward the house and I follow her. One by one, we stomp up the stairs and drop our thawing mittens and boots, gloves and hats, jackets and scarves all over the bathroom floor. From far away, rising from hidden rooms, we hear the adults' voices, laughing and languorous as an ancient river. My cousins, sisters, and I crawl onto my aunt and uncle's vast, perfumed bed, lay our heads on the bottomless pillows, and surrender.

Beyond the windows above the bed, the American night glows with the cold, with the shininess of time and its passage. The dawn is still hours away.

SEVEN

Magloubeh *and the Great Diplomat*

The cousins are coming over! Also various aunties, uncles, maybe some surprise friends, and all I know is we've got to get the house ready. *Yella, yella, yella, imshee.* That means "Let's go!" Uncle Hal always arrives early. We've got to vacuum, straighten up, run around. The refrigerator is already open, which means make the *mezza! Mezza* is appetizers, noshes, little snacks beforehand. It's roasted peanuts in the bowls, sliced cucumbers and tomatoes sprinkled with coarse salt. Sliced salty white cheese and seeded, braided cheese broken into long, loopy pieces. Hummus is whipped in the blender, then decanted with a dash of olive oil across the top. Loaves of Arabic bread. A bowl of olives.

They arrive like mad. Everyone's in the living room and kitchen and everywhere, drinking, crazy laughing, and the air has turned Arabic, a few degrees warmer. And, oh no, the air smells of eggplant and cauliflower, it's *magloubeh*—a dish of rice, meat, and vegetables. I am devastated when I smell it. This is, officially, my most dreaded of all meals in the world. Bud fries the slices of cauliflower so they release a strong, vaguely burnt, bitter scent. The limp slices are then laid out on paper towels to absorb the grassy, fried olive oil. Whenever that smell soaks the air, I know I'll come downstairs to see my father forking up the spitting-hot slices of vegetables, and I'll walk away from this scene feeling martyred and at the mercy of the terrible, sulfur-smoky cauliflower, the bitter, unrewarding eggplant. I used to hate *magloubeh*, but Gram instructed me to never say "hate," so I don't much care for it instead.

I say to Bud, as I always do, knowing beforehand that there's no point to saying anything, "You know, I don't care for *magloubeh*. *At all.*"

He nods without looking at me and starts singing a jaunty jingle, "She doesn't care about *magloubeh*! Oh, she doesn't care about *magloubeh*!"

I walk back out. A stake through my heart.

"START THE PARTY" HUMMUS

1 can (15 ounces) chickpeas	½ cup tahini
2 tablespoons olive oil	½ teaspoon paprika
Juice of 2 lemons	Salt to taste
3 cloves garlic	

Puree all the ingredients to a thick, creamy consistency. Adjust texture by adding small amounts of water.

Serve in a wide, flat bowl with a streak of olive oil on top, along with a basket of warm pita bread for dipping. Black olives, sliced tomatoes, or radishes make a nice dippable garnish.

The room gets crowded and the noise gets louder. Sometimes there's the TV carrying on in the background because there's a war going on. It's America and Vietnam, and the family can't stop watching it. The uncles and cousins want to understand what kind of country this is that they're trying to make lives in.

Our special guest star, Uncle Jack, appears. Uncle Jack is usually arriving from someplace else. He's a teaching fellow at Cornell, but he works in *politics*, as the family says in a hushed, respectful way. He will grow up to be a member of the king's cabinet, one of the drafters of the famously hopeful or unhopeful (depending on who's asked) peace accords between Palestine and Israel, a global diplomat interviewed regularly on the evening news. He's lived in Tennessee with a pet spider monkey, he has traveled all over the world, and he knows how to whittle tiny goggle-eyed animals out of tree limbs with his penknife. Once, he said, he was driving through the desert and a bullet shot through one of his windows and out the other, hissing just past his chin. He just kept driving. Gram says that he is an "instigator" and troublemaker because he's smart and also because he's "bent that way." I know she likes him because when his name comes up, she'll crack a sneaky, slanted grin and call him "the great diplomat" in a way that makes me think she doesn't think he's all that great. She says he thinks he has all the answers. She says, "That man wants to make peace? That man is the exact opposite of peace." He's sitting on the couch with his "tic," the tic that makes it look as if he's winking at you, until you wink back and he says, "No, that's just my tic." Then he goes on winking. He says something provocative about Uncle Jimmy, attributes it to Uncle Hal, and then sits back while Uncle Jimmy and Uncle Hal jump into a fight.

My father is standing in the living room because any second now they're all going to start fighting and that is one of Bud's specialties. Their voices press together and climb, and the argument starts. What is it about? I only half understand. Even though it's just been a year or two since we've returned to America, it's already too long away from Arabic. English is clear as a glass mirror, and Arabic is the silver inside the glass—hidden and essential. The languages show me different things. I hear words I know by heart—war, soldiers, the English, the Israelis, and more, words like *mishakkel*: problems, craziness, turmoil. The voices grow louder, they leap into flames. My father, my uncle, and my adult cousins are all shouting as loud as they can. I can see the pulse in my father's throat.

My father is vivid and dashing; he has an imposing black mustache and a happy, wild look on his face. I wonder if he misses the excitement of his military life, his teenage life of before America. I've seen photographs of him flexing his muscles, standing rigid on looming desert rocks. In America, he has handguns and fanciful silver daggers that he keeps tucked into cases, hidden in secret spots. There is a blue dagger tattooed on his biceps. There are no uniforms or jets for him anymore, and the only war is the one on TV in the living room. He's not an instigator like Uncle Jack or a shrewd businessman like Uncle Danny; he's too earnest, too literal, and too excitable. He cares far too much about everything; he believes in huge, impossible things like fairness, honor, and respect. It will take him years and years to learn how to laugh at himself.

The voices have filled the house, leaping and crackling like a forest fire. They will consume the furniture, the house, the air itself, until it's all burned away, smoldering cinders and just a scorch mark on the ground. Some of my older uncles settle back on the couches, resting, meditatively sipping their drinks. But then some of my young-men cousins sit forward, brows furrowed, elbows on knees, and the argument surges back to life.

"The problem," Cousin Yahia grumbles, "is the damn British. If the damn British hadn't come in and turned the natural order of everything around in all these countries, then things would run better." Cousin Yahia is a graduate student in postcolonial studies at Syracuse University, and he has a great deal to say much of the time.

"Oh, really," says Uncle Jack in his snappy, quick-witted voice. "And just what sort of 'natural order' would you be referring to? The natural order where everyone drives like a maniac and shoots off guns at parties? Why, just the other day, Ghassan was telling me how much he loves his gun!"

Bud sits up. "When did I say that?" He looks alert and confused. "There's nothing wrong with guns!" he declares.

"You see that?" says Uncle Jack "This is what I'm talking about. This is why there will never be real democracy in the Middle East."

"The damn British are the ones who sold us all the guns in the first place," says Uncle Danny.

"I got my gun from my father!" declares Bud.

"The damn British will give you a gun, and while you're standing around shooting it off, they'll be taking over your house and selling it to the neighbors. If that's democracy, then they can keep their damn democracy," says Cousin Yahia.

"Okay, but actually that's not democracy," Cousin Hayder comments.

"Nobody gets my house!" Bud hollers. His face tightens and glows. He looks wild and frightening, but when I sit up in alarm he smiles and says, "Go wash your hands, Ya Ba, dinner's ready."

They call this dish *magloubeh,* which means "upside down," because of the way you invert the pot, so the layers of rice, onions, eggplant, cauliflower, and lamb are all reversed from their positions in the pot. Some cooks make it so the ingredients slip out neat as an upside-down cake, like a terrine or timbale.

Magloubeh is one of the dishes that people think might actually have originated somewhere within the region of Jordan. Before Jordan was created in around 1921 by the French and British and an assorted tribunal of other European men who liked to say they owned it, it was loosely and unattractively called Transjordan. It also had other names and owners before that. There were Assyrians, Nabataeans, Romans, Alexander the so-called Great, Persians, Jews, Christians, Muslims, Crusaders, Mamluks, Turks . . . you can't imagine the comings and goings! All of them stomping over the broadbrowed Jordan Valley and announcing: *This is mine.* But Bud says through all those name changes and political deals and horse trading, there was always this same bunch of Bedouins living there in their goat-hair tents with their wars and their loud arguments and their big mustaches and their music and their prayers and their night stars over the white desert floor and their big pots of upside down.

In the dining room, the fight simmers on even after dinner has appeared on its steaming tray. "In this country, the Arabs are seen only through the lens of politics," Cousin Yahia complains. "The TV says we're oil sheikhs or fundamentalists or terrorists or all three at once. It's all stereotypes! We have no charm or texture! When do we get to have homes and parties and jokes and children? We need a strong, national identity! We're held hostage by ideology, by things like Hollywood and politics and Palestine."

"Just like now this dinner party is being held hostage by Yahia's speech," Uncle Jack says.

Cousin Yahia sits sulking in his straight-backed chair. Last year, his parents, who lived in Jerusalem, vacationed in Jordan for a month and returned to find their home had been requisitioned by a family of Israeli settlers. I hear the same words around the table all the time, rising out of the Arabic: *Engleesee, Amerkee, Israeelee*.

When Uncle Jack sees the *magloubeh,* he laughs and says, "Here it is, our national identity!" He stands and says to Yahia, "You want the Arabs to transcend politics? Then pay a little attention to the culture." He salutes the *magloubeh* and starts singing, "My country, 'tis of thee." Gram slaps the table, stands up, huffs something about no respect, and leaves the room. But the children join in the singing because, well, we know the words. I put my hand over my heart the way the nuns taught me to do for the Pledge of Allegiance, though I don't know why we're singing to the *magloubeh*. The cousins join in, then everyone does, clanking forks and knives in time to the song. "Land-of-the-pilgrim's-pride!   From-ev-ver-rer-ry-moun-tain-side, let-free-dom-ring!"

When we're done, my uncles call to Gram and coax her to the doorway, saying the *magloubeh* won't taste good without her. Uncle Jack gets up, bows, kisses her hand, and calls her his delightful tulip. She glares and swats at him and says, "*You,*" and flounces back down at the table.

We eat, and I do my utmost to avoid the eggplant and the cauliflower, and maybe even the rice and the lamb, which tastes of eggplant and cauliflower. I push the pieces around in a stealthy fashion. The table undergoes its balkanization—women on one side, men on the other—the children forming a private island, remote from the world of grown-ups and their dreary talk. I don't know what my sisters and cousins and I ever talk about, I only know that we can't stop laughing. We watch the adults eat, and we laugh some more. We're not there for the food so much as for the pure electricity of one another's presence: We could subsist on chewing gum and whistling and running in the fields. We're all elbows and faces, big eyes and teeth, holding our forks and knives like shovels.

Suddenly Tammy, one of the American aunties, bursts out, "This is not right! It's not right for you to be saying such things over dinner! You even make fun of our *patriotism*. What will the children learn? All they ever hear from you men is fighting and more fighting. Can't we have some *peace*?" She pushes the straw-colored hair back from her face, her skin damp and raw pink as if she's been bent over a stove all evening. For a moment, all the men are subdued, blinking with wonder.

Gram sniffs. She's not all that impressed with Aunt Tammy. "Flib-bertigibbet," she mutters.

Then Uncle Jack looks at me and says, "Diana, didn't you hear? I believe your auntie would like you to give her the *peas*." And there goes his tic. I sputter and make desperate owl eyes at my cousin Jess, who kicks me under the table. We break out laughing, and it is as bad and funny as wetting our pants. My grandmother—who sits like an international peacekeeping security force between the world of adults and children—turns her dignified head and gives me the evil eye over the rice bowl. She leans over and puts another scoop of *magloubeh* on my plate.

On this particular day, as on so many other days I can think of, the women melt back into the kitchen afterward to do the dishes and gossip. Meanwhile, the men—overfull, overtaxed, with their new, oversize American bodies—lumber into the living room and spread out, everywhere but on the furniture, and fall right asleep, taking up every inch of floor space. There is no way to tell their sleeping forms apart. Great bellies rising, they look innocent and slack as sea animals on rocks.

Their breathing-snoring lifts and falls, gentle as a hidden spring, and again the living room is transformed. Monica, Suzy, Jess, Ed, and

I wander through a great house of sleep—you can feel it on all sides, buoyant and rippling. Jess is fourteen and actively looking for interesting trouble, and Ed and I, a couple of years younger, are essentially at her command. Seven-year-old Monica is a good sport but fundamentally law-abiding. At eight, Suzy keeps her own counsel, careful and painstaking in all things. We creep through the living room, tiptoeing past the slumbering uncles, peering around as if at a gallery of archaeological artifacts.

We stop at our favorite, Uncle Jack the instigator, flat on his stomach and face on the living room floor. We stare at him, wait for him to awaken and start winking or singing or provoking a fight, anything. After a while, Jess says that we are going to play something called A Journey Through Uncle Jack's Body. We squat over him with small plastic toy soldiers that we allow to hover just above his inert form. We start at the heels, and at the rise of his calves we spot enemy forces as they charge down the hillside of his posterior. Oh no! We whisper, "Watch out for the damn British!" We beat them back, but it's all-out war by the time we reach his lower back. The soldiers clash in the air just over his spine. The Zionists appear at the crest of his shoulders, but a spirit of mutual understanding and compromise settles in around his neck, and our armies spread picnic blankets on the back of his head and sit together, eating *magloubeh*.

Cousin Jess directs everything, assigning and reassigning roles according to her whims.

"Here, okay, now you be the Israeli, 'kay?" Jess gives her brother the dashing upright plastic soldier who holds a big machine gun. "He stays over here, by this ear. Now, Diana, you be the Palestinian, 'kay?" She gives me the soldier with the face we melted half-off last summer with a magnifying glass. "You stay by this ear on the other side and just look really scared."

Afterward, my grandmother comes hunting for us and asks what in God's name we're up to, playing so quietly by ourselves. I tell her we were playing A Journey Through Uncle Jack's Body. Her eyes widen and her whole face seems to flatten, then she catches her lower lip in her teeth. "Oh, you were, were you? And did he give you permission? No, I imagine not!" she says in her arch voice. But beneath her stern expression I see what might be suppressed laughter. "Well, then . . ." She turns away and walks to the door. It takes her a moment, then she says, "Well, so much for the great diplomat."

DIPLOMATIC *MAGLOUBEH*
If you really want to make the children happy, add pieces
of chicken and substitute sliced carrot for the eggplant.

¼ cup olive oil
2 large onions
1½ pounds lean boneless
   lamb (or chicken), cut
   into chunks
¼ teaspoon ground
   cinnamon
¼ teaspoon ground
   coriander
¼ teaspoon ground cumin
½ teaspoon ground
   allspice
Salt and freshly ground
   pepper
2 cups beef broth
1 small unpeeled eggplant,

cut into ½-inch rounds,
fried in 6 teaspoons
olive oil until browned
(nonstick pan is nice),
then drained on paper
towels
1 small cauliflower, cut
   in half lengthwise and
   then cut into ½-inch-
   thick slices, fried in
   6 teaspoons olive oil
   until browned, and
   drained on paper towels
1 cup rice
¼ cup pine nuts
2 tablespoons butter

In a heavy saucepan, heat all but a few teaspoons of the oil. Add the onions and sauté until soft and browned. Add the meat and cook, stirring, until evenly browned. Add the spices and broth and bring to a boil. Reduce the heat to low, cover, and simmer for 1 hour, until the meat is tender.

Prepare the fried eggplant and cauliflower and set aside on paper towels.

Coat the bottom of a large cooking pot with the remaining olive oil. Arrange the meat in an even layer in the pot, cover with the eggplant, spread the rice over the eggplant, and spread the cauliflower over the rice. Pour the broth from the cooked meat over everything. Cover the pot and simmer about 40 minutes, until the rice is tender.

Meanwhile, sauté the pine nuts in the butter until lightly browned.

When the meat and rice are done cooking, invert the pot carefully over a serving platter and pour out the ingredients (this recipe will yield a looser, unstructured version, not a layered timbale). Top the meat with the pine nuts. This dish is very good served with yogurt and a cucumber tahini salad. It makes excellent leftovers, too.

SERVES 6.

EIGHT

Country Life

Bud comes home one day and plonks his keys on the brass table by the door. Then he sits across from us—next to the TV that is filled with our dramatic soap opera—and makes an announcement: We're moving back to Jordan. He decided on the drive home from work.

Of course, this is an announcement that has been in the air for years. Behind workdays, picnics and outings, and evenings in front of the TV, there is Bud's feeling that this is all temporary, that we will be leaving America to return to our "true country" any day now. He tells us so whenever we sit down to eat: "In Jordan, we're going to get a big enough table so the company can sit in the kitchen with us!" Sometimes he'll turn angry and frustrated if anyone questions his big Jordan plans; it's easy to bruise his dignity. He can talk himself into a snit just by following one stream in his consciousness to the next, until he remembers something somebody said last week or last month or ten years ago that might possibly have hurt his feelings. He'll be off, stomping upstairs and threatening to go back *home*, "where they really love me." And we won't be sure if he means to take us along at all.

By this point, we have lived in Syracuse for several years, consuming American culture, TV, music, and especially its lavish, oily fast foods—fried fish burgers, fried chicken, and quart-size ice-milk Fribbles from Friendly's restaurant. Bud is fed up with decadent American culture, tedious, anonymous jobs, and most especially with seeing his children grow into stranger-Americans right before his eyes—dressing like them, talking like them, acting like them!

I don't react when he makes his announcement. I've heard this plan so many times, it doesn't seem like a real possibility anymore. It's more like a refrain to a country-western song: *Someday I'll see my old home again.*

But something is different this time. In the ensuing months, while I try to ignore Bud's excitement, everything is sold: the furniture, dishes, the house. My friends, led by Sally Holmes, throw me a surprise going-away party just before school lets out for the summer. They present me with a five-pound album swollen with Polaroids and handmade glitter-dusted cards and personally inscribed farewell poetry surrounded by curlicues of glued-on yarn. The one from Jamie Faraday reads, "I had a friend / She went away / And now I am crying / Tears of icicles." We have moved to Jordan before, but this isn't the same—this time I'm twelve, I have friends, clothes, opinions. And my opinion is: I don't want to move to Jordan.

At the party, my friends keep asking, "Where are you going again?" They gaze at me as if I'm shipping out to the western front.

Jamie Faraday puts her hand on my knee; her eyes are big and refracted with tears. "I'm sorry," she says. "I'm sorry, I'm sorry." She swipes at her shining cylinder of bangs, and they break into pieces. The thought comes to me that she must have willed me out of existence many times already.

Sally Holmes's mother ladles up crystal punch glasses of pink Kool-Aid and pineapple juice for all the girls. Even though this is something I've learned to enjoy, today I can't drink it. It tastes of sugar, stone, and chemicals—the way everything did when I first returned to the States. That fiery reentry comes back to me, the memory of having to re-create myself at seven, at nine, and now again.

It hasn't been easy for me to construct this American self. I've had to observe closely. I have finally acquired hip-hugger jeans and a long shag haircut, in the posthippie fallout look of the seventies. I lie awake at night, trying to imagine Jordan. I retain vivid impressions worked into my body, sharp and inexorable—the whiteness of the streets, the stone houses, the running children. These tokens have always been within me: the scent of mint in my parents' garden, the intricate birdsong, the seeded crust of the bread, and the taste of dried yogurt steeped in olive oil. All of it returns in my dreams. But when I deliberately try to reimagine it, it turns to dust. Two years older than me, my friend Hisham will be almost fifteen by now, but in my imagination he's frozen into a bony, wide-smiling, smart-guy ten-year-old. I've lost my sense of Jordan. If we move back there, I don't know what I'll be any longer.

But nobody asks for the children's opinion. Bud's eyes are focused on an invisible, interior point—the repository of his childhood, the place of innocence and wholeness, a brushstroke of cedar and its lingering perfume.

"When we go back to Jordan," he says, sliding butter-fried eggs onto our plates, "we're going to see the family again. Won't that be great?"

My shoulders slump, heavy and sullen with all the things I'm not allowed to say, like *I thought* we *were the family!* Bud is content now, but that mood is volatile and delicate. To question this decision is to risk his quick temper.

"When we go back to Jordan," Bud continues, stacking piles of toasted pita bread, "we'll have fresh apricot juice and fresh bread. When I was a boy, we made the dough every day and took it to be baked at the bakery every night. It's the only way to eat bread. You'll see your friends Mrs. Haddadin and Hisham, and you'll speak Arabic again. Won't that be great?"

I pick up the bread, put it down. I don't answer.

LOST CHILDHOOD PITA BREAD

1 package yeast	2 teaspoons salt
1 cup water, lukewarm	4 to 6 cups flour
1 teaspoon sugar	2 teaspoons olive oil

In a mixing bowl, sprinkle the yeast into warm water, then stir in the sugar and salt. Let sit for a few minutes, until bubbly.

Place the flour in a large mixing bowl, add the yeast mixture and oil, then combine by hand. Scrape the dough onto a floured surface and knead for about ½ hour, until smooth. Add small amounts of flour if the dough becomes sticky. Form the dough into small, palm-size balls, knead each ball a little, then cover the balls with a towel and let rise until double in size, about 1 hour.

On a floured surface, flatten each ball until about ½ inch thick. Cover and let them rise again, about 1 hour.

Preheat the oven to 450 degrees. Place the flattened balls onto the baking surface (see note).

Bake for 3 to 6 minutes. Watch them very carefully, as they burn quickly.

Let cool on racks. To store, wrap airtight and freeze.

SPECIAL NOTE: The trick to getting the pita bread to puff up and form the hollow pocket inside is to bake them on a heavy preheated surface. Regular baking sheets usually aren't thick enough. A pizza stone works well if you have one. In a pinch you can even use a heavy, oven-safe sauté pan. Whichever you use, it must be preheated to the oven temperature before you cook the dough.

MAKES ABOUT 10 LOAVES.

We finish the school year and pack our remaining belongings into three big steamer trunks to be shipped overseas. If Mom harbors any secret mutinies in her heart, I don't know about them. My father's longing for Jordan is at the center of his identity, which places it at the center of their marriage. Perhaps she believes she must choose between Bud and America. Or perhaps after a few years of suburbia, she really is ready for the adventure. In either case, I have no recollection of my mother resisting the move: She sells the furniture as stoically as she gave away her wedding dress to the nun's charity the last time we moved to Jordan.

At the end of May, Bud flies to Jordan ahead of us to figure out, once again, who we are, where we will live, and what our lives will look like. As our departure date gets closer, I start to lose the feeling in my hands and feet. Life is a sluggish dream as I fold clothes and empty the drawers. I can't stand the taste of food, everything catches in my throat, my skin is too sensitive, and my clothes scratch. I stop eating, sleeping, speaking.

Mrs. Manarelli comes over one day, and she and my mother have a whisper-conversation at the kitchen table about leaving me in the States to live with the Manarellis. I eavesdrop with dreadful hope, biting my nails down to the quick. I imagine sleeping in the lavender-scented guest bedroom, listening to Marco's Monkees 45s through the wall, learning how to knead airy sweet loaves of bread dusted with rosemary. But I know it's impossible. My sisters and I are chief among Bud's reasons for moving back to Jordan. And I feel guilty for this, as if becoming American is a weak-minded decision I've made. A better girl would have embraced the Saturday morning Arabic lessons in the old church basement downtown, would have cheerfully made all the Arabic foods and Arabic coffees her father wanted. I believe that if only I had willed myself more fully Arab in America, all this dislocation might have been averted.

Bud has been away for over a month, and I enter a dull state of lethargy. The panic has subsided into a sort of mute day-drifting through the house. I float, haunting my own life.

Mom resigns her teaching position. Some people come and take our curtains away. We have our tickets, and we leave the day after tomorrow. And just when the house is completely empty, the new buyers plotting out where to put their tomato garden, we receive a surprise cablegram from Jordan: SENDING BACK TRUNKS COMING HOME.

I stand beside my mother, heart stuttering. We reread the scrap of paper about twenty times, both of us holding a corner. "What does it mean?" I ask.

She stares at it. "I do not know."

It means we're not moving to Jordan. Bud comes back. He doesn't want to discuss it. His jaw is set and his eyes have a fierce new light in them, the look of someone who's been shaken awake.

I am swept by relief so powerful that I stand in my empty bedroom doorway gripping the door frame as I feel my knees tremble.

But, oh. This is awkward. We've said good-bye to everyone, sold the house and everything we own. Now what?

We learn that by some crazy, lucky, last minute chance, the art teacher at Mom's former school happens to be spending her summer break and the following school year on leave in London, and we can stay in her place. The five of us pack into her tiny one-bedroom apartment across from the Lakeshore Drive-In, behind O'Connell's Grill. It turns out this is my dream home—everywhere are screens of beads instead of doors, purple-tasseled pillows, pink velour drapes, hot pink shag carpeting, brass elephant incense burners, Buddha statues, and blacklight posters; I am particularly obsessed with the ultrasaturated Maxfield Parrish and audacious Aubrey Beardsley drawings. I sigh and swan-neck around in front of the posters, entranced by the sizzling colors and intimate lines. What's more, the apartment complex has a grand blue slab of pool that we spend the pallid upstate summer in. At night, my sisters and I make our beds on the furry couches in the living room and I doze off while staring at the artwork, the pulsing forms emerging in my sleep.

Bud can't cook in the funny little galley kitchen with the feathered dream-catchers dangling over the stove and the naked Gaia incense burners in the window. He says being in this apartment is like having a fit. So we live on cold tabbouleh salad that Bud keeps stocked in the fridge and fine, greasy onion burgers and curly fries at O'Connell's Grill. Monica, Suzy, and I spin on the stools up front and chat with the gravel-voiced drinkers who slouch over the bar all afternoon. Mom and Bud have murmuring conferences in one of the vinyl booths in back.

Bud has looked vaguely different ever since he returned from Jordan. He lost some weight while he was overseas, and the long, serious slant of his jaw has surfaced. The first flecks of gray dash his sideburns, and he has a new way of gazing into people's eyes. Sometimes it's a little scary to look at him now: He looks back too long, as if he will devour you. I start to flinch at his touch. Mom whispers that he was "very disappointed" in Jordan.

We also have a new family ritual that Bud calls "going for a drive." This entails hours of circling neighborhoods in our Rambler, peering at endless neighborhoods. Families wandering over their fleecy lawns, kids working Big Wheels, men in Bermuda shorts spraying rainbows from the garden hose, all of them stare back at our car. They exude a bland, impassive silence. I believe that if we ever actually rolled to a stop, someone would call the police.

Bud says, "How about this one . . . Evergreen Terrace, how does that sound?" as we turn the corner into another nearly identical cul-de-sac.

"Dad, what are we even doing?" I ask, grouchy about being dragged away from the pool. "Are we really looking for a place to live or are we just fooling around or what?"

"Ooh, just looking, looking all around," he says in his airy way. "Don't you like to see what's out there?"

"Yeah, whatever." I tilt my forehead against the window. One neighborhood pours into the next, seemingly without end or reason. Where does it all lead? Where is the center of all these courts and terraces and cul-de-sacs? My parents no longer have jobs, a house, neighbors. My sisters and I no longer have a school district. We came uprooted that easily. Our Rambler is our home. My throat and eyes burn; something is ignited inside me. I look around the car and survey the backs of their heads: How will I ever take care of all these people?

Late in July, after weeks and weeks of looking around, we set out on what I assume will be another aimless drive. We leave the suburban neighborhoods and drive until the tree-lined lots taper away and we pass acres of yellow-parched weeds. There is nothing but telephone poles, empty roads, and the rolling hills of New York State. Finally we turn off the road and rumble up a long, gravel-popping country driveway. The house is set back among acres of chiming crickets, its long windows sparkling in a plush velvet night, the moon burning over its right shoulder. "Do you like it?" Bud asks us, grinning crazily. He nods as if agreeing with something somebody had said and announces, "That's good, 'cause I already bought it!"

The house is a chunky, modern redwood with traces of Frank Lloyd Wright in the wood-framed rows of windows. The bedrooms are all downstairs, which we are told is a "Californian design." A deck lines the upper half of the house and gives us a view of trees and the long, single road that stretches from us to everyplace else. This house is only twenty miles away from our previous house, but we may as well have moved to Jordan. I can no longer bike to see my friends. I can no longer walk anywhere except down a scalded, shoulderless strip of country road. I wander around the house half-dazed. The countryside feels vast and fabulous, depressing, inspiring, and inescapable: utterly isolated. All around us are waving, pollen-cloudy acres of fields, crickets, streams, maples, lilacs, blue spruces, and cicadas. There's a scary little convenience store way down the long country road at the intersection with the county highway, and a gas station across the street from that. Up the hill there's a public waterworks building, and that's it.

. . .

Euclid is silence and sun spots fried into the carpet and watching the country road for the kids who burn down the gravel on their banana-seat bikes, grime thick as war paint on their faces, their hair slack and unwashed. The boys skid vulture circles and pop wheelies in front of our house of girls. Bud forbids us to go outside and look at them—which my baby sister, Monica, frequently does anyway; she has trouble keeping track of what's forbidden. So I just watch them from my bedroom window.

One day, just a week after we move in, I hear voices outside. I run to the window to see Monica standing in the front yard, chatting with a gang of four boys circling on bikes in the big empty road. They never actually stop, just tilt into their lazy orbit, a vapor of dust hanging over them. Their faces are raw with dirt, and their bikes make screeching noises with every pedal push. Seven-year-old Monica is standing with her hands on her hips, busy telling them everything in the world. I slide open the stiff, wood-framed window and listen to her explaining that the word Bud has pasted in huge red letters on the mailbox is our last name. She tells them the ages of herself and her sisters, the national origins of our parents, their occupations, and a long story about how we'd just sold everything we owned and almost moved to Jordan but then our father changed his mind and moved us here instead.

The boys listen with a grim, determined silence, sawing away on their bikes and apparently communicating telepathically. Occasionally one will throw out a question like "What you call yourselves?" or "You got any candy or cigarettes?" and Monica will go into another extensive answer. They sound, I note with some anxiety, almost as if they're from the South, their vowels flattened, syllables stretched and approximate: "What's at thin' yerr wearin'?"

Eventually, their telepathy clicks again; the meeting is over. With a flick, they turn like a flock of sparrows, pumping down past the four corners and disappearing over a hill.

Monica watches them go as if they are her last friends on earth. I watch, too.

SUBSISTENCE TABBOULEH

*For when everything is falling apart
and there's no time to cook.*

1 cup cracked wheat
   (bulgur, fine-grain)
2 small bunches flat-leaf
   parsley, minced
2 medium cucumbers,
   peeled and chopped

3 medium tomatoes,
   chopped
2 tablespoons olive oil
Juice of 1 small lemon
Salt and freshly ground
   pepper

Wash the bulgur and let it soak in water to cover for ½ hour.
Drain thoroughly and add the vegetables. Add the oil, lemon, and
salt and pepper to taste. Mix well. Cover, and let the tabbouleh
marinate in the refrigerator for a couple of hours.

MAKES 6 TO 8 SERVINGS.

NINE

Runaway

I am twelve, and I can't take it anymore. I can't stand the stillness of this place, the ruthless acres of blowing, dried weeds. It is a hot, still September, the road full of dust and pollen. To soothe myself, I start writing stories in spiral pads while slouching at the dining room table. The stories are all about a girl who is bored and lost and abandoned by her friends and stewing in the middle of nowhere, who spends her time imagining ways to get back at her father for moving her there. One day, I write a story about a girl who gets so frustrated by her life of captivity in the countryside and her cruel, slave-driver father that she runs away to Jordan. Upon rereading the piece, I suddenly realize that this story seems remarkably like my own: I become indignant about what I've written and rear up from the dining room table.

"That's it," I announce. "I've had it with this place, I'm done—I quit!"

My sisters look up hopefully from their Barbie Dream House—both of them half-stunned by the same boredom. "Where you going?" Suzy asks. She generally dislikes snap decisions and impulsive behaviors, but since we've moved to the country things are just a little too slow.

"I can't take it," I quaver. "I'm leaving town."

Monica throws down her stiff-legged doll. "Can we come, too?" She is easily rankled and generally ready for action. Her new motto since moving to this rural boredom is, You're not the boss of me.

In a spontaneous show of solidarity, my sisters walk out with me. Mom and Bud watch from the couch. Bud says, "Hey, where you going? It's almost dinner!"

I roar at them as we thunder down the stairs, "*You don't understand anything!*"

This is all improvisational—I don't know where we are going or how long it'll take us to get there. It's just the three of us walking fast and gloriously righteous along the bare shoulder of Morgan Road. The sunlight glistens on the road and floats a watery mirage before our eyes. An opaque bead of sweat streaks my forearm. After a while, all we can hear is the sound of our feet and our breathing; the sun seems to crackle overhead, and insects sing in the parched weeds.

Throughout my childhood, Bud has informed me that I am "in charge" of my younger sisters, speaking as if they were my employees or personal possessions. He says that if we lived in Jordan, I would be responsible for guiding the shape of their lives, approving of their choices for husbands and other assorted life decisions. I am meant to be their watcher, their mentor, and their activities director. Sometimes I feel I can't bear the weight of this responsibility. (When I am seven, my three-year-old sister, Suzy, vanishes from the front yard and is missing for two frightening hours. Frantic and dazed, Bud scolds that I'm to blame for failing to watch my charge. I fall into a devastated stupor, staring out the car window as my mother drives, until Suzy is found wandering around the next neighborhood.) My sisters become another element in Bud's array of obligations, duties, and family protocols, which makes it so hard for us, as children, to simply be friends. It is almost never possible for us to be together like this away from Bud's scrutiny and expectations. Even though it's strange to be walking along the side of this big empty road like this, on our way to nowhere, it feels a bit like a holiday as well.

"I'm so fed up," I mutter. I pick a stalk of a dried-looking purple weed by the side of the road, smell it, and then throw it down when I remember that I'm angry.

"Yeah, me too," Monica says. She also picks a purple weed, throws it down.

There is the low rumble of a car behind us, gravel popping. We step to one side as we walk, but the rumble lingers. "That's Dad," Suzy says without turning around.

Bud doesn't stop, he just rolls down his window and calls out from behind his steering wheel. "Monica, Monica!" he calls to my youngest sister. "Dinner's almost ready . . . aren't you hungry?"

Monica looks at me—a neat furrow above her clear eyes. I can read her expression, which asks very clearly: *Now, what are we doing out here again?* Her shiny hair falls in spikes across her forehead.

"I'm making grape leaves," Bud croons. "It's your favorite!"

Monica glances back at the car, then looks at me again—mute and helpless. I realize I've already lost. She's a feisty, skeptical seven-year-old, impressive for her headlong fearlessness, but grape leaves truly are her favorite. "Monica," he sings, "there's already butter on the rice!" Monica has been known to eat butter straight from the stick. She sighs and flaps her arms as if it's all too hopeless and inevitable, then veers off and joins Bud in the car. They turn and drive back to the house.

Suzy and I keep walking, but now our walkout feels compromised. And the day is too cheery—it interferes with indignation. Our marching speed slows significantly. Little black crickets chirr and hang in the long grass like musical notation.

"How far do you think we've walked?" Suzy asks. At eight, she is a wise, meditative child, capable of giving herself for hours to intricate school projects—science reports, watercolors, flute practice—much more focused and disciplined than I could ever hope to be.

"Oh, at least a quarter mile," I speculate, silently factoring whether or not dinner is already on the table.

Neither of us stops or looks around, but we can hear the car creep up and then follow us at parade speed for several minutes. Finally, there's a squeak as Bud cranks down his window. "Suzy! Suzy!"

Suzy looks at me. The late afternoon blows her hair into ringlets, covers her eyes with long violet shadows.

"There's also stuffed squash with ground lamb—it's just the way you like it!"

Suzy's face moves into deep deliberation; then her eyes roll up at me. We both know there's no point resisting. "I better go back," she says grimly.

"You better."

"Maybe you should come, too."

I squint toward the sun, try to look rugged and independent. "I know," I say. "But I just can't help it."

"I know," she says.

After the two of them drive away, I walk just a few paces more, then stop on a slight rise and watch the car curl back into our driveway. I grit my teeth. It's just me and my clenched fists and the breathy afternoon light and dreaming clouds. I can't keep going, but I won't give in, either. Grievances roll through my mind: I never wanted to move to Jordan; I never wanted to move to the country; none of this is my fault; and nothing in the world is fair! Since it's a good twenty miles from here to anywhere, I decide to turn back toward the house, then I bypass the driveway and go into the east field, into the dense, maple-sweet trees, their feathery canopies and abundance of branches. I go deep enough to hide. I don't have a plan, I just stand still and silent beneath a single tree. I can smell its nutty, musty bark and ripe scent. I wait to see what will happen.

Bud comes back out of the house, about to get back in the car, when he scans the road and realizes he can't see me kicking along the gravel shoulder. He shields his eyes with his palm and turns, squinting around into the late, coppery-lit fields. He walks down to the end of the driveway, hands on hips. I stifle my laughter, bump into a tree, which leaves sticky resins on my arm. It smells drugged and over-sweet here, like a candy forest. I almost forget why I'm hiding and call out, but something heavy and stubborn and determined inside of me holds me in place. I wait and listen to the high whine of insects in the leaves, and there's a brief flickering high overhead, wings arcing: a lonely mote of sound.

"Ya Ba!" He starts walking south, across the road into the open field, away from me. Instinctively, I take a few guilty steps forward, rustling the leaves.

He couldn't hear this—he's too far away. But he pauses, he seems to sense something. It's a disconcerting thing: I feel afraid of being discovered and afraid of never being found.

From the house comes the briny scent of grape leaves, their trace of salt and the sweet tomatoes they simmer in, their centers of ground lamb and rice, the roasting squashes, their flesh turning buttery in the pan.

Bud walks back up the driveway and into the eastern slope. "You can't hide from your *baba*," he says, and his words settle inside me like something that was already written there. "I'll find you—that's it."

And the weird dread and relief flutters around me, soft as bat wings. I hear it pass over the tops of the trees. I rub my eyes and come out of the woods. He stares at me a second, as if he hasn't really expected me to be there. He is angry, I can tell, but more because of feeling duped now than because I left in the first place.

"Now dinner is late!" He demands, "What do you have to say?"

"Whatever you want me to say," I mutter, infuriated and worn out, and walk past him, back toward the house, knowing there is no way out except through this door that is my father.

The space extends forever inside and outside of this house. We have to import our entertainment, so my parents invite the relatives over every weekend. My mother and aunties churn blenders full of grasshoppers or pink ladies or drink grapey wines from screw-top bottles. Bud experiments with elaborate, ceremonial dishes, sauces from Lebanon, a Moroccan style of preparing fish, a beguiling soup with chickpeas and onion. The men swirl their clear drinks in the living room, serious with man talk and politics, which seems even more serious in this setting, the far-flung philosophical landscape filling the long windows.

"LOUNGING WITH THE LADIES" GRASSHOPPERS

1 ounce crème de menthe	1 ounce heavy cream
1 ounce crème de cacao	

Shake with ice and strain into cocktail glasses *or* mix in a blender with a cup of crushed ice for a gorgeous milk shake effect.

MAKES 2 COCKTAILS.

Jess and Ed, who also live in the country, help me decipher this place. I've felt hoodwinked ever since we moved here, but Jess stands in the long, gradual driveway that extends from the house to the street and nods solemnly at the fields. "This is perfect—you got it just right this time." Suddenly, after weeks of mourning the ice-cream parlor, the movies, the drugstore, there's a better way for me to see this place. If you hang back and gaze at the fields from a distance, they look pretty and empty, yielding nothing. But enter these places and you have a new, fluid perspective, a land of leaves, buzzing walls, heat-struck mirages floating on air. With luck, you'll get so lost that you'll never find your way home again. Maybe you'll be forced to live like Robinson Crusoe in your fort made of twigs, dining on roots and berries and acorns.

We plunge into acres wallowing with cattails. Clouds laze across the sky, and humidity hangs in the tall, rough grass. We're fearless in one another's company, whooping like maniacs, pushing into pussy willows and Queen Anne's lace so high, they nearly close over our heads. Crickets zoom through the air like electrons, and beetles part their shining jackets and ricochet off our arms. Whacking just past a stand of ragged bushes, I come to a stop. There's a trickling light through the leaves—a big drainage ditch. Running through the bottom is a thin, flat creek filled with pollywogs, transparent minnows, water-walkers, bubble-rollers, and millions of roiling, minute, embryonic creatures. It's the primordial stew. We bend over the water and slosh around in it, then turn to examine the drain.

A huge cement pipe juts from the side of the sloping ground like a hidden room in the earth. It's big enough for children to stand in—an irresistible invitation. Jess and Ed have a cement pipe a bit like this at their place, only theirs is narrower and gets dark too quickly, and once you crawl in there you start thinking about webs and spiders and ghouls and flying mummy hands right away. This great tunnel is luxurious in contrast.

"Wanna go in?" Jess asks—a silly question, because of course there isn't anywhere we won't go. Fear is not allowed. Excitement is encouraged and rage is tolerated, but fear is for sissies.

Our voices echo and ripple along the pipe's corrugated sides, the water a narrow trickle under our feet. We walk slowly, studying the place. For a while there's a greenish light glowing at our backs and an innocent, chortling water sound. Then the pipe turns, the light falls away, and almost immediately a rank, brackish smell bloats the air. But turning back doesn't occur to us. We walk along the curving ground, our fingers brushing the slimy cement. It feels as if each step takes us deeper into a trance. Our laughter shimmers and dissolves in my ears. The pipe narrows and we have to crouch. We bump into one another. Now there is nothing ahead but pitch black and we have to decide how curious, and how brave, we might be.

I think that walking in that black pipe takes me as far from my old life as I have ever gone before. Gradually, the redwood house and the life within it begin to dissolve into a dream—the reality is this smelly, reverberating place. We are alone, without names, just our skin and loud breath. I become aware of a distant sound like a hum that vibrates through the tube, into our feet and fingertips. It builds to something like a lower roar, then rushes away in a flood of whispers.

"What was that?" Suzy mumbles. I try to think of an answer, but language feels too far away. All of us have fallen into animal quiet. It isn't a bad feeling. In fact, it's immeasurably comfortable: We will never leave this place again.

Then there is the unmistakable sound of footsteps overhead. It comes to me through my haze that we're walking under the country road. The flood of whispers is the sound of cars passing over. Suddenly I hear my grandmother's voice above our heads, as if she's speaking to us through a pillow. "Children," she says, "where are you?"

Even through the layers of dirt and pavement, I can make out the fine, anxious ripples in her voice. None of us move. An amorphous bubble of time forms in the air. It expands and I watch its transparent body drift through the air. For some reason, it seems as if the children she's calling have nothing at all to do with us; they're people we used to live next door to. "Kids!" Her voice gets louder, more urgent. "Come on, it's time for dinner!" A light hissing breath of something soft and cool emanates from deep in the tunnel and lures me in. We walk farther into the total dark and, quieter now, I hear through the earth my grandmother shouting: "Kids, this isn't funny! Come on now!"

Ed, the conscientious one, observes, "She sounds worried." His voice reverberates along the ribs of the pipe. We all stop for a moment, and I can hear Gram muttering and pacing over our heads. But I have no sympathy for her. In fact, I feel a surge of exhaustion and anger. I'm tired of being dragged from house to house and being told who to be, what to feel, how to behave. I think how lovely it could be to wander down an endless pipe and never return.

Over our heads, Gram huffs and stomps. All at once she releases a string of curse words—the sort of language, she might say, that turns the air black and blue. I'm not sure I've even heard her say "heck" before, and I'm startled into laughter. We all laugh, and the sound opens into something alive, a hiccup echoing a million times over the endless ridges and bends of the pipe.

Gram goes quiet, then shouts, "I can hear you!"

The spell is broken; there is nowhere else to go. But for a moment my hand still moves forward, my fingers drifting over ridges like a braille map. And then the tips of my fingers, the most sensitive points, delicate as antennae, brush lightly against something that is undeniably fur, or possibly hair. I come to a dead halt, so contracted that even the shriek is stuck in my throat. I huff a little, breath scraping, back rigid. Someone stops just short behind me. "Let's leave," an unfamiliar voice, possibly mine, quavers in the dark.

We turn, stumbling over our own feet, laughing with fear, and then just laughing. We are running back, into ourselves, into light, to dinner, to what is known.

MAGICAL *MUHAMMARA*

An enchanting opening dish, this dip or spread is good for when you
want everyone to quit running around and come to the table.

1 tablespoon chili pepper
   flakes
1 teaspoon ground cumin
1½ cups walnuts, roasted
½ cup dried bread crumbs
¼ cup olive oil
2 tablespoons unsweetened
   pomegranate juice

Pinch of salt
½ teaspoon sugar
¼ cup tomato purée
½ teaspoon ground allspice
2 roasted red bell peppers,
   peeled and chopped
Small bunch flat-leaf
   parsley, chopped

Combine all the ingredients, except for the parsley, in a food processor or blender. Purée until smooth.

Spoon the *muhammara* into small bowls and garnish with the chopped parsley. Cover and chill until ready to serve. Before serving, top with drizzle of olive oil and serve with warm pita bread. This dish is also nice spread with *lebeneh* (see page 229).

TEN

Stories, Stories

Bud is a great talker in our family of mostly listeners. He soliloquizes on the history of the Arab-Israeli conflict, beginning with the Bible; delivers a dissertation on free will versus destiny; and offers several exhortations addressing the nature of animals, the difference between men and women, and the meaning of the universe. He tells endless jokes and instructional stories starring his favorite classic Arab character—Jeha the joker. (Jeha borrows his neighbor's pot. A week later he returns it with a second smaller pot and says, "While it was staying with me, your pot gave birth to a baby pot!" The neighbor laughs to himself at Jeha's stupidity but accepts the second pot with pleasure. When Jeha returns a day later to borrow the neighbor's expensive brass table, the man is delighted to loan it out. Several weeks pass with no sign of Jeha, so the neighbor decides to inquire about his table and the prospect of some new table progeny. Tearfully, Jeha says to his neighbor, "I'm so sorry, I have some terrible news, my friend. While your table was visiting with me, it caught a terrible cold and died." At this, the neighbor grows furious and says, "What sort of idiot would believe that a table catches cold?" And Jeha retorts, "What sort of idiot believes that pots can give birth!")

There are also the family narratives, hair-raising tales of Bud running semiwild across Jordan with his tribe of seven (or so) brothers. We hear about our grandfather's dissolute generosity; our grandmother's miraculous home library; the day Bud's brother tried to carry a pig home and his occasionally Muslim father balanced his rifle on the sill of his bedroom window and started firing at his naughty son; the day Bud snuck out to a wedding party without permission and when he came home later that evening his father chased him across the flat rooftops, the sound of their footsteps echoing into the alleys; the time Bud snuck out to witness a public hanging and the weeks of deep-sea nightmares he suffered from afterward.

After we eat, when the kitchen windows glint black with night, Bud rolls away from his plate and begins telling stories of childhood, unimaginable lifetimes ago—fifteen, even twenty years back.

One of our favorites—meaning Bud's favorite—is the story of how his parents came together. He sits at the table, sipping his little cup of coffee, the tiny handle requiring that he bunch his large fingers together in a delicate way. He wipes at his mustache, once, twice, so we know he wants to tell a long story. Finally, he sits back and rests his little cup on his stomach and begins:

"When my father, Saleh, was sixteen or seventeen or eighteen, he was in a caravan with his father and uncles, going across Amman to Palestine. They used to do like that in those days—three hundred camels and horses and all that, full of wheat and barley and sesame. As-Salt was the only city back then, and it took weeks to cross over."

"Why wasn't he in school?" Monica asks, concerned.

He frowns and turns his coffee a little bit, adjusting the rim to exactly the right position. "I think he didn't like school very much. No, in fact, not at all. None of those brothers did. Their parents sent them to boarding schools in Damascus, in Syria, because there weren't any schools in Jordan. Always they used to run away immediately. They would come right back to Jordan. Sometimes they would make it back home before their father got back and be sitting there in the kitchen, waiting for their beating. Anyway!

"One day, when the caravan came into Palestine, Saleh came across a girls' high school. He and his brothers were all hanging around there, looking at the pretty girls. They weren't used to girls. And there was one he liked specially. That was Anissa Zurub, your grandmother. And he and his father and uncles went to her family and asked for her hand in marriage. Only they turned them down! Why? Because your grandmother was educated, brilliant, and perfect, she was going to go to college. She was a sophisticated city girl from Jerusalem. Her father was an Angelic minister."

"Anglican," Mom says.

"Right. And Saleh was just a country bumpkin—a Bedouin! What did he know about the world? Nothing! He was a rough boy with calluses up one side of his body and down the other. Handsome as a black horse, he had a big mustache like I don't know what, and a smile to drive you out of your mind. But education? None! Okay, so of course, Anissa turned down his courtship. She said no, so he had to go home. Fine. So some time goes by, not very much, and the Turks start to prosecute the Arabs all over the Middle East."

"Persecute," Mom says.

"Right. The Turks were after the Christians especially, so the Zurub family had to flee across the border. They ran to Jordan, to As-Salt, the only city. And who owned the best, biggest, oldest house in As-Salt? That's right, the Abu-Jabers! Do you know the Abu-Jabers are responsible for kicking the king out of As-Salt, so the royalty moved the capital of Jordan to Amman? But that's a story for another day. Anyway.

"When the Zurub family got to the Abu-Jaber house, my father, Saleh the handsome bumpkin, was there, ready to fall in love with her again. And so he did that. What happened was Saleh's parents died— some say that the Turks poisoned him—my grandfather Freyeh and his brothers Farah and Farhan—all of them died—maybe by Turks poisoning the well, but also maybe by the typhoid. That is also a possibility. They say the typhoid came and took half of Jordan, you know. If the Turks didn't get you, the typhoid did—"

"Also another story," Mom says.

"Right. So after the parents died, Saleh's oldest sister, Fathee'yeh, she just started matching everybody up. She put together her brothers with some various wives to get those boys out of her hair. And she married Saleh to Anissa, which is how such a smart city girl came to be married to a bumpkin!"

"But did she want to get married to him?" I ask my father. "Were they in love?"

He smiles and leans back in another direction in his seat. "Ya Ba, history is a funny thing. It's a funny, funny thing. And so is love.

That's another funny thing, like history. They're practically the same! I rather to think that she did. I rather to believe in a happy kind of an ending. But who really knows any of it except for Saleh and Anissa, and now they're both gone, God rest their souls. But at least they got married. The end. But you know what's interesting? Aunt Fathee'yeh herself never got married. She was a tough owl, that one, they say she was the true governor of As-Salt, not exactly elected, but you know how that goes. . . ."

Patiently, privately, Mom collects and washes the dishes and Bud keeps my sisters and me at the table with talking. He requires an audience. He leans his elbows on the linoleum table and unravels family history. We get glimmerings of both the sorts of hardships and wealth they grew up with. We get inklings of his cultural values— what a "good girl" behaves like and the ethical responsibilities of children. And we get a full overview on his life plan for himself and for us, which is to buy a restaurant, for us girls to marry our second cousins and have babies, and for these babies to dance around his knees.

He tells of hot, slouchy summers in the fields, a canvas sack full of soft white powder slung around his neck. He and his friends walked between the planted rows and scooped up the powder in their hands to fling over the crops. What was the powder? "Something for the bugs, maybe. We were supposed to tie our scarves over our mouths, but that was too hot." And the powder was so silky and fine, like the elegant French talc his mother bought in Jerusalem, perfect to dig fingers into, the fine grains sparkling under their nails. So pretty, some of the children couldn't resist tasting it. And if it made their fingertips bleed or their tongues blister and their mouths taste of ashes, well, that wasn't so bad.

Another story: Bud's father, Saleh. His personality roared inside of him like a furnace. He needed to have people nearby, to feed them, get them drunk on alcohol and spiraling laughter, to shelter them when they passed out. He used to invite passing strangers into their house, where they would empty the larder with gluttonous feasting. This so infuriated my grandmother that she'd have to sit on one of her many children's beds, grab her knees, and cry out, "That man! That terrible man!" Once, my grandfather—already feeling mellow and sentimental from *araq,* his signature liquor—passed one of the English guards on the road near his house and invited him and his platoon over for a party. To my grandfather's delighted surprise, the man accepted. For an entire day before the British arrived, the whole village had to butcher lambs, pluck chickens, and lug bags of rice, onions, and tomatoes to the house. The intense cooking steamed up every room in their house, wilting all the pages in my grandmother's library—which was a frivolous and vaguely ominous place, to my grandfather's way of thinking, anyway. That night the soldiers came resplendent in their regal uniforms, thronging the little rubble road through Yehdoudeh like a parade down a cow path, hungry and sharp stepping, their English voices bright as spears. At various times during the course of the three long days and nights that the soldiers stayed, my father heard the sound of his mother's voice, coming from her library, keening, "That man! That terrible man!"

Another book of stories: King Hussein days. Somewhere in his dreamy, elastic past, Bud was friends with the king of Jordan. When he was a boy, Bud's family lived in the same hillside neighborhood as the king's family, and Bud and his brothers used to play pickup soccer games with the young, soon-to-be king and his brothers. When he grew up, Bud flew a plane in the king's air force, and he became one of the king's fencing partners. And then there was the rice. As part of his military duty, Bud and his chum Mo Kadeem worked in the king's imperial kitchens. No cooking, though; instead, he and Mo sorted rice, lentils, and *frekeh* (cracked wheat) for hours each week, painstakingly sifting through bushels of grains, flicking out all the tiny bits of stone and grit by hand. These lentils and rice would be used to make great pans of the delicious, simple dish *mjeddrah.*

"It was *as-shugal al-majnoon,*" Bud explains. The work of the crazy man. "Because you go crazy when you do it."

Didn't that upset you, we ask, working as a lowly kitchen helper?

You, a fencer of kings, a pilot of kings, a black-eyed young man with a gleaming, perfumed mustache?

He smiles vaguely; his head lists to one side. "Maybe I liked it. I don't know. It was important work. We kept the king's rice clean! Besides, my father always told me I didn't have the brains to do anything else. He said I should stick to the kitchen because I shouldn't be trusted with a weapon."

Because you had a short temper?

"Because I might accidentally kill myself. He used to knock on my head—" Bud makes a rapping gesture at his temple. "He'd say, 'What's in there? Rocks!' " He snickers and looks down.

Dad, that's terrible!

We can hardly imagine it. What sort of father would say such things about his beloved child? Not the sort of father that Bud is. We can barely imagine it. It's not true, it isn't! we cry, and grab his arms, to pull him up and away from the place of such memories.

But he just shakes his head and says, "It's okay. Mo Kadeem, now, he was the one with all the brains. He had a big, handsome head, like Cary Grant, and he was a genius, smarter than Ibn Battuta. Mo Kadeem was going to Australia someday. He saw in a movie or a book or something that the women there are seven feet high, with arms like swans and hair like lemon trees. He used to say he was going to Australia to get himself such a woman, with skin like an apple, and build a house on top of the world like the Taj Mahal. He used to talk about it all the time, his big-time plans, while we washed all that rice and lentils."

And what did you want to do, Dad?

He smiles his smile full of white, even teeth—not a single cavity. "I wanted to be the one who made the *mjeddrah*."

Whatever happened to Mo Kadeem?

"Mo Kadeem! I wish I knew. I think he must be king of Australia by now," he says in an injured, wistful way. He looks so far off that we try to see what he is looking at—but of course, nothing is actually there.

BUD'S ROYAL *MJEDDRAH*
Clean the lentils carefully, and everyone will love you.

½ cup brown lentils, cleaned, boiled, and drained (reserve the boiling liquid from the lentils)
1 cup cooked rice
1 onion, finely chopped
3 garlic cloves, mashed
3 tablespoons olive oil
1 beef bouillon cube
½ teaspoon ground cumin
Salt and freshly ground pepper

In a mixing bowl, combine the lentils and rice; set aside. In a saucepan, fry the onion and garlic in olive oil until golden brown. Add a little of the cooking liquid from the lentils, then mix in the bouillon, cumin, salt and pepper to taste. Stir the onion mixture into the lentils and rice. Serve with yogurt blended with half a peeled, chopped cucumber and a small bunch of chopped fresh mint.

MAKES 4 TO 6 SERVINGS.

ELEVEN

Immigrants' Kids

In high school, all my friends have euphonious, polysyllabic names: Olga Basilovich, Sonja Soyenka, Yorunda Nogatu, Mahaleani Lahiri. We take as many classes as possible together, and I can still recall the teachers' despair as they are nearly undone by calling attendance, the look of panic that comes over them after picking up the class roster and stumbling horribly through "Diana Abu-Jaber," only to confront "Mahaleani Lahiri." Our lunch bags open and the scent of garlic, fried onions, and tomato sauce rolls out—pierogi, *pelmeni, doro wat,* teriyaki, kielbasas, stir-fries, borscht . . . I become famous for my lunch bags full of garlic-roasted lamb and stuffed grape leaves.

The American girls in my classes are on diets. I first learn about this trend from my friend Kimberly, who is already so narrow and featureless that her skinny jeans barely cling to her hips. She irons her long hair, so there's always a whiff of scorched hair wafting around her shoulders, detectable even over the heady doses of Coty's musk perfume. For weeks at a time she goes on diets where she will live on two avocados a day. And my friends Janie and Kendra are permanently hungry. Everything smells delicious to them. The sight of trays loaded with cafeteria food brings a wanton longing into their faces. But they allow themselves just the barest crumbs: Kendra consumes only diet sodas and the crusts of sandwiches; Janice eats soda crackers and half jars of baby-food applesauce. Usually midlunch one or the other will sniff and glare at her food, there will be a pause like a moment of grieving, and then she'll quickly stand and throw away her minuscule portion, just a few bites taken.

But after school, the two of them will buy big, freezer-frosted tubs of fudge ripple ice cream and devour it with soup spoons while sitting on cement dividers in the middle school parking lot next door. Kendra still fits into her clothes from fifth grade, and even though she's fifteen, Janie brags that she hasn't gotten her period yet. Both of them watch with prim, impassive expressions as my other friends and I eat our lunches. Then Kendra sniffs and balances her chin on her knuckles and gazes across the gray-tiled cafeteria as if she is looking across the ocean, saying with great disdain and perhaps a smidgen of curiosity, "I don't understand how you can so *not care.*"

My immigrant-kid friends are not on diets. Most of us have parents from countries where a certain lushness is considered alluring in a woman. We've grown up in houses redolent with the foods of other places. We cook experimentally at one another's houses, though it's hard to get the others to come out to my remote address since none of us can drive yet. When we do try to cook at my house, my father hovers over our shoulders, sniffing and offering a stream of helpful advice, occasionally prying the spoons from our hands or dashing in extra garlic or pepper.

Olga Basilovich's father is an elderly, gentle, diminutive man from Russia. Olga tells me that when he was a young man, he and his family were shipped to the concentration camps. I have spent entire nights weeping over *Anne Frank: The Diary of a Young Girl,* and I peer closely at Mr. Basilovich the first couple of times I meet him, searching for a sign of his dreadful experience. But his smile is benign and uncomplicated; in conversation, his eyes automatically flutter to the floor. I learn in regular installments from Olga that he escaped the camps and crossed Europe on foot, enduring dramatic perils— towering barbed-wire fences, vicious dogs, gunshots, starvation, and mountaintop exposure. He made his way to America, and once there, he began to try to kill himself.

The first attempt was just after he'd acquired his PhD in molecular biology and had his first university position. He swallowed poison and was thwarted by his wife, who'd come home early and found him curled on the floor. The second time happened not long after Olga was born and involved an at-home hanging, again discovered too soon by his wife.

Our friend Sonja tells me these American suicide stories, not Olga, who is furtive and somewhat prickly. There seem to be invisible quills that lift from her and hold the rest of us at bay. Even though she and I are close, there are things that Olga can't talk about, so her oldest friend, Sonja, tells me. Sonja, of Russian-Catholic descent with a stolid, pragmatic view of the world, is impatient with Olga's evasiveness and Mr. Basilovich's repeated suicide attempts.

Sonja and I linger over the gleaming sinks in the girls' restroom at school as she tells me stories about her friend's father. "Can you imagine?" she whispers. "He walked through whole towns where everyone was totally gone!"

An image of a naked, scorched place called "Europe" opens in my mind: The trees look burnt and stripped as candlewicks. The air is a stirring, sulfurous yellow.

"So creepy."

"But really . . ." Sonja frowns, and her full mouth turns down, her Russian brow-bone high and imperial. "He behaves so irresponsibly! All this suicide! He has children, for heaven's sakes."

I try pulling my hair smooth, give up, and let it *sproing* back. "Maybe he's haunted," I suggest. I think about Olga's own narrow, downturned mouth, her shining, already disappointed eyes, and wonder how much of her father she may have inherited. She has his olive skin and inwardly bent gaze: Among our group of friends, she is the most moody and intriguing.

Sonja flicks back her glossy hair in a single swoop. "Haunted. Sure, he's Russian, he's Jewish. But all of our fathers are haunted. Big deal."

Mr. Basilovich is so quiet and retiring, I scarcely know what his voice sounds like. Then one day when I am visiting Olga, he comes into the kitchen, where the two of us are hanging on the refrigerator door. As if resuming a conversation that had just been interrupted, he walks right up to me and says impatiently, wiping at his tiny mustache, "The cabbages! What about the cabbages?"

I gape at him. This is the most he's said to me through all the bottomless afternoons Olga and I have spent together lounging on their living room floor, awash in a glaze of television reruns. I wonder if this sort of outburst is an effect of his particular brand of insanity, resulting from having walked alone through burnt, abandoned cities. Annoyance flickers over Olga's face: She is easily maddened by her father. She has told me that when he wanders sleepless through their house at night, she too lies awake, mentally wandering after him through dark rooms.

"He's talking about the stuffed cabbage that your dad made last week," Olga says, sighing.

I rack my brain—Olga did come over for dinner, and Bud always sends people home with food, but I have no memory of what we'd eaten. Mr. Basilovich glances at me expectantly. "Was it okay?" I ask.

"Was it okay? Was it okay?" His voice rises, eyebrows jutting. He looks offended.

"I gave him some of the cabbages. He hasn't talked about anything else all week," Olga groans.

"They are beautiful," he says in his Eastern European accent that always strikes me as both ironic and wistful. Each of my friends has parents who grew up speaking different languages from our own, parents who are all too emotional or colorful for comfort. Our fathers ignore or argue with the TV; they sit in Bermuda shorts and black socks at the kitchen table and tell us too much about who they were. They're given to blurting out intense things, like Bud, who will suddenly, ominously observe, "If I live, I live; if I die, I die," or his more succinctly tragic favorite, "*I can't take it.*"

Mr. Basilovich's American wife ghosts around the corner, glancing at him. She is part companion and part keeper. A sort of continual alertness flows in an unbreaking current beneath her skin, with at least one part of her gaze always fixed on her sensitive husband. She quit her own job in order to drive Mr. Basilovich directly to and from work and to bring him his lunches. She watches his face as he falls asleep and wakes him if he falls too far.

"The skin of your father's cooked cabbage is like a flower," he goes on, making a poem of cabbage, wrapped up in a meal that I don't remember eating. His hands sculpt a soft form in the air as if he is describing a woman's body.

"Yeah, my dad says cooked cabbage should be like a lady's skin," I say, then catch myself, distressed that I've actually quoted Bud.

But Mr. Basilovich is pleased by these thoughts of a kindred spirit. "Yes, of course, like the softest skin. The butter, how it works through the cabbage leaves! And the taste of lamb comes next"—he looks delicately at his wife—"like a kiss."

Olga looks away, embarrassed by her father, who has gone in one moment from intellectual and aloof to too sensual and nakedly emotional. "Dad, come on, don't talk about food like that," she says, and folds her arms. "It's just food."

Mr. Basilovich breaks off and stares at their kitchen table, smoothing one palm over its surface, back and forth, a bare trace of a smile on his face. "Yes," he says, "just food." He is different from my father, but I recognize something in him. He never seems to be entirely in the room. His gaze is forever wafting over shoulders and seeking out doorways; he is only partially present.

Mr. Basilovich decides that as an emissary of my father, I must taste the Russian-Polish-Ukrainian-Jewish version of stuffed cabbages, which he calls *golubtsi.* To Olga's astonishment, her scholarly father ties on his wife's apron and rattles through the cupboards, mumbling to himself in one of his other languages; she has never seen him cook before. We watch him through the doorway—me; Stasia, the younger sister; Olga; and her mother—as Mr. Basilovich chops, heats, and stirs, efficient and brisk as a scientist. Olga glances at her mother anxiously.

Twelve-year-old Stasia leans against the refrigerator and nips at the edges of her cuticles, then sighs and fluffs her big Farrah Fawcett hair. "Let's get out of here," she says. The three of us move to her bedroom to listen to music. Olga and Stasia discuss the aggravating weirdness of their father—the mournful, wordless songs he sings in the shower, the drawer full of old, crackling foreign money and photographs of frowning women, with their black eyes and high, slanted cheekbones. "Who are they?" Stasia asks us in annoyance. "He won't tell."

"No, he'll never tell," Olga says.

Somewhere in the midst of the David Bowie album, an aroma starts to bloom around us.

We wander back to the kitchen doorway in time to see Mr. Basilovich pulling a pan out of the oven. It's layered with velvety, glistening packets of cabbage filled with minced beef and carrot. He carefully transfers the cabbages to a platter with a serving spoon, gives us each a fork but no plate, then stands beside the dish, eyes modestly downturned. Olga spears a piece of cabbage and takes a bite. "Oh!" she says. She touches the base of her throat and smiles at her father. "It's wonderful."

Stasia, who has been skeptical, takes a small bite, then another. She blinks and blinks. "Oh, wow," she says.

I slide my fork through the cabbage. It's soft and mellow and evaporates in my mouth, the pork and carrot mildly evanesced, exquisitely intertwined.

"Is it good?" he asks me, and smiles. "Is it good?"

Not long after the day of the ephemeral cabbage, my friend Sonja calls. Olga has told her that their father hasn't left his bed or stopped crying for a week. "Can you imagine?" she says. "Olga says he's been crying in his sleep—his pillows are all soaked." No matter how hard his wife has tried to shake him from his crying dreams, she cannot do it. After two weeks of crying, Mr. Basilovich is hospitalized.

He is kept under sedation for a week. Every day, Olga rushes back to his hospital room right after school, bringing him novels and chocolates, any little treat she can dream up to try to entice her father back to life. "He looks at me," Olga reports from the hospital phone.

"He even tries to smile. But it's like it's hurting him." There is a long pause where I can hear the slip of her breath, the texture of the telephone silence. "His eyes look burned."

A few days later, I get a call from Sonja. I am in the kitchen. My father has just slid a tray of lamb-stuffed cabbages out of the oven for me to bring to my friend's father in the hospital. Sonja tells me that the previous night, just when he seemed to be getting a bit better, joking with the nurses, eating a bite of tuna casserole, Mr. Basilovich had been left unattended for a stray moment between the ongoing visits of friends and family and nurses. He got out of bed, scuffed on his slippers, walked to his sixth-story hospital window, slid it open, and jumped.

"So he finally wins," Sonja says to me in her patient, furious way. "He finally gets what he's wanted all this time."

On the morning of the funeral for Mr. Basilovich, I wake near dawn. I lay out the gray dress I will wear to the service; it drifts like a shadow over my bed. It's early, and I feel restless and edgy. I walk out to the upstairs deck and sit with my back against the wall, still in pajamas, watching the sun glossing over the fields. The night before was cool and wet, and the dawn is coming up warm, twisting arabesques of steam over the road. I have lost myself in studying the ghostly patterns and nurturing a mild sadness under my ribs, when there is a commotion of wings. A white, round pigeon settles on the corner of the deck railing, not more than a foot or so away from me, close enough that I can hear the quiet purring clicks in its throat, the tick of its claws as it turns on the rail.

I hold still, barely breathing, and stare at the bird. It comes so close that I think it will climb up my arm. It turns its profile to me, watching for a long moment with its unblinking eye. Then the wings scatter, flashing it into the clouds. I watch it disappear into the whitening sky and think, for some reason, to wave after it. It is not until some years later that I learn that *golubsti*, the name of Mr. Basilovich's stuffed cabbages, refers to their plump round shape and means, literally, "pigeon."

"IN HONOR OF MR. BASILOVICH" CABBAGE ROLLS

STUFFING

1 cup long-grain rice
1 can (15 ounces)
  chickpeas, drained and
  mashed
½ pound ground beef
1 onion, finely diced

½ teaspoon ground
  cinnamon
½ teaspoon ground cumin
Salt and freshly ground
  pepper
¼ cup water

1 head of cabbage
1½ pounds lamb shoulder or
  shanks

3 cloves garlic, halved

SAUCE

½ cup ketchup
½ cup Worcestershire sauce

½ cup lemon juice
1 cup water

In a medium bowl, combine all the stuffing ingredients.

Rinse and remove the leaves from the cabbage. Blanch the leaves in 2 or 3 batches in boiling water until slightly soft; drain. Trim out stem ends and set aside. Place about 1 tablespoon of the stuffing at the bottom of each leaf, roll once, fold in the sides, then finish rolling.

Place the stem ends and coarsely chopped leftover cabbage leaves on the bottom of a 4-quart pot. Place the lamb over the cabbage pieces and scatter half of the garlic cloves over this. Place the cabbage rolls over the lamb and scatter the remaining garlic cloves among the rolls. Stir together the sauce ingredients and pour over all. Bring to a boil, and then simmer for 2 hours. Turn out onto a platter or tray.

The cabbage rolls are very good served with plain yogurt and a salad.

SERVES ABOUT 6.

TWELVE

Restaurant of Our Dreams

One day I wake up and there's that crazy old energy in the house again. Bud is excited, amplified, larger than life. He sings at us from the kitchen, "Oh, who wants a nice egg or three?" Improvising as he goes, "a nice egg, not an ugly one, not a grumpy one, not a low-down mean and miserable one." His grin cracks his face, then he laughs quietly, sneakily, nodding and inviting us to join this insider joke, whatever it is. Mom just smiles and rolls her eyes as though she knows what the joke is and it's pretty corny and she's not telling. All afternoon there are long, animated phone conversations in Arabic. Later these are followed by middle-of-the-night calls from overseas.

The next morning, Monica and Suzy congregate on my bed, staring with their serious eyes. I loll back, sighing, and say, "It's one of two things: We are either moving back to Jordan again or . . . it's another restaurant."

Bud's earlier efforts were more tentative, an ambitious dreaming out loud: "I've got to run a place of my own." Various friends and relatives chimed in, egging him on: "Sure, Gus, that'd be great. We'll help out!"

At least that's the way the process is described to me when I get older. On two, three, or maybe more prior occasions, Bud has picked out a restaurant for sale, called meetings with his affluent cronies, and lined up investors, only to have them back out at the eleventh hour, the deals dribbling apart just before they sign the lease. I imagine their crises of faith: Well, it was fun to talk about, but . . . talk is just talk, and what does Gus really know about running a business?

These are all dispatches from the adult world, however, a place I know remarkably little about. I catch only shreds of family gossip and retain little of that. When I eventually move out on my own into the world, my family history is forever coming as a shock: the secret medical conditions, the broken marriages, the police reports, the cousin who finagled having a blank diploma folder handed to him at his college graduation ceremony so his parents wouldn't know he hadn't been to a class in years.

This time, Bud tells us, it's different. The place he plans to buy is *perfect, perfect, perfect* (excellent location, good foot traffic, high visibility, loyal clientele). A can't-miss. The owner is selling his treasured restaurant at a clearance price because he and his wife—the head chef—are getting a divorce. Bud is ecstatic as he describes his family utopia: "I will be in back, creating! You and your sisters will be out front, taking the orders and making the customers happy and laughing." He sits back and studies the ceiling. "It's going to be running together like this—" He interlaces his fingers. "A perfect running-together machine!" Mom opens her mouth, looks as though she's forgotten what she was going to say, closes it.

I scowl. I'm in my second year of junior high, and none of my friends have jobs. I'm not sure what exactly he has in mind for my younger sisters, but he isn't overly concerned with the child labor laws. "I notice that no one asked the local slaves for their opinions," I say, pouting.

Bud looks startled, then bursts into laughter. "Oh ho ho, good one. Like they have slaves in America!"

Family summits take place. There are more phone calls from Jordan. I learn that Bud still has a parcel or two of inherited land in Jordan that he's going to sell. This is momentous—a final exchange. It's the first time I've known Bud to be willing to put his new country before his homeland.

Bud's excitement over the restaurant is palpable. It will be a real breakthrough, an amazing, modern combination of Arabic and American food, he says. It's the mixture that I grew up with, the only sort of cooking that makes sense to me. Bud says that first we need to make a field trip and investigate what the "other guys" are offering. At this point in time, the only Arabic restaurant in Syracuse is a little joint called King David up on Marshall Street, the student-clogged thoroughfare on the cusp of Syracuse University. King David is eternally crammed with college kids—Arab and non-Arab alike. It is small and intriguing, filled with Persian carpets and Arabic music, its windows sweaty with condensation. You pass its front door through a fragrant mist of garlic and olive oil. The brother runs the cash register, and the sister is the genius in the kitchen. I adore it there and always order the same thing—a tender falafel sandwich in pita, tabbouleh salad, and sweet apricot nectar to drink.

One Saturday, Bud and I go "undercover" for lunch at King David, which doesn't seem to be any different from the way we usually eat lunch there. Bud goes into his routine: He rejects the first two tables we're shown, and after we're finally settled he waits for one of the Arab student-waiters to come over and launches into a torrent of Arabic greetings—how are you, how are your parents, you look healthy, may you prosper—as if they've been friends all their lives. When they get around to discussing, finally, what we'd like to eat, Bud says, "Oh, you know, nothing, really. Just put me a little of this, a little of that—" And he gestures humbly at the table, suggesting he'd be happy with a crust of stale bread.

What happens is what always happens. The owner leans out of the kitchen, wipes back her hair, and waves to us. Dishes fill the tabletop, and the waiter brings bottomless baskets of pita bread. We will never be able to finish it all—that's the point. We are meant to be overwhelmed, stuffed to the gills, groaning. There's a way to say "a lot" in Arabic, but no way to say "too much."

Our waiter is an SU student. Bud quickly ascertains that his name is Waleed, he's from Lebanon, he's majoring in engineering, he's twenty-two years old, and he's not yet married.

"Why not?" Bud demands. I tighten my lips and look away. "Life is short and marriage is a pleasure. It's like food," Bud says. "Why are you going to drink water when you can drink tea?"

"But water is the greatest drink of all," Waleed parries.

Bud nods and picks up a falafel, examining it as if it's a fallen apple blossom. "The strongest wisdom is the wisdom of the body."

Waleed hugs his serving tray to his chest and says, "But the greatest wisdom is the wisdom of Allah."

Waleed bows and goes off to the kitchen to find one more dish to fill the last inch of space on our table. Bud looks after him a moment, then returns his attention to the table. He bites into the falafel, and I know what he is tasting—the deep, smoky, slightly charred warmth, the crumbling outer crust giving way to the tender, mealy, spicy interior. He nods and shakes a thoughtful finger in the air. "When we get our restaurant, Waleed will come to work for us."

Waleed brings out two more dishes: succulent tomatoes filled with spiced ground chicken, and dainty, budlike artichokes steamed in lemon and garlic.

"I can't take it!" Bud sputters happily, and fans his hand over the filled tabletop to signal that things are out of control. "It's impossible—there's no room. Now you're just going crazy."

Waleed tilts a smile in my direction, bringing me to attention. He nudges, nudges, dish lapping dish, until like the miracle of loaves and fishes, what is small is made large: The little space expands until the dishes fit. "In this world, there is always more room," Waleed says. "Thanks be to God."

"You see?" Bud leans in my direction after Waleed has left, indicates all the plates covering the table, lifts his eyebrows. "An engineering student!" He studies the food, nodding with great satisfaction. "Just wait till we have our restaurant."

VERY FRIED FALAFELS

2 cups dried chickpeas, soaked in water overnight and drained	1 teaspoon ground cumin
	1 teaspoon ground coriander
3 cloves garlic, crushed	1 teaspoon oregano
¼ cup sesame seeds	2 teaspoons baking powder
¼ cup finely chopped flat-leaf parsley	½ teaspoon cayenne pepper
	¼ teaspoon freshly ground
2 teaspoons salt	black pepper

Purée all the ingredients in a food processor. Let the mixture
stand for 1 hour. Form the mixture into little patties or balls about
the size of walnuts. Deep-fry the falafel in oil until golden brown.
Drain on paper towels.

SERVES 6.

When we get our restaurant, I know what I'm going to wear. I besiege
Mom with questions about my waitressing uniform; she rubs her temples and agrees to anything. She says I can wear red patent-leather boots
and a pleated skirt above my knees. My little sisters, it's decided, will
work back in the kitchen, where they won't be so obvious. Bud says this
place has a bar, and right away I imagine low lights twirling with cigarette smoke, the clink of ice in glasses, murmurous laughter, black velvet booths, and luxuriant platters of food. I get interested.

The plans build. We discuss menus. Bud envisions Arabic-fusion
food—though no one calls it that at the time—Arabic, American,
and French! Maybe Italian. Why not Italian? Look at Libya! The Italians occupied Libya, and now they've got all kinds of pasta in their
lentils. Smart Libyans!

Bud's outlook brightens. He seems less withered by his long workdays as an administrator in the local hospital, where his main duty is to
sit at a big desk listening to a stream of employee complaints. We talk
about the restaurant every night at the dinner table. According to Bud,
this golden place, no mere restaurant, will be a Shangri-la that finally
heals the old wound between East and West. All languages will be spoken
here, all religions honored. And the food will be pure and true as the first
food, the kind that weighed down golden boughs and shone in the wind.

A business of one's own—at last!

"You see this *bamia?*" he says to us, holding up a chunk of okra
stewed in tomato on his fork. "Americans are nervous with *bamia*
because they fear the slime. You know how to take away the slime?"

My sisters and I shake our heads.

"You have to boil it good first and then you fry it! And sometimes
you reverse it. How many people you think know about *that*?"

We marvel. Not many. Hardly anybody.

"When we get our restaurant," he says, and eats his bite of okra, "it will be full of secrets like this."

Mom moves around the edge of the kitchen table, a stack of dirty dishes in her hands, an expression on her face as though she's trying to decipher some inscription on the kitchen cabinets. But it's too old, unknown, and the dishes are muttering to her. She doesn't say anything.

There are weeks and then months of debates, schemes, and outlines. The phone rings at all hours. You never know when you'll lift the receiver to the hiss of the overseas connection. Incredibly, Bud's relatives seem to be convinced by his business plan this time. Several have even promised to buy shares in the place. Who could fail to be moved by Bud's exultant rhapsodizing? His voice bounces; he seems to give off a hum.

After much negotiation with lawyers, real estate agents, and the gloomy owner, whose disconcerting gaze lingers on Bud long after conversation has ceased, they work out the last details and agree on a signing date. To celebrate on the night before he is due to go in and sign the lease, Bud prepares a grand dinner starring a golden chicken *msukhan*. This is the traditional Palestinian dish, which owes its ravishing succulence to a few simple ingredients—chicken, onions, and so much olive oil that the chicken is nearly poached in it, turning its flesh soft and amber as a silk purse.

"Do you see this chicken, girls?" he asks as we break off tender bites with our forks. "Do you know what it's saying to us?"

No, what, Dad?

"It's saying, 'I am more delicious than anything. People will come from everywhere to taste me. I am the queen of all!' " He sighs and gazes fondly at the queen. "Only here in America can such a thing as this happen," he says. "I used to be crazy—back in the days when I wanted to go back to Jordan. I was like a baby who only wants to be with his mother. But now!" He shakes a finger. "A person grows up, he looks around, he sees with his eyes . . . and his head . . . and his feet. You see with every part."

"What do you see, Dad?"

He flares his open hand to encompass the entire kitchen. "You see America the beautiful. It's right here. And it's telling you: Come here, open a restaurant, be who you are. America is like Mo Kadeem, it knows what it wants and it says to go get it. I have been crazy to want to go back home. You know what Jordan says to me? It says, Be who I tell you to be!"

The day of the signing arrives bright and fresh. I'm brimming with excitement. Mom props her elbows on the kitchen table, composed and watchful, part of her suspended. This is Bud's restaurant, but she will own it, too, help pay for it and run it. We are all characters in my father's restaurant dream.

It's a Friday and Bud promises he will take us to see the place this weekend. First he and Mom are driving to the restaurant after work to sign the paperwork. "We'll be home before six, and then, you know what—Cosmo's pizza!" he says, his voice lifted with glee. "This is the last time I won't have to cook for a living." My sisters and I wait around the house in a state of nervous exhaustion, wrung out with anticipation.

We watch *Dark Shadows* on TV; the floating severed head is on the loose again. But we talk through the whole show, lounging all over the big half-moon couch in the living room, our bodies slack, as if it's too much work to even hold ourselves upright. "What do you think it's gonna be like?" one of us says for the eighth or ninth time, hands strumming the cushions. "Is it gonna be great or is Dad crazy?"

The light changes, and reflections from the fields in our big windows drift over the TV screen. We run out of questions and stare at *Electric Company, Wild Wild West, The Brady Bunch.* When the evening news comes and goes, we start to stare at the windows. The long twilight sifts like hookah smoke into the house. Where are they?

It's nighttime when Mom and Bud get back. The car rolls impossibly slowly up the driveway. We sit up, then wait, motionless, listening to the crunch of tires on gravel, the pop and ping of tiny stones under the car. Our parents come in slowly, their footsteps deliberate, as if there is too much gravity in the air. They fumble with the keys at the door. We sit there, listening. Bud is too quiet. He always has something to say. Whether he's happy or sad, cooking, shaving, or driving, he's always talking about something. But tonight he doesn't say a word, just goes straight upstairs to bed.

Without his dinner.

Mom sits at the kitchen table with us and rubs her forehead with her fingers for a while, and then she says, "I had a feeling about this, right from the start."

We lean in. "What happened?"

She shakes her head as if she'd like to cross out all the past weeks and months of big hopes. She explains that the restaurant had been very successful, but once the owner's chef-wife left him for their produce supplier, he no longer had the heart to run his business. He wanted to do away with painful reminders of what they'd had together, and he priced the restaurant cheaply just to move it along. Bud liked the inky blue backdrop of this story, the folds of passion and betrayal, which made the place feel more exciting and elusive. But passion, Mom knew, does not necessarily provide the optimum conditions for business transactions. Apparently, after months of separation, word got down to the wife in her love nest in Florida that the restaurant was being sold. And it seems she'd had a change of heart. She'd taken the next flight back to Syracuse and reclaimed her husband, their home, and their restaurant. Which is only to be expected when you consider that, whatever it is, knowing that someone else wants something always makes that thing more alluring.

When Mom and Bud had walked into the restaurant, the owner, whom they'd known to be chronically melancholy, his chest sunken and neck curled, now met them chin first, his arm wrapped around a slim blond woman in a lilac pantsuit, his wife. He refused to hand over the keys. He beamed and shook his head. "Sorry," he said over and over, grinning hugely. "No sale, no sale. We changed our minds."

At first Bud also laughed, as if it were all a huge merry, *Candid Camera*-style prank. He's kidding, right? That's how these crazy Americans are! But the owner just kept grinning until Bud became distraught, flushed, eyes stunned with panic. He shook, he demanded, he shouted. He threw a fork across the dining room. He grabbed one of the tables as though he were going to run out the door with it. He was outraged, incredulous, but he had no words for any of it. In the old country, he might have known what to say—called upon his brothers and uncles, made threats, called for retribution—but here nothing was clear. He knew none of the American language of lawyers and court and lawsuits. That was only what people said on TV. All he knew was that, here and now, at the very moment of grasping it, his life's dream had turned to dust in his hands.

"I don't believe it," I say to Mom, my forearms flat on the table. "Can they do that?"

Mom shrugs. "I don't know. I guess they did."

"But—but—" My hands tighten and my ears buzz. The kitchen looks woozy and soft. I hadn't expected this. I'm surprised by how disappointed I feel. "But it isn't fair!"

She turns her steady blue eyes to me. This is the way she holds to things, lightly, knowing to let such stuff pass on and through. Neither Bud nor I can do this. We seize up, our insides tightening fiercely around our desires. I stare at the corners of the ceiling as if the answer will be written there, in the rough plaster swirls. Better not to have dreams at all, I think in a surge of bitterness, than to feel this way. Better not to know what could have been. "I could tell as soon as I saw them," Mom says almost apologetically. "There was just no way."

I feel Bud's presence, turning in their bedroom, sleeping away his broken dreams, lost in the thin gray air of loss and disappointment.

PERFECTLY TENDER *BAMIA*

½ cup olive oil

6 medium onions, quartered

4 garlic cloves

1 pound okra, trimmed

3 large tomatoes, chopped

1 can (15 ounces) chicken broth

Juice from 1 lemon

In a saucepan, heat the oil over moderate heat, add the onions, and sauté until translucent. Add the garlic and okra and stir until the okra is soft. Add the tomatoes and stir a few minutes. Add the broth and bring to a boil. Reduce the heat to low, cover, and simmer about 30 minutes. Sprinkle with the lemon juice, cover, and simmer another 10 minutes.

Serve alongside a golden chicken *msukhan* or a nice lamb kibbeh.

SERVES 6.

THIRTEEN

The Language of Baklava

Auntie Aya is in town. You can tell by the way all the uncles and older cousins drive over to the Route 57 Chalet, a mile from my parents' house. It's a grim cinder-block motel the color of dust, but she picked it out on the drive in from the airport. "There"—finger to the window—"that's where I want to stay." The uncles and cousins come back from her hotel with their once graying mustaches and sideburns miraculously transformed to a gleaming black; they also walk stiffly upright, brittle with pain, their backs arched, arms lifted a few inches, dainty as ballerinas.

"She does the cupping," Bud tells us in a lowered voice that edges between pride and embarrassment. This is one of Aya's great medical specialties. The procedure involves lighting small tapers placed inside little glass cups, which are then inverted over the afflicted body part. The heat of the doused flame creates a suction, raising cruel red welts on the skin. These welts are considered openings, escape passages for dark fevers and spirits to pass through on their way out of the body. Aya's patients are covered with a rash of circular welts after she treats them, and they're in so much pain that for a while even the sheerest fiber of a fine Damascene cotton shirt is too much to bear.

Bud shakes his head and says they're all totally *majnoon*—crazy. But then he too goes out and returns with his mustache—until very recently steel gray—now finer, blacker, and shinier than any he's ever had in his life. "Her medicine, it's from the real old-time Bedu," he confides, tugging at his new, improved mustache. Auntie Aya, the family matriarch, has lived alone in the desert for years in her "country retreat," a lyrical stone-and-marble house that one of her suitors had built for her. She knows the ways of the desert people, the

Bedouins—including the magical, beautifying, and medicinal uses of herbs, minerals, and elements.

Bud has not seen the desert for a long time. He has been living in apartments, town houses, two-family homes, ranch homes, suburban manors with attached garages, and bungalows. He is a modern guy. He senses that the evil eye, and its malevolent force of envy, vengeance, and greed, is not really modern or *civilized.* But still he keeps the prayer beads draped around his rearview mirror to ward off the evil eye, *just in case* anyone might be harboring dark or covetous thoughts toward his 1975 Rambler. He refuses to submit to the cupping, but he eats parsley, "to bring money," and he makes secret gestures with his hand when he thinks someone has looked at him "the wrong way."

Bud has many unique treatments that he's unaware aren't standard medical procedure all over the States. He removes dust from our eyes by licking them clean, and he rubs a cut clove of garlic over a bee sting, a piece of onion over a mosquito bite.

Besides my aunt's exploits with herbs and cosmetics, she is also, like most Bedu, a bit of a bonesetter, an exorcist, and a general practitioner. She works extensively with leeches, specialized teas, and earthy spices that she has ground in her own mortar. She apprenticed under Sitt Arjah, or the Limping Lady, the gifted midwife of Yehdoudeh who delivered Aya and the many little brothers who followed her. My aunt also loves the fall fashions at J. C. Penney and feels strongly that the nails should match the lips and the shoes must, if at all possible, match the purse.

The first time I ever met Aunt Aya was in Amman when I was eight years old. After a boring lunch with some relatives in a dull, grand house devoid of children, I'd escaped into the kitchen to get some water, expecting to see a maid, and run into Aya instead. She was sitting like an empress at the kitchen table, a burning Pall Mall between her index and middle fingers, the beetle-shelled scarlet nails glimmering. She hadn't sat with us at lunch, even though this was apparently her house. I realized with a burst of understanding that she was escaping from the relatives as well. She looked me over, her eyes fierce inside thick wings of black eyeliner, lips pointed and lacquered an uncompromising red, hair a shimmering, coal black tower, and skin powdered white.

I think we stared at each other a full minute before either of us spoke. Auntie Aya finally gestured a little with the cigarette and said, "Go ahead, then, let me see you walk across the room."

I had the sense that I was auditioning for the role of a lifetime, and I put everything I had into it. I settled on something between a swoon and a glide, attempting to use every muscle in my body while pretending for some reason to be waving my own smoldering cigarette. When I finally made it across the room this way, I touched the wall like a swimmer and shimmied back to the other side again.

"Mm-hm, mm-hm," she said. She took a deep drag on the Pall Mall, her eyes slivering narrow and wet, the cigarette ember glowing. Then came a long, steamy exhale, after which she said, "I see you haven't a bone in your body."

Bud laughs anxiously and averts his eyes when one of his brothers returns from Auntie Aya, but I know that Bud has also consulted her on treatments. One night, I overhear him murmur to his sister over the phone, asking if she ever sees the spirit of their father. Because, he says, he has. He has spotted him wandering through the kitchen at night. He describes the ghost looming over the refrigerator door, as if he would like to peek inside—but how can a ghost open a refrigerator? A fiery thrill runs from my nape through my wrists. He's afraid that his father is hungry, the same father he fed spoon by spoon during his last days on the earth. Bud asks, Is this possible? If so, what should I feed him? How? I strain to listen, desperate to know the answer, but it's hard to make out his whispered Arabic. A few days later, I find a small glass full of watery *araq* beside a small loaf of bread on the window ledge in the dining room.

This is Auntie's first visit to this country in years, and she is not used to things. She, my mother, Monica, Suzy, and I patrol the shopping malls, where Aya is upset by fashion offenders—particularly the ones in stretch pants or matching pastel sweat suits. "Now, will you look at that?" she flares up, startling a woman in a tight green sweat suit. "Isn't that just a shame? Why does she want to squeeze herself into something like a little pork sausage? Why must she do it in that color? Will nothing else satisfy her?"

Mom steers us quickly into the food court. There, Aya samples my Orange Julius with a parfait spoon, looks astounded, and pronounces it inedible. She rests her chin on her fist and sighs. "In Jordan," she comments, "not many can afford fashion, so it isn't such an issue. But in America, where anyone can afford anything, *why this*?" she laments, gazing at the sea of jeans and sweat suits. "Why?"

Aunt Aya happens to have arrived at the time of the Long War between me and Bud. This war started sometime after I turned thirteen, around the day that Bud came home early from work, got the mail first, and found a tattletale midterm report enumerating my many crimes in Algebra 1, including talking in class, passing notes, cutting up, failing the first quiz, and general lazy, goon-headed good-for-nothingness. When the school bus pulled up in front of our house that afternoon, I spotted Bud from the bus window. He was standing at the bottom of the driveway, waiting.

He flapped the white letter in the air as I walked up, ranting that this time I'd done it—I'd really, really done it. He called the parents of one of the girls I'd giggled with throughout algebra and told them that their daughter, Molly, was a "criminal" and a "bad influence" and to keep her away from his daughter. He tore the school letter into confetti, threw the pieces into the air, grabbed his hair, and shouted, "That's it! Finish! No more! I can't take it!" He was sending me back to Jordan, he couldn't take one more second of any of it.

For as long as I'd known him, there were times when my father's emotions roared and threatened to incinerate him and everyone else in the room. Bud would come home in a bad mood from his latest stressful, impossible job—as a court bailiff, carpet salesman, hospital custodian, department store security guard—go to the upstairs bedroom, and storm around over our heads, cursing and stomping and yelling to himself until he'd yelled it all out. He was trapped, destitute in the American dream. Then he'd come back down to take us out for ice cream. These episodes were like electrical storms, breaking with ferocity and passing swiftly. This wasn't a problem for me until I hit thirteen. Then it was as if the chemical composition of the air in our house had changed. Something made Bud edgy and frantic and paranoid, and something made me skulk in my room for hours on end.

Our fights roll like thunder through the house. It's the way I'm dressed, the late hour I returned home, a bad mark in school. Frequently it will be about something as subtle as a mere glance or my "attitude."

"Look at the expression on her!" Bud cries out midfight if I pout or roll my eyes. "*Look* at the belligerence—it's written all over her!"

In the end, the cause of the fight is always the same: the astonishing fact that I'm growing up. Worse, this happens to be going on in America, where to Bud's mind girls are famous for such stunts. He blames my whole adolescence on the United States and believes that in Jordan the problem would be solved.

"You say one more word like that," he threatens, pointing—I may have said a sulky "Fine" in response to his "How was school?"—"and I'm sending you back home to Jordan! You'll go live with Auntie Aya. She'll straighten you out a hundred percent."

"I'll never go back there. You can't make me," I retort like a movie tough guy, driven by the same surge of rage as Bud's. "That isn't my home. I don't care what you say. My home is *here.*"

"You say this to your father." Bud's face glows, his hands rise in the air. "You deny your ancestors and culture and your whole family!"

"*My* family isn't Jordanian," I throw back at him, the refrain of my adolescence. "My family is American!"

He opens his mouth, pulls at his hair, squeezes shut his eyes. He runs into the next room, as if trying to escape from me, then suddenly bends, seizes one of the fluted dining room chairs, and flings it across the room so hard that it shatters against the wall.

. . .

I remember the home of certain well-to-do cousins in Amman where the girls were indeed polite, docile, and obedient to their father, treating him more like an official in the house than a family member. These daughters attended the private girls' school with its coal gray uniforms and regimented, straight-backed rows of chairs. They kept their voices low and discreet, bowed their heads, brought their father slippers, cookies, and books, then scurried away, relieved of duty. There was no joshing, no in-depth reading in the bathroom, no flying off the top stairs, and no father in the kitchen. They weren't friends, they were employees. But my father sees only the polished, lowered tops of the girls' heads and the tranquil, limpid air in their house. He doesn't notice the expression on their faces.

So every week and then every day, my father and I cross words and burnt colors fly over our faces. The tension between us lowers the ceiling, draws in the walls, makes the floor glow—too hot to walk on. When I come home one day and my auntie is waiting in the kitchen, the blood seems to fall from my head in a sheet. My first thought is that she's come to take me away. Aunt Aya looks me up and down and up again and says, "*Habeebti,* you look like the terrible ghost of the Black Valley."

She gestures for me to sit, as if it is I who has once again burst into her kitchen, then she sits across from me at the kitchen table, studying my face closely. She turns my hands over, looks at a lock of my hair, frowns, and asks why I'm so thin and white anyway.

I chew at the edge of a nail for a second, studying the mica speckles in the linoleum floor. Suddenly I am telling her what, at the time, I think the problem is: that Bud wants to ship me back to Jordan. Because somehow, somewhere along the line, I've gone bad. Just because I argue with him relentlessly, it doesn't mean that some very big part of me isn't convinced that he must be right. He is, after all, the father.

Her kohl-lined eyes widen and her scarlet mouth falls open. She is sixty, yet her hair is like polished onyx and her eyes are wine black. Her clothes are bright and tropical, given to drifting on the breeze, and she bedecks herself with armfuls of ringing golden bangles.

"Oh, that is all dog-headed nonsense," she says. "Look at you—" She seizes my hand and flaps it in the air. "You're soft as a fish. What are you going to do in Jordan? What would they do with you?"

She instructs me to stay right where I am, and then she bustles to the front entryway, comes back with a suitcase, and lays it flat on the kitchen table. She unzips the long, whining zipper and the top flaps back, releasing a pungent puff of dust. Inside the suitcase are dozens of small plastic and paper bags filled with all sorts of dried herbs, shrunken buds, and dark spices. "Lucky that Mr. Customs Man didn't look in this bag!" she says, chuckling. She sprinkles a few pinches from certain containers into a pan of water and makes me a cup of what she calls "shaking tea." "For when you need to calm down and figure things out," she says.

It's a tawny brown liquid. I inhale, and a mist fills my sinuses and chest. It mingles with the brown melancholy inside of me. It tastes a bit like bark and earth and tears, yet somehow it's delicious. It releases particles of sleeplessness and sadness embedded within me. I sigh, my eyes well, my nose runs, my mouth waters. I want more. But Aunt Aya says, "That's enough," and puts her hand over mine. She examines the empty cup for some sort of sign, then sighs, clicks her tongue, and puts the cup in the sink.

SHAKING TEA INFUSION (MODERN VERSION)

1 cup water
1 small piece dried ginger
¼ teaspoon whole cloves
1 cinnamon stick
1 teaspoon anise seeds
   (optional)

1 teaspoon sugar
Pinch salt
2 teaspoons chopped
   almonds or pistachios

In a saucepan, cover and gently simmer all the ingredients except the nuts for 10 minutes. Strain into a nice mug and garnish with the nuts. Serve with sugar or honey.

MAKES 1 SERVING.

"Okay," she says. "I recommend that we bake."

"Fine," I say, then shock myself by saying, "As long as it isn't Arabic."

She lifts a taut brow.

I lean forward, perverse and obstinate. There is a fine, nictitating tremor in my right hand. I narrow my eyes and say, "I hate Arabic food!" Then I look away quickly, afraid to see her reaction and frightened of my terrible words. Worse even, it seems at that moment, than saying, "I'm not an Arab." It is like a rush of cold air after holding in my breath for too long. I am dizzy.

Auntie Aya sits back down across from me, slaps her hand flat on the linoleum, and says, "Fine, I'm not so impressed. I hate it, too!"

I stare at her. My breath chugs in my chest. I'd expected—I realize now—to be punished for saying such a thing. But that's not what is happening. Aya's face is direct and bold. She tosses back a few strands of hair, then looks at me. "But how do you feel about baklava?"

Something large and heavy opens its wings and begins to lift from my rib cage. Baklava?

"The Arabs say *baklawa,* of course, but the Greeks call it 'baklava.' I can't imagine what the Turks call it. And I don't know who made it first, but we can call it baklava since we both hate Arabic food."

I consider this. "Fine," I say.

Aunt Aya's cooking is so good, they say she can tempt angels out of the trees. It's too good, some of my aunties say, it's not natural. For some reason, no one can remember her recipes after she demonstrates her dishes, and she never writes them down. If you write them, Aya says, they lose their power. I have been warned by some of the other family not to eat her food, told that it's magical, a disruptive force.

"When you're old enough to know better," she says as we skim the liquid butter spoon by spoon, "you'll teach some man how to cook with you. And you'll see what happens then," she says, nodding and lowering her eyelids.

I stop, my spoon full of pale butter foam. "Why, what happens then?"

"Ahh," she says, her lashes sinking over the dark mercury of her eyes. "Ahh."

I look at the foam in my spoon before I spill it into the bowl.

Aunt Aya closes up her practice at the Route 57 Chalet. For a week, she comes to our house every day before my parents get home from work. We spend the afternoons together baking voluptuous pastries from a variety of ethnicities. We don't actually start with baklava, which she says is too "sensitive" at the moment. Our dough rolls out into cream puffs, layered cakes, tortes, *kolaches,* cookies. This, she says, is my tutorial in "womanliness," designed to help me make my womanly way in the world. The freezer is filled with desserts.

"Marry, don't marry," Auntie Aya says as we unfold layers of dough to make an apple strudel. "Just don't have your babies unless it's *absolutely necessary.*"

"How do I know if it's necessary?"

She stops and stares ahead, her hands gloved in flour. "Ask yourself, Do I want a baby or do I want to make a cake? The answer will come to you like bells ringing." She flickers her fingers in the air by her ear. "For me, almost always, the answer was *cake.*"

I am silent as I stare hard at the cup glittering with sugar. This is advice, but it feels more like pressing my ear to the wall. I don't want her to notice how closely I listen, or she might stop talking. What she says rings inside me like a spoon in a crystal glass. After years of assuming that the purpose of all this cooking and working—the purpose of everything, really—was to produce and grow babies, this is the first intimation I have heard of another way through life. It is the first time I've really understood that my aunt, with her houses filled with friends and siblings and servants and lovers, does not have children of her own.

"And your father! I know. Nobody can talk to that man. Well, your father does not know everything. He thinks he does, but I'm his older sister and I say no. Jordan is not the place he thinks it is. It won't save him; it can't even save itself." She sprinkles a layer of shaved chocolate into the filling for the cream puffs and adds, "It's never a bad idea to put a secret in your filling."

MONA LISA CREAM PUFFS

FILLING

2 cups heavy cream

½ package instant vanilla
   pudding

CHOUX PASTRY

1 cup water

½ cup butter

1 cup flour

¼ teaspoon salt

4 large eggs

2 tablespoons confectioner's
   sugar

TOPPING

1 dark chocolate bar

Preheat the oven to 350 degrees. Stir together the filling ingredients and put aside to set.

Bring the water to a boil in a saucepan. Add the butter and boil until melted. Add the flour and salt all at once and stir until it forms a dough, then scrape into a mixing bowl. Add the eggs one by one and beat in with a wooden spoon until smooth.

Scoop heaping tablespoonfuls onto a cookie sheet. Bake 20 minutes, until lightly brown. Let cool, then split open each pastry into equal halves.

Spoon the filling onto the bottom half of each pastry, shave the chocolate over the filling, then top with the other half of the pastry. You can also conserve some of the chocolate bar, melt it, and pour this over the top of the cream puff, for those who like a crowning touch.

MAKES 8 TO 10 CREAM PUFFS.

"Make sure to boil the attar syrup clear, then add the essence of rose so it will bloom," she says, stirring the pan of sweet syrup. She leans against the oven and folds her arms. "If you're going to kiss a boy, try to remember to eat a little parsley first. Also, think of a compliment for his mother. That's always good."

"Never let anyone tell you what to say or feel or think. No exceptions. If you can't say it out loud, then write it on a piece of paper."

She tosses some spices into a dry pan. "Heat up your spice before you add it to the mix so it will have something to say."

While clarifying butter, she brings her eye close to the skimming spoon, not missing a sliver of foam, and says, "We clean the butter to remind ourselves of the way our lives should be—light, delicate, and pure."

"The thing about cinnamon and ginger—they're pretty, yes, but they also bite, which is more interesting and can be dangerous."

"When a man tells you something, I don't care what it is, look at his eyes and hands. Don't worry too much about the words. If you can't see his eyes or his hands, don't believe any of it."

. . .

"High heels are good, but don't forget how to run."

"You can be yourself, whoever that is, like these Americans are always saying. But once in a while, it's better to be a mirage."

"How do you do that?" I ask, beating flour off my hands and apron.

"Ahh," says my aunt. "You must allow it to occur."

"People say food is a way to remember the past. Never mind about that. Food is a way to forget."

She is showing me how to make the phyllo dough that constitutes the foundation of so many Middle Eastern pastries. We work standing over the table, wrapping the dough around long, narrow wooden spindles to press out the exquisitely fine, papery sheets. This part of the process had always been invisible to me. As far as I knew, phyllo originated in waxed paper columns in freezer cribs.

"Food is not sweetness and families and little flying hearts. Look at this!" she cries, holding up a spindle. "Food is aggravation and too much work and hurting your back and trapping the women inside like slaves."

From my hunch over the table, I stare up at her.

"Food is robbery. Did you know that?" She stands straight, a handprint of flour at the base of her throat. "Let's say your country hasn't existed for very long at all. Just say. Then you announce to the world, yes!" She slaps her chest—another bloom of flour. "My people invented baklava! And there you have it, an instant history, a name."

"But—Dad says . . ." I struggle, for once in my life, to remember what he says. "Dad says that everyone invented baklava." It occurs to me only now to wonder what that means.

Aunt Aya rolls her eyes. "Your *father*? He's the worst of the worst. He thinks he cooks and eats Arabic food, but these walnuts weren't grown from Jordanian earth and this butter wasn't made from Jordanian lambs. He is eating the shadow of a memory. He cooks to remember, but the more he eats, the more he forgets."

I bite the edge of my lip. Somewhere on the horizon line of consciousness, I sense my ancient loyalty to Bud stir. I hesitate, then test an opinion. "That seems sort of . . . well, dramatic."

"Dramatic? You think food isn't dramatic!" she demands, wheeling on me. "You want drama—how about peace in the Middle East?" She yanks the apron from her waist and flings it at the back of the chair. "Fine, I'll tell you how to do it. Watch." She sits down, straightens her forearms on the kitchen table, laces her fingers together, and stares at me, her heavy lids drawn back.

I wait. I wrap my hands around my waist. "I don't think I—"

"Who am I?" she snaps. "I am America, Israel, England! What am I doing?" She waits another long moment, her eyes shining. "I'm shutting up and *listening*." She draws the last word out so it hisses through the air. "I am the presidents, the kings, the prime ministers, the highs and the mighties—L-I-S-T-E-N!" She spells the word in the air. "The woman who made the baklava has something to say to you! Voilà. You see? Now what am I doing?" She picks up an imaginary plate, lifts something from it, and takes an invisible bite. Then she closes her eyes and smiles and says, "Mmm . . . that is such delicious Arabic-Jordanian-Lebanese-Palestinian *baklawa*. Thank you so much for sharing it with us! Please will you come to our home now and have some of our food?" She puts down the plate and brushes imaginary crumbs from her fingers. "So now what did I just do?"

"You ate some *baklawa*?"

She curls her hand as if making a point so essential, it can be held only in the tips of the fingers. "I looked, I tasted, I spoke kindly and truthfully. I invited. You know what else? I keep doing it. I don't stop if it doesn't work on the first or the second or the third try. And like that!" She snaps the apron from the chair into the air, leaving a poof of flour like a wish. "There is your peace."

. . .

One day near the end of her visit, Aunt Aya comes over early before I get home from school and bakes something special. She hoists the big round tray from the oven onto the table. It's a baklava made with our homemade phyllo. "I asked around," she says. "There are reports that baklava originated in Anatolia—so we're safe. It's still not Arabic."

Baklava is her specialty. The layers turn flaky and buttery in the oven, but the real glory of this pastry as interpreted by my aunt is its central core of sweet, mild pistachios that roasts and develops during baking. The whole pastry is then sweetened and perfumed like a baby with an attar dashed with sprinklings of orange blossom and rose-water. When I inhale Auntie Aya's baklava, I press my hand to my sternum, as if I am smelling something too dear for this world. The scent contains the mysteries of time, loss, and grief, as well as promises of journeys and rebirth. I pick up a piece and taste it. I eat and eat. The baklava is so good, it gives me a new way of tasting Arabic food. It is like a poem about the deeply bred luxuries of Eastern cultures.

Auntie Aya stands over me, watching me eat; she offers no advice.

That evening, the last before she returns to Jordan, Aunt Aya eats with us one more time. The family's conversation is lighter and airier than it has been in months. There's a froth of laughter in the atmosphere, and not a single topic of debate is broached. When Aunt Aya comes forth with the tray of baklava, newly reheated with just a few tiny pieces missing, everyone sits forward and inhales.

"My sister the magic maker," Bud says after eating a piece. He applauds and half rises from his seat to bow. It is magic: How could a pastry so dense with ingredients, so rich with nuts, be so light on the tongue?

I am thinking about Aya's words—about how a mirage sometimes seems better than reality—when Aunt Aya abruptly pushes her chair from the table. "So, brother, are you enjoying our food?" she asks in a not entirely conversational way. Bud blinks. "Good! Because as you know, eating is a form of listening, and I have something to tell you." She flattens her hands on the table and says, "If you ever say anything more about sending your daughter back to Jordan to live—oh! I will honestly never speak to you again. In fact, I will just go out that door right now and that will be that."

Then she stands and walks toward the door.

I am in for it now. I look at Bud. Astonished, he blinks again, his last bite of baklava still between his fingers. A deep crease forms between his brows. I think, This is going to make things a hundred thousand times worse for me.

She stops before the door, turns. "I'm going now!" she says. I'm about to bolt from the room.

Bud looks across the table, and for a moment, the smoke between us seems to subside. His look is tender, almost shy. It is as if we see each other in a way we'd forgotten or lost track of as I'd gotten older. It is a moment of recognition. And I do not know exactly how it's come to pass.

"I would never send my daughter away," he says.

Neck rigid and fingertips flared, Aya returns to the table and sits back down.

"This is such delicious *baklawa*," I say to my auntie. "Thank you so much for sharing it with us."

"You're welcome," she says formally. Then she smiles in a weak, relieved sort of way and pats Bud's cheeks. He is smiling, pink with pleasure.

"May I have more now?" Bud asks.

"Of course you may have more, my sweetest little brother. You may have all that you want. I made it for you."

I am home for good.

POETIC BAKLAVA
For when you need to serenade someone.

SYRUP

2 cups sugar

1 cup water

Splash of lemon juice

1 teaspoon orange blossom
water (see page 58)

1 pound walnuts

1 cup sugar

1 teaspoon ground
cinnamon

1 box phyllo dough, defrosted

1 pound butter, clarified
(melted and with the top
layer skimmed off)

In a saucepan, boil all the syrup ingredients until the mixture turns clear. Cover the syrup and set aside in the refrigerator to cool.

In a food processor, grind together the walnuts, sugar, and cinnamon to a fine, sandy consistency. Set aside.

Preheat the oven to 300 degrees.

Carefully unfold the phyllo dough, making sure not to crack or tear it. Keep it covered with a piece of waxed paper to help prevent it from drying out.

Butter the bottom of a shallow baking pan. You can also use a cookie sheet that has at least an inch-high lip. Carefully unpeel the first sheet of phyllo and lay it flat and smooth in the bottom of the pan. Brush with the clarified butter. Continue layering sheets of phyllo dough and brushing each sheet with butter until you've used half the dough.

Spread the nuts-and-sugar mixture over the dough.

Place another sheet of dough on the mixture and butter it. Continue layering and buttering dough until you've used up the rest.

Using a sharp knife, carefully cut through the baklava in long, straight lines to form diamonds or squares (about 2 inches long).

Bake for about 50 minutes or until golden brown. Pour the cooled syrup over the hot baklava. Eat when ready!

FOURTEEN

Bad American Girl

I t's after dinner when the doorbell rings. As usual, I'm in my lair of a bedroom with a screen of rose beads hiding the entrance. Around me are my purple floor-length curtains, half a dozen mobiles, several blacklight posters, and my pink shag-rug bedspread. Every surface is covered with strawberry-scented votive candles. I'm sprawled across my bed with pad and pen, loose-leaf papers fanned over the covers, writing an inspirational piece about a man who makes a pair of wings out of beer pull tabs and flies away from his oppressive parents. I sigh and write and stare furiously at the wall and sigh and write a little more. I ignore the chiming doorbell. It will just be another non-English-speaking cousin who's newly arrived unannounced from overseas.

I can hear my sisters go out to the front entranceway. I know they're peeping through the little spyglass window in the top of the front door, but they don't open it. Their voices clang together as they nervously debate whether to open the door or go get Dad. Finally, the door opens and there are more voices, speaking *English*. I look up and frown. Suzy runs to my room. Her shoulders and arms are taut with panic. She pushes back her curly dark hair. "A boy," she says. "Here. For *you*." She runs back to the hallway.

I peer around the corner. There, larger than life, is Ray Jansen from Advanced Placement English class. He is fingering the hinge on the doorjamb as if he's admiring the fine workmanship. My breath roars as though I've dropped from a high place into a lake. The ironclad rule in our house is: No boys. Bud has drilled these rules into my sisters and me: Who are you? Good-Arab-girls. Who aren't you? Bad-boy-crazy-American-girls. Doesn't Ray Jansen know this?

I walk to the front door on watery, bouncy knees. I'm vaguely hoping he's here to raise money for the Euclid volunteer firemen. He's a sweet-natured boy with a loose, daring smile, a foreshadowing of a mustache on his upper lip, and easy black eyes. He lives down the road in one of the crooked tar-papered houses, where there's always a passel of unwatched little kids. Ray works on cars and keeps a wrench and a red bandanna in his back pocket. He's probably the closest I've ever come to a cowboy.

He is bold and a little dashing. His picture was in the *Liverpool-Salina Review* for helping put out the fire at a local pool hall and dragging out a man who was too drunk to walk. Ray would make a perfect object of infatuation if such a thing could occur to me. Instead, I'm grimly adding up the way he flirts with me in English, how just the other day in class, he stood arched over me as I sat at my desk, his arm barely brushing mine, his breath grazing my hair, as he helped me write a book report. Now the lights in our hallway seem to flare as I get it. That wasn't just to get a closer look at my paper.

He thinks I'm an American girl.

His grin is a little lopsided. "Hey, Di, I just happened to be in the neighborhood—"

"Hi, Ray." I'm trying to keep my voice natural and neutral—oh sure, cowboys turn up at our front door all the time!—but my jaw feels tight. Ray's smile dims. I can feel Bud sailing up behind me.

"Yes, sir," Bud is saying, drawn up and straight backed, voice an octave lower, as if Ray is a salesman whom Bud is about to dismiss. "What can I do for you?"

Ray's expression broadens and flattens. He stammers something about going over our English homework.

"English homework?" Bud says in a strained voice. He looks at me. "Do you know this man?"

The air is thin and unbreathable, like something from the far side of Mars. "Well, yeah," I say. I can barely hear my own voice. "He's in my English class. And . . . he wants to go to law school." *Pathetic.* I can't meet Ray's eye, but he doesn't correct me.

"Law school?" Bud mumbles. The information about English and law school makes him edgy—I can tell he's trying to work out if this is educational and respectable or not.

Next thing I know, we've all somehow made it upstairs and into the living room. I have no idea how this comes to pass. Events seem to ooze together. The whole family is up there with us. Our living room is a long, window-banked rectangle divided into two seating areas. Bud instructs my sisters to watch something on TV. Monica, after a long, incredulous gawk at Ray, flips on *Truth or Consequences* and Bob Barker's wry, avuncular voice ripples through the room beneath waves of canned laughter. The blue vapor light washes over the back wall. Bud seats us in the opposite end of the room. Mom hovers near the hallway, looking as though she'd love to catch a bus out of town. She gently asks if Ray would like something to drink. He searches her face for a moment, then says anything is fine.

A dreamy moist heat rises from my skin. A boy in the house! It's like fumbling into a Dalí painting—all the clocks slither off the wall, and Bud's smile looks as if it's cut out of a magazine. We're all well mannered, but the living room floor is spongy. Bud sits forward in his recliner, elbows propped attentively on his knees. He sighs, nods, shakes his lowered head, as if someone has just told him a really good one. He looks up in a patient, aw-shucks way and says that he better explain some things to Ray. Then he flaps his hands on his knees, pushes up, and goes into the kitchen.

I follow him, feeling doomed yet curious. I'm not sure if I've ever been in this much trouble before. I keep forgetting that none of it was my idea in the first place. Interspersed with a sense of doom is the feeling that I've just won a raffle: A boy, here, for me! In the kitchen, Mom busies herself with pouring soda. Bud starts rooting through the refrigerator, mumbling something that sounds like ancient incantations under his breath, sliding out one Tupperware bowl after another. He begins spooning leftovers onto a plate: some rice, salad, a big slice of stuffed kibbeh, the crisp wheaty bulgur layers fragrant with ground lamb and spices, all of it still fresh from dinner. I stand by uselessly, arms dangling, then trail after him as he brings it back out into the living room and sets it on the carved brass table between him and Ray, a challenge.

Bud doesn't have any intention of actually letting Ray eat. After placing the platter full of food before Ray, Bud leans back in his armchair and tips his head at an insouciant angle. "So, sir, who are your people?"

Ray looks up from the plate. "My people?" He squints, picks up a fork, turns his head slightly to one side.

Bud pushes on. "What is your trade?"

"Well, I . . . I volunteer for the fire department, and I fix some cars for people. I'm mostly still in high school."

Bud nods gravely, considering this information. "Where are your people from?"

"Well . . . I—" Ray gestures vaguely toward the windows. "I guess Granny and Grandpa are living right up the road there, outside of Baldwinsville."

Where the houses are broken down and heaped with junk, where people live in abandoned buses, where the roads dissolve into gravel. I gaze at him: my tragic hero.

As the food rests and Ray sips his sweating glass of 7-Up, Bud leans forward and sighs. "All right. You see, sir, I have to explain something to you," he says evenly. "This is something very easy for you to understand. My daughters are good Arab girls."

I feel a paroxysm of lethal embarrassment. My sisters sit up on the couch. Suzy telegraphs sympathetic looks to my side of the living room; Monica hides her face in her hands, then looks out between her fingers. Ray's glance slips toward me, checking to see if Bud is kidding or not. Bud is just getting warmed up. "My girls are not like these American girls." His face tightens. "Not like these girls that you're used to." With this accusation, he rolls even farther forward, his voice ascending. "My daughters stay home like good girls, and do their homework and help their mother. They're going to marry the men that I tell them to marry—good Arab men. Doctors and lawyers. Maybe an engineer, *maybe*. My daughters don't 'go out.' They don't go to 'parties' or 'do drugs' or 'run around.' " He's getting louder, as mad as if Ray had in fact proclaimed that we go right out and do those dreadful things regularly. "So I don't know why *you* come here, walking into *my house* and looking at *my daughters,* but I can tell you right now, sir, you have the *wrong idea.*"

"Yes, sir," Ray whispers.

I feel an old fury rising in me. I've heard Bud's speech many times before, but listening to it in the clear, public presence of a stranger makes it excruciating. Bud has been shaping and containing the direction of my life as long as I can remember, but never before has it seemed to matter so much. I don't know a thing about Ray Jansen, I only half recognized him at the door, but suddenly he seems like the only thing in my life that has ever really mattered at all.

Bud grows impassioned—combating legions of invisible American boys—cowboys!—attempting to steal his daughters. "I don't know where you got this great big idea," he continues, gesturing over our heads, "that you can just come into my house—the home of Ghassan Abu-Jaber—come to my home uninvited, talk to my daughters, and—and—and—" Whatever it is that Bud thinks Ray was intending to do is too horrible to put into actual words. Ray shrinks from it, creeping back into the seams of his chair.

There is a crackling pause like the second before the execution. Suddenly, Bud stands and Ray seizes the moment. "Well, thanks for everything, sir, s'long!" He's on his feet and moving fast down the stairs toward the front door.

"That's right," Bud growls. "That's right. Time to go home now, you. Go back to your people and your girls and your—your—*cars!*" He follows Ray all the way down the stairs, shouting, "Go on now, time to go home!" The sounds of *Truth or Consequences* follow them to the door.

I don't let myself look out the front window. I know I will only see Bud banishing from our property the sole man in the world who will ever be interested in me. I can't believe any of this has happened. I am not prepared to accept that life can be so unfair. I tremble with indignation and furious excitement: A boy liked me! My father chased him away!

When Bud comes back in he looks invigorated, as if he's just gone for a jog. There's an expansive mellowness settling over him, as if he's preparing to be tolerant about the whole sordid affair. I can barely contain myself. I glare at him while he settles into his armchair, puts up his feet, nods to himself, and plucks up the paper. I finally burst out, "How could you, how could you?" my voice a pure, scorching wave. "Don't you care about me at all? Don't you care about my feelings?"

Bud looks at Mom in astonishment. "What? What feelings?" he says.

"It's not fair!"

He looks utterly blank. He looks at Mom.

I appeal to my mother, who, I know, was raised by a reliably American mother. "What about you, Mom?" I say. "Didn't you go out on dates? Didn't you go to malt shops with boys and wear poodle skirts and go to your prom and everything? What about that?"

She allows this, nodding. "It's true, but if your father feels so strongly about this matter, I think we should respect that."

I am abandoned. My mouth is open, my indignation shimmers. I swing my focus between the two of them. "Why didn't you just lock me into some prison in Jordan when you had the chance?"

Bud thumps the arm of the upholstered chair, infuriated all over again. "I wanted to!"

"I wish you had. It'd be better than here."

Bud is incredulous. It's as if he can't even see me. He widens his eyes, but he can't make my features out. "Did you hear that?" he asks Mom. "Look at her—look at that belligerence. In Jordan, daughters never look at their fathers like that. If I looked at my father like that— my father would beat us every day! You don't know what a family is!" He's shaking his finger at me, his voice a rampaging force. He'll go all night long and I'll stay up, too, and we'll burn down everything in our path.

We fight to the brink of exhaustion. Bud's logic is free-form, leaping from half memories to accusations to wild conclusions. There are few connections between any of it, so it's almost impossible to fight back. He makes speeches about what a bad daughter I am, we all are, all daughters in the world are. He recalls moments of grief and suffering at my hands, offenses that I've utterly forgotten or didn't know about in the first place. "Do you think I've forgotten about the day you told me to 'never mind'?" he demands. "Do you think I forgot about that?" He's relentless.

But I can't hold on to my anger as I tire. It seeps out of me in wisps, leaving me in a sort of trance. I slump in my chair as all of it falls away from me—Ray, freedom, the future. Eventually I'm so tired that I'd give it all away in exchange for a chance to go to bed. I end the fight in the most expedient way I know how: I let my face crumple, my chin caves in, and the warm, ignominious tears come. Bud, from his family of tough boys, is stupefied by the sight of female tears. He waves his hands in the air, a little frightened, and the spell is broken. "There, there," he says. "We'll forget the whole thing."

I rub my eyes and stand to go. My throat aches from anger and from crying. Then I notice something on the table. The plate. It's there like a message in a bottle. Apparently, at some point during my father's earlier speeches, Ray managed to eat the food that Bud had set out. The rice and okra have been scooped up, the crisp lamb kibbeh is gone. He did it somehow, without anyone noticing. The sight of Ray's empty plate is so potent that I hold still inside myself and don't even let myself smile. And I know then that there are all sorts of things that can be done that don't require anyone's permission.

COWBOY KIBBEH

STUFFING

1 onion, minced	½ pound ground lamb
2 teaspoons olive oil	Salt and freshly ground
½ cup pine nuts	pepper
1 cup medium bulgur	1 onion, minced
1 pound ground lamb	Salt and freshly ground
1 cup water	pepper

TOPPING

2 medium tomatoes, sliced
  thin (optional)

  Soak the bulgur in water to cover for 2 hours. Drain well and
set aside.

  Preheat the oven to 350 degrees.

  Prepare the stuffing: In a small saucepan, sauté the onion in
olive oil until lightly browned; transfer to a bowl and set aside.
Sauté the pine nuts in the same oil; transfer to the bowl. Sauté the
lamb in the remaining oil with salt and pepper. Drain off the fat
and then combine in the bowl with the onions and pine nuts; set
aside.

  In a large bowl, mix together the bulgur, lamb, water, and
onion, seasoning with salt and pepper. Press half of the mixture in
the bottom of a baking dish. Sprinkle the stuffing over this.
Spread the second half of the bulgur mixture over the stuffing and
press down lightly. Top with tomato slices if desired. Bake for 45
minutes at 350 degrees, then remove and cut into squares.

MAKES 4 TO 6 SERVINGS.

The next day, Ray passes me a note in English and I meet him after
class in the library. We pick a large, polished wooden table near the
card catalog and sit at a right angle from each other, our joined
hands resting on the amber-colored table beside a stack of books. At
first I feel frightened and excited, my breath rippling through me
like electric sparks. But then I realize I don't feel guilty at all, not
one bit, and no one in the library cares that we are holding hands
anyway.

  The whispering, watery sounds of the room are soothing to me.
We don't talk very much, so I'm able to study the way our fingers
knit together. I look at the black tufts of hair above Ray's knuckles
and the neat, smooth trim of his nails and a few dark lines of grease
near his palms—the kind that remain even after you've scrubbed and

scrubbed. I marvel at how natural it feels to link hands with this boy, a stranger.

We avoid talking about the previous night, instead discussing our homework, our eccentric substitute English teacher, the trouble Ray is having with his Thunderbird. Finally he looks at me through a fine spray of hair over his forehead and says, "But you know what? I really liked that food your dad gave me to eat last night. Especially that sort of crunchy one? With the tomatoes?"

I have to suppress a nervous burst of laughter. "The lamb kibbeh?"

"Yeah," he says, his eyes a little far away. "That was the *best thing*."

Ray and I never progress beyond holding hands, and I don't really see much of him after that day. Once I've established that I'm brave enough for secret meetings and hand holding, I don't feel especially interested in Ray anymore. But oddly enough, he seems to feel that he and Bud have struck up a friendship. If Ray is driving by while Bud is out on his riding mower, he'll honk and wave and Bud will wave back. Sometimes he'll pull over, and he and Bud will chat like old pals.

Bud will come into the house looking for cucumbers and cheese, salted nuts and tomatoes. "Nice boy, that Raymond," he'll say. "A real good kid."

FIFTEEN

Food and Art

Our regular English teacher, Mrs. Loprienzo, goes on maternity leave, and when the substitute takes over, everything changes. It turns out that Mr. Sims, a man with an innocent, simple-minded expression, has a fondness for modern classics. My English class veers away from studying the ruthlessly dull Leatherstocking tales and begins reading works that were written in the same century in which we were born. Mr. Sims brings in cases of new books, one of which is an anthology with the words *Here and Now* on the cover. These are full-bodied, difficult, modern works. I want to crawl into these books and live there.

One afternoon, Mr. Sims brings in an oversize book and reads twenty pages of *The Waste Land* to us in a theatrical, puffed-up voice, gesturing with one open hand as if to tap the ideas floating around his head. I don't understand most of what I'm hearing, but I feel it. I'm entranced and distracted by the writings of Sylvia Plath, Ezra Pound, James Joyce, F. Scott Fitzgerald, thrilled by Faulkner, Tennessee Williams, and Edna St. Vincent Millay, startled by John Dos Passos, Flannery O'Connor, and William Carlos Williams. One of the books that most intrigues me is *The Autobiography of Alice B. Toklas,* replete with Stein's descriptions of salons and dinners full of painters and writers. I've grown up within the curve of dinner parties; the years of inviting and cooking vibrate behind the pages as I read Stein's descriptions of a witty, artistic community. What seemed parental and dully natural to me now becomes charged with possibility. I glimpse the electricity of the dinner party, the way that one might join the perfect yet incongruous worlds of eating and thinking, food and art.

Inspired, I ditto off fragrant blue hand-printed invitations to come to my house and read literary works, to perform and "converse." Across the bottom I've written, "A light French Picnic will be served." I bestow these invitations upon a selection of friends whom I have deemed sophisticated and urbane enough to invite. This group consists of my three closest girlfriends, Olga, Sonja, and Mahaleani, and the three American boys with long hair in my English class.

We get to the house before my parents get home from work, so I can sidle my friends in the front door, through the house, and out the back door. We sprawl in the long, blowsy backyard grass, and my sisters watch us from the kitchen window. Suzy opens the back door. "You know that Dad's going to be home soon," she says. They don't know what to make of this. I haven't told anyone I was planning to do this, so no one has had a chance to tell me not to. Boys have always been forbidden in the house, but nonetheless there we are, sitting together in a circle, reading aloud. I'm hoping that Bud will back down from making a scene in front of a group.

We sit cross-legged while Jay Franklin strums his yellow guitar. Jay wears his hair in an unbroken oily sheath, propped to one side of the rim of his glasses. He closes his eyes and leans into his song: a quavering plea. The spring sun heats the grass, releasing its sweet, starchy scent. I close my eyes halfway and the light reddens my lashes. It wouldn't be so hard to imagine myself falling for Jay Franklin. Why not? He isn't obviously good-looking, but he has wonderful, watery blue eyes and Coke-bottle glasses, and he's brave enough to sing this awful stuff to us in his feeble, half-shattered voice. I think he must be sensitive and, therefore, completely different from Bud.

I'm almost sixteen now, and circuits of feeling run through me. What I think I want is love. I want to be in love, to be set loose in a mystery. I lean back into the scent of dandelion dust, the sun-cooked dirt and grass, and Jay's fragile singing sounds lush and promising. Something in that sound and that sweep and that light is just what I want, and exactly the thing I'm not to have. Boys. Their hands and voices and minds, hidden and uncharted.

Next comes Jerry Depiza's reading of a short story that renders in minute, Escher-like detail a scene in which a man bullies his young son into shooting a deer. It's a drippy yarn, meant to be read through tears, but I'm enchanted. It may be the first story I've actually known to exist outside of a classroom. Finally, Martin Chapelle gives an impassioned reading from *The Communist Manifesto* that I ignore. Olga opts out of the performance; she has already decided that she's a conceptual artist who will make assemblages out of things like kitchen appliances. And my other two girlfriends shake their heads when I ask them to read. "We're the audience," Sonja says. "Somebody has to listen."

They look at me expectantly, and I feel the gravity of my hostess-performer role. First I try to bribe the audience by bringing forth the French picnic from a Styrofoam cooler. The menu is inspired by M. F. K. Fisher's descriptions of meals in the Alps and on the French Riviera, but it is influenced more specifically by the availability of ingredients in upstate New York. The sandwiches are meant to be composed of a little Brie and prosciutto tucked inside buttered baguettes. But the closest I could come to baguettes at a moment's notice are the spongy loaves in paper bags that the Super Duper Supermarket calls "Italian bread," the only unsliced bread in the store. The kindly grocer with the bristling eyebrows at the Greek import market downtown unearthed some prosciutto—at stunning expense—but no Brie. He did, however, have fresh wet balls of a white cheese that he advised me to place sliced on the bread with fresh tomato and basil leaves and dark green olive oil, so this is what we do. There is also supposed to be a foie gras pâté and cornichons and whole-grain mustard, but, finding none of these items at the Super Duper, I guiltily substitute chips and French onion dip. Dessert is based on our French teacher's junior year abroad in Aix-en-Provence, when he learned to eat slim black bars of good chocolate upon a baguette. Our version: Hershey's and more Italian bread.

IMPROVISATION SANDWICHES

For when you want them to keep their minds on the art.

6 long, slim baguettes
Unsalted butter
½ pound prosciutto, thinly
    sliced
½ pound Brie, cut into thin
    slices

Fresh basil leaves or
rosemary, chopped
(optional: if you're
feeling fancy)

Split open the baguettes with a serrated knife. Spread the insides well with butter. Layer each baguette with prosciutto, and then Brie slices. Top with fresh herbs, if using.

Serve with a nice, creamy pâté and little cornichons—if you can find them where you live.

SERVES 6.

I slip some loose-leaf pages out of a manila envelope. While my audience eats, I read them a story that I've been rewriting for years, a seven-page opus about, yes, the man who constructs a pair of getaway wings out of pull-off beer tabs. I don't know if it's more frightening to invite a mixed group of boys and girls to the house or to read my work to them. The pages rattle in my fingers, and I can't seem to remember how to read and breathe at the same time. I am on high alert, prickling with the expectation of Bud bursting out of the back door at any moment and scattering us like wild birds. The boys are oblivious to my state, but my three immigrant-kid girlfriends are also on alert, their gestures crisp and light. I notice Mahaleani eyeing the back door, Olga and Sonja twisting their hair, nipping at their nails. They all know Bud, and they've all heard Bud's speech as well as their own parents' versions. When I invited my Indian friend, Mahaleani, to my literary salon, she stared at the printed invitation, then looked up and said, "You're inviting boys?"

"And girls, too!"

"To your actual house?"

"Why not?" I said fake defiantly. I wrapped my arms high around my rib cage.

"Right, right, why not? Great question," she said grimly. "Just don't tell my father, either."

I keep reading my story, as if I'm not possessed by hyperconsciousness. I can't help myself. I take risks—going out with friends, letting my room go to ruin, throwing a literary salon in the backyard. Over and over again, I just let go. What choice do I have? Everything presses down on me—the walls are too close, our house is too crowded. I snarl at everyone in the family, guarding every boundary, half-crazed for privacy and retreat. Because of this, of course, I'm constantly in trouble. Bud grabs his head and rants, beginning with the trauma of his arrival in America and finishing with the trauma of his eldest daughter, her ingratitude, her outrageous rebellion, her basic badness.

Still, occasionally, miracles happen, small moments of grace where I dive into space and Bud doesn't notice.

When I finish reading my story, I don't even say, "the end," I just start to stuff the papers back into the envelope as if I'm hiding evidence. My friends smile, begin to clap, and then the back door opens. I don't look up. Bud comes out and sits on the back porch, the wooden boards creaking. "Well, something big is going on here," he says. "Something, something, something!"

Everyone glances at me. My lungs ache. What was I thinking? I stare at the pages in my hands, the curled, smudged edges, the hand-printed words and blurring blue lines. I've heard this tone of voice before, the careful neutrality as Bud studies the situation. Wind washes through the maples and birches, stirring them around; I cannot imagine that I will not always be here, sitting on the grass under this long scrutiny, waiting.

The step creaks again as Bud shifts his weight. He says pointedly, "So. Are you studying?"

Without any prompting from me, in one of those miraculous moments of group telepathy, my friends say, "Yes!"

"What are you studying?" Bud asks, hope and skepticism in his voice.

"English literature," Jerry Depiza volunteers at the same time that Sonja is saying, "Science."

"Social studies," Martin Chapelle adds.

"We're talking about applying to law school," Mahaleani adds. "Or medical."

Bud turns his head and looks at me out of the corner of his eye, as if this gives him X-ray vision: I catch my lip in my teeth.

Then Jay Franklin delicately steers his hair behind one ear with a finger and says, "Diana told us you make your own hummus." Even the wind hum in the trees stops. He pronounces it the way you pronounce the stuff you put in with potting soil. But the fact that in Syracuse, in 1976, Jay Franklin knows what hummus is at all is like a little star falling down into our backyard. Eventually it will be everywhere, in tiny plastic tubs doctored up with roasted peppers and spinach. But at the moment, nobody knows what hummus is.

My father's face becomes tender as he focuses on Jay, and I think this might be the first time he's ever really looked at a young American male. Or at least the first time he's ever looked at one without thinking *molester* or *rapist*. "You know hummus?" he asks in a low, ardent voice.

It turns out that Jay's parents were Peace Corps workers in Turkey. Jay also knows about pita bread, falafel, and "the eggplant stuff."

Bud and Jay form an instant food connection. The others lean back while those two hunch forward, chattering. We try to act casual and discuss poetry. But we're amateurs at high art talk, and Bud and Jay drown us out with their excited discussion of tahini sauce.

Bud stands abruptly, dusts off his pants, and with no further ado gestures for Jay to follow him up the back steps. The husks of my French picnic—seeded bread crusts, strips of prosciutto—are left to curl up in the sun. I want to call after Jay, tell him he doesn't have to go! But, like an enchanted child in a German fairy tale, he seems to have forgotten about his past life. Jay actually wants to go in and see the kitchen. The two of them tramp up the steps, and soon we hear the sounds of pots rattling and cupboards opening. The other boys don't know what to make of this, and we give up on high art and start whispering about whatever the hell might be going on in the kitchen. The guys get bored and decide to bicycle home without their friend Jay, who is now pacing around inside, wearing an apron. I want them to stay longer, but it's getting near dinnertime and I realize to my horror that my French picnic was not enough food. Everyone is sixteen or so and hungry—appetite has overcome art.

My girlfriends have a more optimistic view of things. "Your dad actually invited a guy into your house," Mahaleani says. "That's a miracle!"

She's right. Jay Franklin and Bud are making something in the kitchen, nattering on like old friends. Bud has stolen my boyfriend.

Jay and my father prepare dinner that evening. They make hummus, rice, olives with chili paste, and a lightly braised chicken with thyme and onions. Jay sits and eats with us, the first nonfamily American boy ever to do so. He and Bud discuss varieties of foods—my father's love of *tagines* and couscous, Jay's recent discovery of mole, their mutual unhappiness with instant rice.

"This is great chicken, Jay," I say, trying to reclaim his attention.

He nods absently and flips back his long shank of hair. "Is sumac a traditional Arabic spice?" he asks Bud.

"Really, it's so good!" I crane my face toward Jay.

He and Bud trade an indulgent, knowing look.

"Isn't it funny how people never seem to write about food in novels?" I soldier on, determined to have some art tonight. "In—in—*Howards End*, for example, they're always talking about houses and money, but you'd think that nobody ever ate back then or something. . . ."

My sisters are mute and stupefied, blinking at me as if I'm speaking Swahili. No doubt they wonder if I've noticed that there's this boy in the room. "Of course, now, Hemingway—he's very good at writing about drinking and parties, of course."

Jay looks as though he isn't sure who I am. I stir tiny meandering paths through my baba ghanouj with the tines of my fork. It seems at that moment that there will never be a way to have both E. M. Forster and baba ghanouj at the same table. Art settles to the floor of my mind like bits of snow in a snow globe.

But Bud perks up. "That reminds me!" he says brightly. He takes out his special bottle of *araq* so he and Jay can drink a toast to themselves. "Here's to cooking lots of nice food with your friends," my father says.

"Perfect," Jay says. They touch glasses. I don't drink *araq* myself.

I see the light of pleasure and acceptance and approval in my father's eyes, and I realize, with some regret, that I can never have anything to do with Jay Franklin again.

A PERFECT GLASS OF *ARAQ*
For making the perfect toast.

Ice	1 bottle good Lebanese *araq*
Highball glasses	Water

Place a few pieces of ice in glass. Pour 1 ounce or so of *araq* over this. Top off with about 2 ounces of water. The drink will turn milky once the water is added.

A traditional Arabic toast is "*Sahtain!*" or "Double health!" said to encourage good appetites of all sorts.

I learn a valuable lesson about strategy from Jay Franklin. At the end of my junior year of high school, I discover a boy named Sam Ralston who is willing to take me to the prom. By this time, I am as anxious to go on a date as some other young people are to lose their virginity. Sam is in my advanced English class, an honors student and hockey star, on his way to Harvard to prepare for medical school. He has a cheery blank stare, the genial mindlessness of one who expects to inherit the earth. Under ordinary circumstances, a "date" like the prom, involving myself alone in a car with a boy, would have been out of the question. But I'd learned from Jay that you just have to ask the right question in the right way. It happens that red-haired, blue-eyed Sam is actually Samer Abdul-Rami. His immigrant grandfather changed the family name to Ralston. Samer is half Lebanese.

I approach Bud while holding a tray of Arabic coffee and date-stuffed cookies. "So, Daddy, is it okay if Samer Abdul-Rami takes me to the prom?"

"A what?"

I repeat the question slowly, carefully vocalizing Sam's full name with elaborate Middle Eastern calligraphic flourishes.

Bud's eyebrows descend, then lift, then descend again. He looks as if he is trying to solve an algebra puzzle. He takes a sip of coffee and scrutinizes the tiny cup as if he's never seen it before, then asks slowly, "You're asking—you want—what's his name?"

Now I repeat it nonchalantly.

"Who are his people?"

"From Lebanon."

"And what is his father's trade?"

"Electrical engineer."

"Christian or Muslim?"

"Christian."

"And his grades are?"

"Perfect. He's the class valedictorian. The guidance counselor's office can confirm that."

His eyes narrow, then widen, then narrow. Bud gets on the phone with his second cousin who works as an engineer at the power company. They have a long discussion in Arabic. Somehow they ascertain that Sam's father works in the same office as one of Bud's second cousin's friends' daughters-in-law and that the report is that he's "a good guy." He may also be the nephew of Bud's aunt's cousin—a surprise bonus. Bud hangs up. He takes a bite of cookie and looks pensively through our picture window. He sighs. It is a sigh that is deep and blue streaked, reminiscent of late, bright, cedar-scented nights over the fig trees and olive groves. Finally he nods, first to himself, then to the world, and says, "Okay, why not?"

"STOLEN BOYFRIEND" BABA GHANOUJ

2 medium eggplants, cut in half lengthwise
½ cup tahini
3 tablespoons olive oil
3 cloves garlic, crushed
Juice of 3 lemons
Salt and freshly ground pepper

Preheat the oven to 425 degrees. On an oiled baking pan, roast the eggplant cut side down for 20 minutes, until the eggplant is very soft and tender. Scoop out the pulp. Place in a large bowl and mash with a large fork or spoon.

In a medium bowl, mix the tahini, olive oil, garlic, lemon juice, and salt and pepper to taste, and then add water for creamier consistency. Stir into the mashed eggplant. If a smoother consistency is desired, you can blend the ingredients in a food processor.

Garnish with tomato slices or sliced cucumber. Serve with a dash of olive oil on warm pita bread.

SIXTEEN

Candy and Lebeneh

When my alarm goes off in the morning, I stare holes through the ceiling, trying to think up reasons why I ought to go to school that day. Maybe it's turkey chili day in the cafeteria or animal balloon day in art class. I wander zombie style through high school. Each week, my social studies teacher, Mr. Bushnutt, scowls, leans his wide backside against his desk, and spends the period reading us *National Enquirer* stories about his favorite television stars. I'm in my junior year, but I can't take it anymore. The beige walls, the scent of linoleum and used lockers, the shrill bell between classes—high school is sucking the air out of me.

Perhaps it's due to my mournful slouch through the halls, but one day my guidance counselor casually mentions that with enough credits, it is sometimes possible to skip one's senior year of high school and go directly to college. I've become convinced that *college* is where my life will begin. I start collecting stacks of university brochures and spreading the glossy images of red-brick, ivy-sided campuses across the table at breakfast. Bud touches the gleaming pamphlets, leaving fingerprints. "So—this is a college?" he says in a dazed church voice. Bud barely wants to let me out of the house at all. But the very notion of college leaves him a little breathless. After intense negotiation, he agrees to let me skip my senior year of high school, but only on condition that I attend the State University of New York in Oswego, thirty miles up the road from us, where Uncle Hal and Aunt Rachel teach. Where I will stay at the all-girls dorm. Where the family will keep an eye on me. Isn't that wonderful?

When we get to campus, Bud looks across the crowded school bookstore and intuits that the manager is a Palestinian immigrant.

He grins, introduces himself, and flings one arm across the man's shoulders. Then they walk off toward the man's office. When they come back, I learn that I have a job, starting now. I'm going to work for minimum wage at the campus Sweet Shoppe, a big open counter that turns out to be at the hub of the university's social life in the heart of the student union building.

At the Sweet Shoppe we sell newspapers, cigarettes, girlie magazines, and candy. The floor-to-ceiling shelves are crowded with old-fashioned glass jars with shiny metal lids that need constant polishing. There are two antiquated weighted scales that we measure the candy into, piece by piece, using sugar-dusted metal scoops; then we slide the pieces into white paper bags. We sell quarter, half, and whole pounds of candy, and I get so used to the incremental measurements that I can tell by feel what small things weigh. If we like someone, we dribble in extra.

The dull prefab candy arrives directly from the factory in cartons that smell of old chocolate, waxed paper, cardboard, and dust. But there's a great variety—malt balls, chocolate turtles, nonpareils, fireballs, double-dipped peanuts, orange jellies, sugar-coated fruit slices, English toffee, gumdrops, peanut clusters, jawbreakers, and so on. We sell the candies my grandmother grew up with, Mary Janes, butterscotches, and Bit-O-Honeys. Even the cash register is old-fashioned—the manual keys *thwack* like a typewriter's, and I have to think about how to make change.

Most of my work hours are scheduled before afternoon classes. Early in the morning, I cut across the cool compound of the student union, past sleepy commuter students sunk into chairs, nodding over coffees, staring at notes. The metal grating rumbles up with a crash, and the first wave of Sweet Shoppe aroma makes my stomach trip. I settle into one of the tall chairs on rolling casters behind the counter. We are instructed to leap to attention whenever a customer appears, but some of my co-workers manage to work entire shifts while rolling themselves around.

We have our regulars—sugar junkies who arrive at eight a.m., angling toward the counter as soon as they push through the big glass doors at the front of the union, a draft of cold wind, lakefront rain, or early snow washing in behind them. The junkies are usually bored or lonely, homesick and stressed out, looking for easy comfort, their eyes a smidgen off kilter. They come by to mope around our counter. I sell them expensive whole cartons of Winstons, Salems, and Marlboros, newspapers, and *Playboys*. They confide how excited they are about candy fruit slices. They buy bags of rubbery Swedish fish and pay for them with crisp twenties. All I ever seem to have in my pocket are crumpled singles and silver.

The school is unequally divided between the generally less moneyed, less sophisticated upstaters like myself, and the downstaters who come from New York City and Long Island. We all have the same conversations over and over. A student leans over the counter, peering into the dim candy cave, then looks at me mournfully and asks, "Where you from?"

"Upstate."

"Upstate! You're from here!"

"Yeah. Where're you from?"

"The Island."

"You like it here?"

"Yeah, it's not my parents' house. You?"

"Same."

My parents, thank heavens, are paying my tuition and board, but I never have any cash. I discover that my co-workers consider nibbling from the jars a way to supplement their food budget. Dorrie, the Sweet Shoppe manager, is an unhappy, overweight single mother who wears the same baggy sweatpants and shirt to work every day—a "townie." She says we're supposed to eat only the broken candies and stale remnants, but Dorrie stays locked up in her closetlike office in back, reading dog-eared romance novels, one hand fishing around in a bag of peanut clusters while on the other side of the door her staff has contests to see who can catch the most M&M's in their mouths.

My parents have bought me a year's worth of breakfast, lunch, and dinner at the loathsome dormitory dining hall. My floormates and I go en masse to cafeteria-style meals where we are served trays of glutinous soups, curling gray steaks, and tissuey salads. One day I am so appalled by the state of the bacon and eggs at breakfast that I write my first ever food review on a paper napkin, then sit down with the dining hall manager and read my tirade aloud. He listens, his head nodding with laughter, his school ring clacking against the linoleum table as he slaps it in amusement. He mumbles over it, rereading: "Hey—trichinosis—big word!" Then he asks if he can keep the napkin as a souvenir and walks away, stuffing it in his back pocket.

After a few weeks of food misery, I start skipping dining hall meals and snacking liberally at the Sweet Shoppe. It's not enough food, but it's not the regime of enforced starvation that some of my dormmates are on. Within my first months at college, on two different occasions I see girls—stick creatures—pass out from hunger. I adore eating well and will eat less than well if necessary, but the dining hall with its lifeless taupe sauces and tepid ingredients leaves me appetiteless. Bud calls every day and asks, "What are they feeding you there?"

"Flank steak, mac 'n' cheese, chicken à la king," I say glumly, twining the phone cord around my wrist.

"Sounds good!" he says too enthusiastically. "Is that all one thing?"

By midterm exams, I'm living on candy. Occasionally my dormmates order a pizza and I consume a little protein, but aside from that it's chocolate almonds, jelly beans, and nonpareils. I start to lose weight. My tongue feels stripped and scalded from eating so much sugar, my teeth ache, my skin looks ghoulish, and there are hollow blue crescents under my eyes. I complete this look by wearing black sleeveless T-shirts featuring punk bands—the Sex Pistols, the Ramones, the Clash—and black stovepipe jeans. I sit in my poetry class, my blood fizzy and acidic. I bounce in my chair, a rushing sugar jig, foot wagging, teeth clicking, until people get annoyed and grab me, trying to press me down into my seat. Three minutes later, I start bouncing again.

. . .

Two or three times a month, I unfasten my safety-pin necklace, put on
a cotton blouse and corduroys, and take the hour-long bus ride back
to my parents' house. But something inexplicable begins to happen
on these visits. Bud prepares big special meals, all my favorites—
roasted chicken, shish kabobs, grape leaves. I eat and talk with abandon, inflated with college ideas and new classes, helping myself to
seconds and thirds. But hours later, after dinner and dessert and
dishes and more dessert, at some point late at night, deep asleep in
my bed, I'm awakened by molten nausea. It comes with a dreadful
disorientation—the sense that something is deeply wrong yet completely unidentifiable. It is such a primordial sensation that it seems
in those waking moments that I've never lived without it.

I spend the wee hours of the night staggering between my bedroom and the bathroom, vomiting, then retching. My body is racked,
helpless, reduced to rubble. Usually it's just as the dawn is beginning
to turn watery and pale that I'm able to collapse back into sleep. I
awaken late in the morning, shaky but stabilized.

My mother, who has heard me creeping around in the night,
smooths back my hair. She is a marvelous nurse, showing up with
ginger ale and saltines, broth and magazines. "Poor you," she says. "I
hope it's not your father's cooking!"

"It couldn't be—nobody else got sick," I groan.

She places a cool washcloth on my forehead. "Or it's just some
weird bug. Probably you're a little run-down from all your studying."

The nausea begins to occur with such regularity on my visits
home that I wonder if this mysterious virus is somehow embedded in
the walls of my old room. I consider that it might be psychosomatic,
since it happens only when I return home. But the sickness is so
immense, crashing over and swamping my whole body, that I can't
imagine it's something that comes simply from my mind. That seems
much too clean and abstract for this pitching agony.

Aside from the nausea, my visits home are unremarkable. Rather, what is remarkable about them is that I no longer feel edgy and impatient with everyone. I'm no longer driven to hide behind the double set of beaded curtains in my bedroom doorway. I feel this relief especially with Bud. The sizzling stress between the two of us has dissipated. We're calmer and more genial around each other. All the usual old flash points of debate topics like dating and boys, women's rights, and Middle Eastern politics seem beside the point. Instead, I sit sideways in the kitchen chair and, newly curious, ask Bud about his life.

"Tell me again—how did your youngest brother die?"

"Oh." Bud shakes his head with the memory. "They put leeches on him—but his appendix still burst open. Terrible thing. I couldn't watch."

"How did they take out Uncle Hal's tonsils?"

"Oh." He rolls his eyes. "No nice drugs forty years ago. The barber was also the dentist. He came at Hal"—Bud lifts his hands into claws—"with a great big pair of scissors!"

If I'm steering the conversation to safety, neither of us notices. Bud is glad to visit the past with me, and sometimes it feels as if we are both in there in the old place. Our conversations are journeys. We lose ourselves in former lives. I half wonder if Jordan would exist if Bud weren't here.

Barely a month into the semester, the mornings are charged with sharp, clean filaments of winter air. By October, I can look out of my eighth-floor window and view the campus grounds all the way to the start of Lake Ontario glowing in a crystal ice sheet. Light snow glitters in the air. For some reason, I miss my childhood. It's a subtler, more ancient form of homesickness that I find absorbing, a delicious sadness.

In late October, Hillel, the Jewish student organization, papers the hallways with posters for a Jewish Foods Day as well as a menu that includes a number of the foods I grew up with. The poster features the Middle Eastern dishes that I think of as the Trinity: falafel, hummus, and baba ghanouj. I study the sign and recall Aunt Aya's teachings on the origins of dishes. Does falafel belong to a nation? A culture? I stand in the corridor, hands on my hips, mulling over the poster.

Whatever the nationality or religion, I'm excited about this event. I've never heard of anyone outside of our family serving such dishes—especially falafel, which is a messy, deep-fried affair. Better to leave falafel sandwiches to the guys with the full-body aprons selling it from carts.

I try to convince a number of my dormmates to attend Jewish Foods Week with me. But the girls in my all-girls dorm are turning out to be finicky, hothouse flowers. They spend hours lined up in the mirror-lined bathrooms, blow-drying their hair to glassy straightness, painting their toenails, or lolling in bed eating ice cream and pizza. In the end, I manage to entice only Elise, who happens to be Jewish, and to harangue my two roommates into submission. Annie is a stolid, good-natured Irish-Catholic girl from working-class Long Island. She owns two pairs of jeans and six T-shirts and wears her long brown hair parted cleanly down the middle so that it hangs in two shanks on her shoulders. Courtney is a strawberry-blond southern debutante with sticky mascaraed lashes. She is engaged to the former captain of her high school football team. "I don't like anything new, pretty much ever," she says in her buttery accent. But, grudgingly, they agree to go.

We travel together in a clutch to the cafeteria in the student union building, where Hillel has set up a small assemblage of caterer's chafing dishes and orange heat lamps against one wall. Besides the falafel, hummus, and baba ghanouj, there's an okra stew and a plate of sinewy chunks of beef they're calling *shawerma*. Alongside all of this is a tub full of three-bean salad. We join the sparse crowd, sliding trays through the line. Exuberant student workers with shining dark eyes mill around, greeting everyone individually with a handshake and a bright "Shalom!" But two older men standing glumly behind the tubs and dishing out the food are muttering in Arabic, discussing the three-bean salad:

"I can't explain it."

"But what is it? I didn't bring it."

"I think that might be the Jewish food."

"But where did it come from?"

"The Super Duper Market."

After we settle at our table, Courtney, her eyes continuously damp from her contacts, looks around and whispers, "Is everyone here really Jewish?"

"Courtney, half the kids at this school are Jewish," Annie says.

"They are?"

"And Diana's Arabic!"

Courtney stares at me as if I've been hiding something.

Elise examines her plate of food, then finally samples some cucumber salad; she praises it lavishly and encourages the rest of us to dive in. Annie, pleased by the break from the dining hall fare, says the hummus reminds her of peanut butter and scoops her pita bread through the dip in wide streaks, then goes back for more. Courtney daintily pokes at the falafel, rolling it around without managing to break the fried crust, and I have to resist the urge to slap her hand. She refuses to touch her food with anything but metal utensils.

The truth is that the food on our trays looks lumpen and uninspiring. It's been steamed to death under the heat lamps. The hummus is dull as clay, the baba ghanouj thick and bitter. The dried-out falafel crumbles on impact with the bread, and there isn't any tahini sauce or chopped tabbouleh to spruce things up. Even the three-bean salad releases a viscous, mucilaginous fluid that I scrape to the edge of my plate. I feel too disappointed to eat more than a bite or two.

"Well, really, Diana," Courtney says, "I don't know what you expect me to do with this Jewish food. I'm not even Jewish."

I grind my molars together and stab a cucumber slice. I glance at the two gloomy Arab men behind the chafing dishes and lower my eyes, irrationally worried that they might somehow know me.

Now Courtney looks thoughtful. "They should have an Episcopalian food week, too. I wonder if they ever do that here?"

Elise snorts. "Oh, and what would that be, Courtney? Sugar

peeps?" Courtney is renowned in the dorm for subsisting on marsh-mallow chicks.

"I'm just saying, I don't see the point of getting all high and mighty about food anyway," she says, her voice singed with hurt. "I mean, since when is food religious? It's not like it can make you hear angels or something."

Elise and I are both looking at her. Elise takes a big bite of falafel and says, "I feel sorry for you."

Suddenly reinvigorated, I scoop up one of the hard little falafels in a corner of pita and take a bite, expecting it will taste as bad as it looks. And while it's cold and overcooked, I still taste fried chickpeas, the golden, mellow fundament of falafel, and, embedded deeper within, the sun-soaked air of Jordan. The taste is clear and direct as emotion, glowing inside me, keenly edged with longing—a wallop of a feeling. Reassured, I look up and say, "I've heard angels at dinner."

"Does this taste like angels to you?" Annie asks me, grinning.

"Y'all are like religious fanatics," Courtney says with a fastidious sniff. She puts down her fork and knife. "And I'm not hungry."

Before I'd left for college, Bud sat me down at the kitchen table, cleared his throat, and dictated a list of rules that I had to write out on a legal pad. These rules consisted of things I wasn't allowed to do:

No staying out late.

No parties.

No silliness.

No boys.

"What does that mean, exactly?" I'd asked.

"It means what it means!" he'd thundered. "No boys!"

As it turns out, the list of rules gets "lost," which happens on a wintry morning, the air as clean and bright as peppermint. I take the elevator to the top of my dorm, exit through the heavy service door, stand on the gravel roof, and slowly, happily, begin shredding the list. I allow these pieces to be blown from my hands and scattered far and wide, past the edge of the building, beyond the curve of the earth.

Days later, I begin dating a boy who calls himself a "punk rocker." Timmy Fussell wears a necklace of safety pins and pretends to play guitar with a band called the Nervous Robots. He doesn't actually know how to play guitar—his fingers never touch the strings—but the band keeps him because they think he makes the show "lively." I've seen the Nervous Robots perform twice, both performances ending in drunken, indecipherable arguments between the bassist and the drummer, and there is some doubt about whether the group still exists after that. Timmy is from the same part of Syracuse I am, and in fact, I'd heard of his family before we'd met. His mother, Louise, kept a little meat smoker in her garage that made her famous in town. There is even a local celebration named after her, Louise Fest, complete with T-shirts bearing her name. Once a year, Louise rolls the rattling, shuddering, sawed-off smoker out of her garage and down to the local public green and smokes grease-slathered ribs for everyone. Exactly the sort of food my father would say is *haram*: taboo.

Timmy looks like a banty rooster. He has snappy blue eyes and yellow hair that sticks up from the back of his head in a ruff. He always looks a little sickly, with his shock-white skin, inflamed knuckles, and hairless, glutinous chest. He's in his second year at college but hasn't attended any classes I know of. He first picks me out at the large communal dining hall linking the boys' and girls' dorms, waving across the room as if we know each other. When, curious, I slide my tray down next to his, he begins narrating a brief history of punk rock and concludes by saying he thinks I'd make a "good punk." Timmy starts saving seats for me at every meal. Each time he waves as soon as I wander into the chaotic hall. He's interesting and arresting, and he pursues me with an ardor that I find, at sixteen, irresistible. After a few weeks, we start to meet at the one artsy coffeehouse in Oswego, the Lowlife Café, a decrepit joint with a sour, rotting reek that seems to be sliding by increments into the Oswego River just beneath its windows.

Local musicians spread out their instruments and play guitar rocking back and forth in a chair or standing, bouncing loose-jointed, singing on the squat platform at the front of the café. Some-times Timmy's friends let him come up and accompany them on his tambourine. Some of the musicians are off-key, but a few possess clear, sparkling voices or a tender, refined ability to play guitar. Inside, the radiators hiss and the music arcs along the wooden ribs of the old building and down through rickety floorboards. I sit at a table near the stage and pour a misty stream of sugar from the glass canister into my cappuccino, sweetening it into candy. I love the chocolaty-roasted coffees rich and airy with steamed milk, the inverse of my father's blunt, black Arabic coffee.

My days of candy and nights of cappuccino, the music and the boyfriend are all my own. There is nothing here that Bud knows about or would approve of. And there is nothing better than being surrounded by this complicated atmosphere of music, old wooden furniture, high, dark windows, and plumes of steam from the cap-puccino machine. The night belongs to me alone. It is a creature of my own invention—a new, seductive country.

My dormitory will be closed for a month during Christmas break. At this point, I've made several short visits home and gotten sick. It doesn't happen on every visit, but it happens enough that I start to anticipate the symptoms almost every evening of every visit: the subcutaneous, creeping sensation of nausea, its rising, unignorable bloom in the gut, the sweating palms and clammy mouth. After weeks of candy, I crave my father's cooking; I meditate on it during my silent rides back home. But I never know what will happen. I may eat the big welcome-home dinners only to wake in the predawn to throw up again and again. I begin to mourn the food even before I eat it, wondering, Will I keep it down this time?

It's a frigid night when I return home for Christmas break—too cold to snow, a startling clarity to the air. I drag my bags into my bed-room and look around wistfully. My parents have had it with driving for miles to get groceries. They're tired of being shocked awake in the early dawn by gunshots from hunters lost in the backyard. They've decided to sell the country home and move into a brick house back in the suburbs that we moved away from five years ago. This will be the last Christmas we spend here. For all my moping about the isolation when I lived here, I've grown to love the thought of this house. It's become a romantic Walden fantasy in my imagination.

My bedroom is blue from the early winter moon. Through the frost-stenciled window I can hear rushing fir boughs and the creak of icicles tightening. I gaze into the dim mirror above my dresser: chopped hair, shadowy eyes, hollow cheeks. I feel fragile, almost translucent. Suzy has been occupying my room while I've been away. I can see her refined touches—some of my old blacklight posters, strawberry candles, and whirling mobiles have been cleared away in favor of a painted parasol, a straw hat, and a lot more light and air. I feel ghostly, not fully returned.

I sit in the living room before dinner and contemplate the dwarf plastic evergreen blinking on the end table; there's a lilt of snow sighing past the living room windows. I realize, in this confluence of sweet, brief return and loss, that I think I miss Timmy. I hadn't expected this. I'd already started cataloging his imperfections before leaving on break. His teeth are small yellow squares, his breath has a fishy cat food edge, and the whole tambourine-playing routine has lost its charm. Over the past several weeks, while he's stood on-stage, wagging and snapping the tambourine between hand and hip, I've fidgeted in the audience, uncertain if my father's disapproval is enough of a reason to date someone. I'd contemplated breaking up with Timmy before the holidays but had gotten preoccupied with packing. And now, far from the actual Timmy, the idea of Timmy isn't too bad. It gives me a focal point. Ours has not been a terribly romantic relationship—we've barely even kissed—but it is not so much Timmy that I miss as my late nights of music and cappuccino. A month is a long time to be away from my new, barely constructed life. So I give myself to this secret grief. I intend to pine for Timmy, write him agonized letters every night, and regularly sneak him calls, leaning into the rhythm of his breathing.

But tonight I put aside my longing and wash up for dinner. For my first night back, we're having chicken *fatteh*—a layered dish of toasted bread, chicken, onion, spices, and pine nuts covered with a velvety yogurt sauce. It's so lush and lovely, I eat recklessly, like an amnesiac, with no awareness of anything but the table, the sweet sadness of return, and the moon hanging like a sigh just beyond the long dark fields.

HOMECOMING *FATTEH*

2 cups plain yogurt
4- to 6-pound whole
   chicken
6 tablespoons olive oil
Juice of 1 lemon
½ teaspoon ground cloves
1 teaspoon ground
   cinnamon
1 teaspoon ground cardamom
Salt and freshly ground
   pepper

1 large onion, coarsely
   chopped
1 cup uncooked rice
2 cups chicken broth
2 loaves pita bread, cut in
   pieces
4 cloves garlic, crushed
½ cup chopped flat-leaf
   parsley
¼ cup toasted pine nuts

Place the yogurt in a double layer of cheesecloth, tie the ends to the kitchen faucet, and let drain into the sink for about 1 hour, until thickened.

Preheat the oven to 350 degrees. Place the chicken in a baking dish and drizzle with 3 tablespoons of the olive oil and the lemon juice. Mix the spices in a small dish and sprinkle over the chicken; surround it with the onion pieces. Cover the chicken with foil and bake for 1 hour. Remove the foil and let the chicken brown in the oven for 5 minutes.

Meanwhile, cook the rice in the chicken broth.

Fry the pieces of pita bread in the remaining oil until crisp and brown.

Stir the crushed garlic into the thickened yogurt. Line a baking dish with the fried bread and place the cooked rice on the bread.

Cut the chicken into pieces and lay them on the rice, then cover the chicken, rice, and bread with the garlic yogurt. Sprinkle the parsley and pine nuts over the top and serve.

MAKES 4 SERVINGS.

During the meal, Bud decides it's time to evaluate what all this American schooling has made of me. He gives me big spoonfuls of *fatteh*, insists that I take more broccoli, and heaps the rice onto my plate. Then he sits in his spot opposite me, frowns, and says, "Ya Ba, now tell me again. Say it slow. What is your major?"

I look at my sisters. They've become even better allies since I've been away at college, funnier, smarter, and more entertaining than when I was at home. On the verge of starting high school, Suzy has grown poised and graceful, her dark, regal eyes watchful. Monica is still in junior high. She's charged up, too wired to gain an ounce of weight, a wise-guy grin on her lips. They squint snake eyes at Bud, but he doesn't notice. Suzy tries to deflect him by saying, "Can we just eat? She'll tell you later—the broccoli's getting cold!"

Bud waves his fork at me. "She can chew and talk."

I huff and fan myself as if it's all too much for me to think about. "I hardly just finished my first semester. I barely know where the dining hall is, much less what my major will be." I scoop up a big forkful of *fatteh* and say, "Hey, Dad, this is fantastic—I could eat this whole tray!"

He points his fork at me. "Okay, okay, sure, but what do you think your major is *going* to be?"

Bud didn't go to college—how does he even know about majors? I feel harried, and finally I blurt out, "Well then, I guess English, probably." Then I bite the inside of my mouth. I focus all my powers of concentration on trying to spear a pine nut with my fork.

Bud inhales deeply through his nose. This was not the correct answer. The correct answer is medicine, law, maybe engineering. He has always told me to make my own money and to have a trade. Not to depend on a man for anything. Now he shakes his head as if he's trying to clear it. He says, "English? You already speak English!"

"English literature," Mom says.

He squints at this, then says, "I knew that." He glares at the table. "And I don't think I like it."

Foolishly, I sigh.

He draws his head back. "Are you telling me that English literature is a *trade*? Are you telling me that it's going to give you food and a house? Why don't you just run out in the streets and start drinking and smoking cigars and going around with strange men while you're at it?"

"What's that got to do with anything?" I cry.

"What's anything got to do with anything!" he retorts. His eyes are so wide, they look peeled. He shoves back his chair, the rubber stoppers on the legs making a terrible shriek against the linoleum. He jabs one finger against his temple. "You think I don't remember anything, but *I remember everything*!" And with that he storms from the room.

That night I'm awakened by roiling nausea. Over the following three and a half weeks of vacation, I have several more terrible bouts with vomiting. I sweat and shudder over the toilet, nose running, the bitter shock of bile burning my mouth and sinuses. While I'm home on break, I read a magazine article that suggests that people store specialized and symbolic sorts of pain in different body parts—tight chest, throbbing head, achy back—each limb betraying something about the condition of our lives. If this is so, then there is nothing more uncannily, ineffably wrong than the condition of nausea. There is no part of me that can stand apart and watch it happen. I turn inside out, my body physically rejecting the food. A rejection of something more powerful than food.

Bud doesn't ask any more questions about my major during that break, but now my visit feels less a truce than a standoff. Bud and I sit silently in the living room together. He naps or falls into trances under the newspaper, but I sense that he is still monitoring me, his gaze edging over the top of the paper, appraising me. I stare at the TV and train my thoughts on missing my boyfriend. Then, in my peripheral vision, I'll see the edge of the newspaper go limp and I'll snap to attention, saying, "*What.*"

Bud's face goes slack and innocent. "What—what?" he says. Then, indignant, "*What!*"

When I sense that Bud is about to start asking questions about college, my intentions, my trade, or anything remotely related to such topics, I flee to my room, fed up and misunderstood, aching to be back at school, wishing away the few remaining days of my vacation. I begin another florid, top-secret love letter to Timmy, "Being away from you is ABSOLUTE AGONY," and follow that with, "Here at home, the lunatic is running the asylum. . . ." The letters are all complaints. I stash them in my suitcase, thinking I will give them to Timmy once we're reunited. As it turns out, I will never do so. When I next actually lay eyes on him at school, I will be so stunned by the difference between my memory of Timmy and the reality of Timmy that I'll feel a little surge of rage, as if he'd deliberately tricked me, and end things there and then.

One night, not long before I'm to return to school, I wake in the early morning night. I am instinctively clenched, my mouth clamped shut, anticipating the nausea that usually wakes me at such an hour. But that's not it. I gradually sense a pale lavender light pulsing through my bedroom curtains. I sit up, curious and oddly hopeful, and swing my feet out of bed. The colored air makes me feel buoyant and soft, as if I'm floating to the window. Outside, the immense country night is ribboned with eerie streaks; unearthly tones rise like smoke signals from the horizon. What am I seeing? I don't know how long I stand there, looking. The light makes a photographic negative of the world—blackening the snowfields and rinsing open the night so it looks pure and violet, like moonlit sand—and this seems to have the effect of dissolving time itself, turning it one-dimensional, slight as breath.

I've read about moments in books where the author says that while one is contemplating the physical world, a sort of veil is lifted and there is a glimpse of the infinite. For me it's the reverse. The light roots me to the floor, the window, the snow-shaking, windy sky. It pulls me immediately and irresistibly into the senses, the physical world, and I feel a startling cellular jolt of exquisite love and connection to the people who lie asleep in the purple lights and in all the sleepy, snowbound houses around us. It is like a benediction. I sense the distances between places, the country house and suburbs, even between America and Jordan, start to disintegrate. Geography turns liquid. There is something in us connecting every person to every other person.

After some time, the lights diffuse and I turn away from the windows. I realize that I am very hungry. Instead of returning to bed, I go upstairs, cross the night canyon of the living room, and head into the kitchen, where the refrigerator waits for me, humming.

The white door gives with a kiss of suction. Its glass shelves are crowded with the leftovers from our big meals. There are bowls of stuffed grape leaves, roasted chicken with garlic, and lamb kibbeh. But I see what I want tucked in back in a plain white soup bowl— yogurt *lebeneh*. It is the simplest dish in the world: yogurt that's been drained and thickened so it's mild and rich as cream. You eat it with a little salt and a drizzle of good olive oil on top, and you scoop it up with a loaf of warmed pita bread. I sit alone at the kitchen table in the afterglow of the spotlit winter night and dip pieces of bread into a dish of *lebeneh*.

Tonight, this is the purest food in the world. Mother's milk. It is the sort of food that can't be replaced by anything else.

For my remaining time at home, I sleep the nights from beginning to end. The nausea has stopped as mysteriously as it started. I sleep soundly and dreamlessly, and I wake with a good taste in my mouth.

SEVENTEEN

A New World

After graduating from college, I take lots of small jobs—waiting tables, cooking chili, eggs, steak, and hash browns over spattering grills, or wheeling office chairs around a variety of cloud-carpeted offices, carrying manila folders in both arms. I try marrying a sweet boy from my writing class—I can't see any other way of leaving my parents' home. But I can't be married with much success, it seems, because during my twenties so much of me still belongs to my parents. And also because I'd grown up in confinement and now there is no part of me that can bear anything like more confinement. I don't feel married at all, not one bit, even though I do enjoy eating lunch with the boy. So one day after washing the dishes, I sigh and say, "Yeah, I'm gonna take off now." He and I split up in a very friendly, sociable sort of way. Not until much later—beyond the ending point of this very book—do I own enough of myself to know how to marry for the good, pure sake of marriage and not for the sake of running off.

The one thing I'd taught myself in my childhood confinement is the thing that stays with me through college, work, and marriage, and that is to write. I learned that no one can stop me or make me tell the story any differently from the precise, exact, ruthless way I want to tell it.

I publish two poems in my senior year of college, and I remember the pure, physical pleasure of seeing my voice caught and pressed into print for the first time. I'm nervous about showing the poems to my parents because, of course, even with the validation and liberation of publishing, the next new fear is waiting for me around the corner. What if nobody likes it? What if they're angry or hurt or upset by what I've written? But at least I have the one good fortune of an immigrant's child—to write in a language my father doesn't read fluently. Bud says he loves the poems.

I give up on all the little jobs and go to graduate school, trying to find the trail that will take me to a writing life. I try to learn how to write by sinking myself into reading. My attic apartment is so full of novels, I have to go out onto the little balcony to read them. And I do, one by one, closely, painstakingly, examining the unconscious elements of style as closely as an apprentice observing a watchmaker or blacksmith, studying her masters. Not long before I graduate, my parents go on a vacation to Hawaii. First, Bud wanders away from a group tour because he believes he hears "the voice of the earth" calling to him ecstatically. He falls behind the walking group (Mom is up ahead, socializing with the others), then scales a fence, climbs over a few ridges and hills, and finally comes upon a small impoverished village where he spends the day eating barbecued chicken, drinking beer, and chatting with his new best friends in the world. When Mom finally realizes that Bud is missing, the group has to spend the rest of the day and part of the night searching for him.

The second thing that happens is that Mom comes home with a present she's bought for me in Hawaii: a necklace of deep azure beads sparked with white flecks, lapis, in honor of my completed dissertation—a collection of short stories I've titled *Lapis Lazuli.* We sit on the edge of my couch in my rickety, cramped graduate student apartment and she drapes the exquisite beads over my head. The necklace is like a dash of light, by far the nicest thing in the whole apartment. I feel anointed, recognized in the deepest possible way. We laugh over the story of Bud and "the voice of the earth." I know that she is telling me—as she has in her subtle ways over the years—that I shall be a writer.

When my first novel, *Arabian Jazz,* is published six years later, my parents attend my readings in Syracuse and bring their friends. They laugh at the funny parts and look sad at the sad parts and applaud wildly, sitting in the front row with five copies each stacked on their laps. Mom tells me it is great, just great, great! When the question-and-answer session begins, Bud waves his arm from side to side. After I call on him—"Yes, Dad?"—he stands and turns to the audience.

"I just want you all to know that's *my daughter*." He points at me, in case they might've missed me standing there at the podium. "And I don't know where she got all these ideas in this book, but she really did!"

Then he invites the audience over to his house for dinner.

Each event is one piece in the path of claiming myself. As I begin to teach and publish, I begin to own a little more of my own story. I buy a car, move to the West Coast. Bud watches me with pride but also something like confusion: I am at the microphone, I am holding the pen—this is not the way he would tell the story! And maybe there is a little sadness there as well—the sadness that comes from watching something new grow out of your hands, knowing that to let it grow you have to open your hands.

"INVITE THE AUDIENCE" TOMATO CHICKEN *MENSAF*
A crowd-pleasing variation on classic lamb (or goat) mensaf.

1 chicken, cut up and skinned
1 can (28 ounces) tomatoes
½ teaspoon ground cinnamon
Salt and pepper
2 medium onions, chopped
2 tablespoons olive oil
1 cup uncooked rice
2 cups chicken broth
½ cup pine nuts
4 tablespoons butter
5 loaves pita bread, torn into pieces (my parents use slices of white bread instead)

Place the chicken in a large cooking pot and add water to cover. Simmer for 20 minutes, skimming off the fat.

Place the tomatoes, cinnamon, salt, and pepper in the pot with the chicken and simmer for 30 minutes.

In a small frying pan, sauté the onions in the olive oil until tender. Add the onions to the chicken and continue to simmer.

Simmer the rice in the chicken broth until the liquid is absorbed, about 20 minutes.

Sauté the pine nuts in the butter until they are lightly brown and fragrant.

Place the pieces of bread over a large serving dish. Spread the cooked rice over the bread. Place the chicken on the rice and pour half of the onions and tomato sauce over this; save the other half in a serving dish. Top with the sautéed pine nuts.

Some people who can't get enough of a good thing also add a few extra pats of butter here and there before, and even after, serving.

MAKES 4 SERVINGS.

EIGHTEEN

The Best Cook in the Family

It takes twenty years for me to get back to Jordan. After college and graduate school, there is debt, travel, debt, teaching, debt, and work and debt and work—so much that I lose sight of myself. I have published a novel, but my life doesn't exactly crack open, the angels don't pour down. There is still debt and work. After nine years of teaching, I decide to apply for a Fulbright fellowship to live in Amman, Jordan. I write in my application that I want to do research for a new novel. But after I drop it in the mailbox, I walk away with a dull, chilled, grayish sensation in my stomach. I don't entirely understand why I've written this proposal. When I receive the grant, instead of plotting my novel, I start wondering what on earth I'm going to do with myself in Amman.

My sense of connection to Jordan has been winnowed down by time, my memory of the place gone soft and silvery as a piece of driftwood. My Jordanian relatives continue to move in and out of America—virtually all of Bud's brothers have moved back to Jordan over the years—and Bud continues to talk about Jordan as if we've just left it. But I no longer catch traces of its scent or the rushing sense of its light in the summer. I'm an American, with only a few lingering suggestions of another place in my nature: I stuff the teapot with fresh mint; I use obscure aphorisms to illustrate points; sometimes I invite too many people over for dinner—more guests than there are chairs to seat them. I want people to come without invitation, walk in the door and lean over the counter while they inhale the garlic, and eat too much at dinner.

My flight to Jordan goes in two legs: America to Britain is filled with people in business dress and a smattering of tourists. At Heathrow, it takes me some time to locate the gate for the flight to Amman.

It turns out to be at the end of a long, crowded corridor filled with tourists from Spain and Portugal. As I get closer, I notice what I think is a marching band in black uniforms milling around the Jetway. Not until I'm almost at the gate do I realize I'm actually looking at a group of women in *hejjab*—the long black veil that covers the hair and circles the face. I step back into the busy concourse, staring at the women in the gate; my hands feel cold and slick. That is when I first understand that I'm really going to Jordan. I remember passing the dark, liquid forms of veiled women in the streets of Amman. Some of them had slots in their veils for the eyes; occasionally there were some whose faces were entirely covered, elusive as living shadows.

On the flight, I'm mildly disappointed to be seated next to a businessman who disappears into his newspaper and a mist of lemony cologne. I'd love to talk to somebody about just about anything. We stop in Beirut to let some passengers disembark. There's a layover, but we aren't allowed to get off the plane, just invited to stand and stretch. I go to the door of the plane and look out into the glowing Lebanese sky. There are several languorous soldiers with iridescent automatic weapons tilted against their shoulders, standing at the foot of the stairs—guarding us or guarding Lebanon, I'm not sure which. The physical fact of those oiled, insectlike weapons disturbs the air and causes an instant physical contraction. I shrink away from the luxurious blue sky, back into the cave of the plane.

During the same stop, some of my fellow passengers consult compasses and unfurl their prayer rugs in the central aisle of the plane. The businessman beside me takes the pages of the newspaper he'd been studying and lays them out on the floor. They pray there in the middle of everything.

After growing up with Bud's idea that Jordan is our truest, essential home, a part of me has come to believe it. My grant proposal describes a novel that I will write about characters undergoing ambitious self-excavation, recovery, and reconciliation as they move between countries. It is set in both America and the Middle East, and it is meant to draw together my own deep cultural ambivalences—to try to look right at the conundrum of being *Arab-American*. Arab and American.

But what I think is a project proposal is really the crude outline for the process I want for myself. Sometimes it's too intimidating to look at things directly, to think, Now for the first time I will go to live in Jordan, I will choose it freely, and I will see if this place has anything at all to do with me. The airplane door *thunks* shut for the last leg of the trip. As the plane taxis down the runway, the fear that perhaps I don't belong in Jordan at all begins to fill me, overtaking my knees, my hands, my breath. It tightens like a net. I try to breathe deeply. There's the sound of rustling papers. A woman across the aisle unwraps an elaborate portable meal of lamb, onions, squash. I inhale the scent of rice with fried nuts and cinnamon and feel calmer.

The pilot comes on the intercom and announces in French, Arabic, and English that for our takeoff out of Beirut the lights must be extinguished. The aisle lights, the overhead lights, the little private reading lights all go out. I hear passengers exchanging theories about why this is done. Their voices seem like confidences in the dark. One passenger says it's simply easier for navigation at night, but another says it's so bored, armed teenagers—or freedom fighters—on the ground won't be tempted to shoot at the planes. There is pitch-blackness as we roar down the runway, and when we lift off, I feel invisible, lighter than the unlit air, rising into the night, a transparent blackness.

Just before I left for Jordan, my mother unearthed an old family photograph. It shows a lineup of devil-eyed, dusty-skinny, scaly-kneed boys. My father is down toward the smaller end of the range. There were too many rough little boys to count—how could my grandmother keep track of them all?

"You know, there's a streak of insanity in the Abu-Jaber family," Mom said. Her voice was strained when we first discussed the trip: I would go off for a year in another country. And not just any country, of course, but the place that pulled at the seams of their marriage, the very fabric of our family life.

She ran her fingers along the edge of the old photographs. These were the tiny black-and-white snapshots, trimmed in wavy white borders, of Bud's before life, the place where even Mom could not go. In them, he posed Tarzan style, sylph skinny, on the rocks at Ma'in, a Jordanian hot springs. The mist in the air and the gray tones of the little photographs made everything look smoky and prehistoric. Dad scampered over the boulders, shouting, "Flash Gordon—hooray!" Or he pointed his finger fencing style, scratching out the mark of Zorro in the air—his other hand held back and skyward as if for balance. In another pile, Mom's old snapshots showed her sitting neatly in white knee socks and a Brownie uniform, bangs combed demurely over her forehead, trimmed straight above the eyebrows. Her pale eyes were sweet, luminous, and innocent—still blissfully unaware of the leaping Zorro on the other side of the world.

My mother is the voice of sanity in our family—for which I love her beyond all reckoning. She has always held the same job as a reading teacher, she wears soft, unfussy clothes and shoes, keeps her hair cropped close, relies on a firm, brick-colored lipstick. But on that day, just a week before my departure, she tucked the photographs back in the envelope—such a slim container for a legacy. She sighed and tapped the edge of the envelope. She would have liked to tell me not to go, I realized, but she also wouldn't let herself do it. She wasn't like her own mother, who insisted on her own way even when she knew it was impossible. Mom knew that I needed to do this and that she couldn't follow me. The TV news program swirled with startling images of the Middle East: angry men holding guns, frightened women scurrying under beetle black veils. There was this to consider, and then there was also the fact that it seemed nothing short of a miracle that Bud was still managing to live in America, that his homesickness hadn't torn him—and us—to pieces.

As we sat there, contemplating the envelope of photos, I wished Mom would tell me not to go.

She frowned at the envelope as if she were concentrating very hard. I bit the inside of my lower lip. If she had told me not to go, would that have stopped me? Very possibly. Instead, she finally shook her head and said, "You'd better pack some fancy clothes—they love dressing up for dinner over there."

. . .

My family is full of snappy dressers, big dreamers, holy fools, drug addicts, riot starters, layabouts, poets, con men, gurus, murderers, gamblers, diplomats, tyrants, professors, vicious gossips, magicians, toughs, snobs, petty thieves, big crooks, rich guys, mesmerists, gigolos, and fancy idiots.

The women wear too much makeup and jewelry, their heels are too high, they have too much hair, and they flaunt their beauty like a torch, even after it's burnt out and fallen to cinders. The men lie and charm and steal—especially from one another. The Abu-Jaber women run away from their men, deer-wild, into the night.

There's very little in the way of middle management in this family, very little domestication, serenity, or respectability.

What's more, they're proud of it.

I don't know if these attributes are just a reflection of all families or more particularly of the Abu-Jabers. Because, let's face it, they can also be party starters, big spenders, yarn spinners, magnetic, and plain exciting. Arabs and Americans alike can't quite seem to resist their spell, can't help but get tangled up with them, fall for their schemes, defend their outrages, adopt their illegitimate children, bail them out of jail, and listen to their sob stories.

When I get to Jordan, that same bunch of shifty-eyed, crook-grinning uncles is there, three times as big as those skinny boys used to be, their faces pure reflections of years of wisecracking, drinking, and self-destructing. Some of them lived in the States long enough to have three careers and raise their children to adulthood, but one by one the brothers all were eventually called back, as if drawn by the very essence of blood. And now they call me back as well. Americans never think I look Middle Eastern, but in Jordan, the people who know my family say, "Oh yes, I can tell you're an Abu-Jaber."

If I ask how they can tell, they roll their eyes, chuckle wryly, and say, Well, you have that thing, the way you laugh and walk and that way you have.

I ask my Jordanian friend Mai what that means and she says, "You know, it's that crazy Abu-Jaber way. You're all like that!"

Two things take place as soon as I get to Amman. The first is that my American friends are seized with curiosity about this place that I have gone off to, and one after another, they schedule visits. The other thing is that every day there is the tinny ring of my little telephone on the kitchen wall and then the rumbly, accented voices of my many uncles, calling me to their tables. Uncle Jack is having a dinner party at their city house, but Uncle Hal wants a party at his house in the country. Uncle Frankie proposes a small meal at their place near the embassy, but Uncle Danny wants a big feast at his desert retreat. When, in addition to all the other invitations, I accept an early invitation to Uncle Rafiq's house, a controversy arises, as Uncle Rafiq is not a true uncle, but the son of my grandfather's brother. As such, he is considered something of an outlander, a meddlesome pot stirrer, and—I'm informed by an auntie—I should have waited several more months to go to his house if I was going to insist on seeing him at all.

After an elaborate, multicourse meal at his palatial home on a street lined with soughing trees, Rafiq takes me aside and tells me that my grandfather was "single-handedly responsible for the downfall of the Abu-Jaber family." He doesn't elaborate on this statement, but he does grin and abruptly wander off alone into another drawing room, as if he has finally delivered the message he's held in his pocket for sixty years.

My uncles' dinners are massive, and each one takes up half a day. One must arrive early for the *mezza* course. The style of the *mezza* reflects the personality of the host. At some homes, there are special breads and dips made sumptuous with olive oil, fried nuts, fresh herbs, and so on. At other places, like my Uncle Hal's big country house, it's roasted nuts, olives, fresh whole tomatoes, cheeses and cucumbers, and a knife. Always there is *araq*.

So much food. It's hard to imagine how much food there is. This is a country crowded with Palestinian refugees who were pushed along with parents and grandparents across the border, where so many people are hungry, where there are demonstrations in the street when the price of bread rises by a few pennies. Food is one of the primary values in Jordan. The country isn't wealthy enough to pretend it doesn't matter or to imagine that dieting and slenderness are signs of beauty and virtue. There are stories in Jordan about men placing an anklet around their new wife's slim ankle with the expectation that if she's happy, she will fatten during the marriage until the anklet is tight. Eating her way into captivity, Gram says tartly when she hears this story.

According to my father, when he was a child, he and his brothers would gang around the dinner table until his mother and sister would appear with a platter of chicken at the head of the table and pass it into a sea of boys' hands.

"By the time it got down to me and the other little brothers, we'd be lucky to get a wing or a back," Bud said.

In my uncles' houses, they lean over me while I eat and cry out in despair, "Is that all you're having? Are you shy? Shall I help you?" They lift handfuls of food to my lips, urging me, "*Min eedi*," or pile heaps of rice and chunks of meat onto my plate. For every bite I take, they add three spoonfuls. I learn to eat very slowly.

I come back to my rented apartment after each of these events angry with myself for losing another day and vowing to get more work done tomorrow. I stare hard at the telephone when it rings. I'm supposed to be working on my novel, but within a few weeks of arrival, I realize that I'm not even trying. I avoid the stack of loose, smudgy pages. The phone jangles with invitations. If I don't answer, people stand on the lawn in front of my apartment building and shout up to my third-floor window or come upstairs and rattle my doorknob, calling to me to let them in. After the meals, the uncles call again and demand, "What do you think? Do I make the best eggplant? Was it better than Uncle Jack's eggplant? Who is the best cook in this family?"

And I say, "You, Uncle, you're the best cook in the family!"

. . .

Most of the uncles are good cooks. But there is one bad cook: Bachelor-Uncle Omar, who is actually my father's cousin. They call him "Bachelor Omar" because he was turned down for marriage approximately twelve times, each time after he'd cooked for his bride-to-be. His technique isn't bad, but his ingredients are terrible. While he has many charms and talents, my bachelor-uncle is cheap— brilliantly, relentlessly, stunningly cheap. His refrigerator, like my grandmother's refrigerator in New Jersey, is packed full of oozing, aging food. He will buy the gristliest, yellowest, most unchewable lamb, then cook and serve generous quantities of it. He's quite well-off, he has advanced degrees in mathematics and architecture, he's entertaining and warm, but he will serve you festering meat.

I invite Uncle Omar out for dinners. He refuses loudly, adamantly, trumpeting that restaurants are for sissies, dandies, and fancy idiots. He says, "Why should we go out to these ridiculous places when there is food a hundred times better at home!"

About a month after arriving in Jordan, I receive my first visitor from America—my single, pretty friend Tess. Bachelor-Uncle calls right away. "I want you both to come to dinner tonight. What does your friend look like?"

"But—" I cannot come up with a convincing dodge under pressure. I stammer and sweat and avoid looking at my reflection in the edge of the china cabinet mirror. "She—she—just got here!"

Tess looks up from the jumble of clothes spilling out of the suitcase onto her bed, tosses her heavy yellow hair over one shoulder, and waves at the phone.

"Then she is hungry!"

I reluctantly convey the invitation to Tess, and she is delighted. I warn her that the evening might be a little nonconformist, but this pleases her. She is twenty-four years old, on her first overseas vacation, and she says she wants to have experiences. "I'm ready to see the real Jordan," she says earnestly.

Bachelor-Uncle begins courting Tess immediately. He whisks her sweater from her shoulders as soon as we walk in, tosses it on a distant piece of furniture, and begins lecturing on art, philosophy, and his theories of class and economics. Tess nods, stunned into silence. His home is spacious yet formal, full of serious drawing rooms and tall, straight-backed chairs. But he takes us right into the kitchen, which is literally steaming with oven heat, and seats us at the kitchen table. The glass cabinet doors are beaded with condensation. "You know why people are poor?" he says, rummaging through his refrigerator. "Because they give away their possessions."

"Well, now," Tess ventures. "I mean, I can't imagine that *poor people*—"

"It's true!" my uncle insists. "They do! They throw away perfectly good furniture and dishes! They get rid of all their clothes! Look at this—" He plucks at his paisley shirt with the cat-face buttons. "I found *this* at a Goodwill in New Jersey twelve years ago. Still like new!"

Before dinner is served, Bachelor-Uncle announces that there will be a brief musical recital. He leads us into a shadowy room that is Victorian in its arch expansiveness. It is lined with shelves of moldering books, its corners filled with battered musical instruments. He seats us side by side on a starchy, unforgiving chaise and sits directly opposite us on a wooden stool. After picking up a bow, he accompanies himself on cello, swaying back into the sawing bow, singing a dirgelike melody that seems to dip ever deeper with each dark chord: "Do not forsake me, oh, my da-a-a-arling—" These seem to be the only words to the song, which he sings in a grim voice, over and over again. Then he stands and bows. Just as I'm about to stand, he moves to the piano. Tess clasps her hands together, not quite applauding, more as if she's trying to grab hold of something. "You're so talented!"

He nods, then puts one hand to his chest, lowers his head, and looks up at her. "Why, yes, I really am."

After a few more renditions of the same song on a few more grieving instruments, it is time to eat. He has cooked all day, he says. He returns us to the linoleum kitchen table, drags open the oven door, and pulls out a big, sumptuous tray of chicken *msukhan,* which I eye with a cautious optimism. He positions the tray and holds up a big carving knife like a conquering hero, but then he cries out and goes back to the fridge. From the deep of the deeps of the frost-crusted box, he unearths a decrepit chunk of roasted beef that's been stewing, forgotten in some sort of brine for so long that it looks like a huge dill pickle. He carves it into three hearty chunks and places one on each of our plates. "Now what about *that*?" he asks, nodding as we gaze upon the glistening hunks. "Can't have you saying I let you walk away from here hungry, now, can I?"

I do a sort of Morse code signal to Tess with lowered eyelids and raised eyebrows. As soon as Bachelor-Uncle goes off to the pantry, wondering where he put that case of orange soda he found by the side of the road, I pluck the pickled beef from all our plates and scrape it into the garbage, camouflaging it under some sodden lettuce leaves. When my uncle returns, he stops in his tracks, dumbfounded to see that the roast has vanished.

I say, "We liked the roast so much, we ate yours as well."

He smiles broadly, beatifically. He leans toward Tess, dips his head to one side, and says tenderly, "And do you know that last week one of my neighbors was hounding me to throw it away? He thought it was too old!"

The next morning, Bachelor-Uncle will call and ask to speak to his "future wife." My fingers ice up, my chest stiffens; I will hear the tiny expectant lilt of his breath as he waits. I will hand the phone to Tess as she smiles a bright, surprised smile, and when she puts the receiver to her ear, I will watch her eyes blink wide and her porcelain skin turn mulberry red. "I—I'm so honored," she will say. "But I—I—I—we just met!" She will stare at me like someone drowning, and when I take the phone from her, he will be gone.

But tonight, all is calm. After the meal, we sit out on the veranda and meditate on the white cup of the crescent moon. The desert landscape around us is clean as a tabletop. The call to prayers sifts through the powdery air, making us quiet and softhearted. My uncle recites romantic poetry from the Bedouin poets, then nods as if he's told us a secret. He leans forward, elbows on knees, gazing at us dreamily, and says, "Okay, now tell me, honestly, which of us uncles is the best cook?"

CHICKEN *MSUKHAN* FOR RICHER OR POORER

2 chickens, cut up
½ cup plus 3 tablespoons
    olive oil
½ cup pine nuts
4 medium onions, chopped

1 teaspoon salt
4 tablespoons ground
    sumac*
2 loaves pita bread

Preheat the oven to 400 degrees.

In a large baking dish, arrange the chicken pieces and drizzle ½ cup of the olive oil over all. Bake for 30 minutes.

In a medium frying pan, sauté the pine nuts in 2 tablespoons of the olive oil over medium heat until lightly brown. Scoop out the nuts with a slotted spoon and set aside. Mix the chopped onion with the salt and sumac, place in the pan used for the nuts, and sauté in the remaining 1 tablespoon of olive oil until the onions are translucent.

Split open the pita bread and line a baking dish with the insides up. Cover the bread with half of the onion mixture. Place the baked chicken pieces over this. Cover with the rest of the onion mixture and heat under the broiler for 5 to 10 minutes. Sprinkle the pine nuts over the top.

Serve with yogurt, rice, and salad.

MAKES 6 SERVINGS.

*Sumac is a popular spice in Middle Eastern cuisine; it has a pleasantly sour flavor and may be sprinkled over grilled meats and salads.

I've been living and not-working in Jordan for five months. I have all but given up on my writing. When I'd begun the novel in the States, I'd set large swaths of the story in the Middle East. Back then it was an imaginary, literary sort of setting, full of abstract gestures, airless and scentless. Now I am swamped by smells and sounds. The dust of Amman shines in my morning windows in twenty different colors and tastes of clay and salt, and I wake to the sound of car horns, crying door-to-door knife sharpeners, flat bells, the disgruntled blat of goats wandering across the backyard. The call to prayers floods the same windows at night and patterns arabesques in my sleep. Jordan towers over me, dashing metaphors and plot out of my head. The neglected novel is barely a little spot of guilt in the back of my mind.

One morning, I get a call from my uncle Nazeem. I don't know him very well, in part because he wasn't among the younger generation of brothers, including my father, who had gone off to America to seek their fortunes. He stayed behind on the land, accumulating his fortune very efficiently, and he almost never traveled anywhere. So his English is fairly haphazard. He knows a lot of English words, just not necessarily in any particular order, his sentences veering into and out of meaning like a drunk driver trying to find the road. I'm on alert when I hear his voice on the phone early one morning, saying, "Diana? Is you?"

"Yes—uh, Uncle Nazeem?"

"Is time."

"It's—?"

"You come to lunch, inside of my house, it is today, it is the time." Click.

It happens that my friend Audrey is visiting at the time—the fifth American friend in as many months. In preparation for lunch, Audrey and I change out of jeans. Jordanian high society is a dress-up culture. The women wear full complements of makeup, designer dresses, and feathery gabardine slacks from Italy. The men wear creamy silk ties and fine, tropical-weight wool suits. Since Nazeem is one of the richest and toniest of the uncles, his parties are showy and extravagant. Audrey and I do our best, working from our easygoing American wardrobes.

Even so, when we arrive, we're still taken aback by the women who look as though they're dressed for the Academy Awards with their sequined lapels and slinky skirts and gleaming high heels. The men wear primrose boutonnieres.

Audrey, a university administrator who is very aware of correct appearances, is upset. She swipes at the skirt of her plain cotton sundress. "I didn't know this was a special occasion!" she says. "Why didn't you warn me?"

But the occasion is lunch.

Covering the banquet table is a vast *mezza* course, as intricate and complex as a tiled mosaic. My cousin Habeeb, an aspiring filmmaker, videotapes the food while murmuring an intense narrative description: "Here we have the charming baby aubergines dipped in seven spices and fried with egg and sweetbreads—a soft yet unsentimental dish. Oh, look over there! Honey-and-pine-nut tarts, straight from the hand of the creator. . . ." There are glittering bits of meats, dips, and vegetables prepared with audacious, artistic streaks of olive oil as fresh and more intensely flavored than any classical sauce. There are tiny, jewel-like eggplants, tomatoes darker than rubies, and onions sweeter than milk. Audrey sighs and eats and sighs.

She sits straight up in her chair when I warn her that these are only the appetizers. "There's more?" she says. She looks at me sideways, trying to see if I'm joking.

I'd forgotten to warn her about "hospitality." Hospitality to the Jordanians is more than a virtue; it's a sacrament and exaltation. It's risky to compliment anyone here on anything—their shirt, for example—as they're apt to push it on you in the middle of a dinner party. One of my American friends has an entire man's suit, three inches too short and two inches too wide—hanging in his bedroom closet owing to a carelessly offered compliment to one of my Jordanian relatives. I instruct Audrey to eat slowly, as I have learned to, to lean away from the plate, to chew each morsel as

though your life depends on it, letting entire minutes go by in animated conversation before turning your attention to the next bite.
If you don't empty your plate, it can't be refilled so quickly. Audrey
tries to follow my lead. But despite her propriety and caution, she
also has satiny chestnut hair, sleepy eyes, and pillowy lips. There is
something accidentally seductive about her slow chewing. The
uncles are all entranced watching her eat. Poor Audrey is repeatedly
given more lamb chops, the uncles stretching over the table with
big silver spoons to tip fresh dollops of stuffed squash onto her
plate. They ignore her pleas to stop. "Well! With us she is flirt,"
Uncle Nazeem says with great satisfaction, fanning himself with his
napkin.

Like all my uncles, Uncle Nazeem is a flirt. He's also a dandy; he
preens and gazes into mirrors. His natty Italian suits always include a
vest, pocket watch, and silk handkerchief. He combs his white hair
with intense focus, smoothing both palms straight back along the
sides of his head. In my family, Arab hair that's curly or kinky is
frowned upon. So hair is carefully and frequently combed, pomaded,
perfumed, tugged, and monitored. Uncle Nazeem always has one
hand floating at the side of his head as if to keep his scalp on alert.

At dinner, Uncle Nazeem sits with his brothers at one end of the
long table while my aunties and the children sit at the other. Audrey
and I have gotten stranded across from each other, guest-of-honor
style, in the midst of the uncles. Audrey is seated between the two
biggest flirts, Uncle Nazeem and Bachelor-Uncle, who vie for her
attention by fighting over the serving spoon. She tries to distract
them by attempting actual conversation.

"This is incredible food!" she exclaims to Uncle Nazeem, who
puffs up to twice his size. His wife, the actual cook, is too far away to
hear the compliment.

"Aha, you think this is good?" says Bachelor-Uncle, rising to the
challenge. "You'll come to my house tomorrow!"

"Ha, eat and learn," Uncle Nazeem rejoins.

"But this squash," Audrey persists bravely, "this stuffed squash is
especially wonderful."

"Oh ho, she likes the stuffed squash!" Uncle Jack, the great diplomat, announces to the table, his voice melting with innuendo. "We haven't seen anyone like that around here for a while." My uncles flicker to attention, turning toward Audrey with renewed interest.

Audrey shoots me the look of someone who isn't sure if the ground has just moved. I would like to be able to lean across the table and tell her that in certain quarters, the Arabic word for squash is also slang for certain female anatomy. But the table is as wide as a river, and every noise ricochets off the marble floors and crystal chandeliers. Instead I try to muster what I imagine might be a pleasant, relaxed smile and chirp, "Audrey loves all sorts of Arabic cooking, like shish kabob and falafel and, um . . ."

"Oh, really? And stuffed squash?" That's Uncle Jack again.

"Yes, yes . . ." Audrey soldiers on. "Did he stuff the squash himself?"

I bite my lips.

"Oh, my God," says Uncle Jack. "Are you kidding? Nazeem is an amazing stuffer of squash."

"Yes," Bachelor-Uncle joins in, choking on his own laughter. "He's a grade-A squash stuffer."

Audrey's face is beet red, confounded; she can't figure it out. "You mean he makes a lot of stuffed squash?"

The uncles are wheezing and twisting with laughter. Bachelor-Uncle's face gleams. "Are you kidding? He's stuffed hundreds of squashes, probably thousands!"

"Big, little!"

"Old, young, shriveled, cute!"

Tears are streaming down their faces; they pound the table so the dishes jump. "All decent squashes run in fear when they see Nazeem coming!"

"We bow down to his awesome squash-stuffing power!" Bachelor-Uncle screams. Then he crashes out of his chair to the ground and the whole room shakes. He's laughing so hard, I think he's going to burst a purplish vein glistening in his forehead.

Uncle Nazeem's Egyptian housekeeper, Antonia, bursts through the kitchen door. She is so old that her back is nearly parallel to the floor and her face is scrawled over with deep, soft wrinkles. She sizes up the situation, then slaps the top of Bachelor-Uncle's head, and he gasps laughter right back into his lungs. Still facing the floor, she unleashes a torrent of Arabic invective. I can't understand a single word. All I know is that all my uncles are suddenly sitting straight in their chairs, facing ahead, a few of them wiping away tears, but no one is so much as smiling. Antonia slams back through the same door, and we're not served a single bite more for lunch.

INNUENDO SQUASH

FILLING

¼ cup rice	½ teaspoon salt
¼ pound ground beef	½ teaspoon freshly ground
4 tablespoons olive oil	pepper
1 tablespoon dried	½ teaspoon ground cinnamon
mint	½ cup chicken broth
9 medium yellow or green	1 large can (29 ounces)
squashes, washed	tomato purée
thoroughly	3 cloves garlic, crushed

In a medium bowl, combine all the filling ingredients and set aside.

Trim off the squash stems. Cut 1 inch off the tops of the squashes and save for later.

Scoop out the inside of each squash with a serrated spoon or *mengara,** being careful not to cut through the squash. Dispose of the inside and wash again.

*The *mengara* is a special coring tool for scooping out the insides of squashes, cucumbers, and the like.

Fill the squashes loosely halfway up. Close the top of the squash with the squash tops cut to fit. Make sure tops are tightly closed so the rice mixture will not come out.

In a medium cooking pot, place the filled squashes, add the tomato purée and the garlic, then cover and boil for 5 to 10 minutes. Lower the heat and simmer for another 45 minutes.

MAKES 4 SERVINGS.

NINETEEN

House of Crying

Great-Uncle Jimmy is the richest of all. His wealth is like a golden drapery tossed over everything. The sweeping steps to his front door are made of a veined pearlescent marble, the air in his house smells like water, and he seems to have trained green parrots to laugh in his trees and flame-colored songbirds to sing in his windows. Smooth Damascene robes and brilliant white Egyptian cottons sheathe his wattled, alligatory neck. I note with interest that the older and wealthier he gets, the more he resembles a lizard. His thyroidal eyes bulge, his gray lips jut, and his hair gleams, stroked back in long, oiled shards like a reptilian crest.

Bud called me from the States to tell me not to accept Jimmy's invitation. He has refused to speak to his uncle in over ten years, although Great-Uncle Jimmy appears to be unaware of this fact. Despite Bud's ambivalences and ongoing feuds with certain family members, he still likes most of his relatives. Jimmy is one of the few relations my father still holds a grudge against; even the delicate patina of distance and time can't soften it. When I ask Bud why he feels this way, he squints and tucks in his chin, as if there is something before him that he can't bring into focus. Then he says, slowly, "He makes me upset." I do know that Jimmy's personality has always seemed remote. I feel his eyes glaze past me at get-togethers, consigning me to a generic category: one of "the kids." I assume that Jimmy is just another problem uncle, too rich for his own good. After he bought his first hamburger franchise, he officially changed his name from Jamil to Jimmy, a name he wears as jauntily as the brass-colored toupee he sometimes affects, perched at a rakish angle on top of his silver hair, beret style. "There is something wrong in that house," Bud tells me tersely, our transatlantic connection hissing as if ocean waves are actually lapping over the cable.

"What is it?" I press the receiver against my head so hard that my ear hurts. I stare at the cover of the Amman phone book, filled with its weird Anglicized spellings of Arabic names. "Why don't you want us to go?"

Audrey sits slumped back in one of my straight chrome chairs, her eyes unfocused. She was ready to cut her vacation short following the lunch at Uncle Nazeem's house, but after a nice trip to the ruins at Petra, she has regained some of her good humor.

Bud lowers his voice so I can barely distinguish it from the ocean hiss: "If you have to go—" His voice sinks back into the static.

"What? Dad—I can't—"

"Don't eat the food!"

It's evident that a battalion of Sri Lankan maids is running Jimmy and Auntie Selma's house, along with their beleaguered Egyptian "houseboy," Roni, a seventy-two-year-old man whom they shout for and order around all day.

"Now you will see what real Jordanian cooking is about," Uncle Jimmy assures us, tipping his highball glass in our direction. "Prepare yourselves." Then he bellows for Roni to refill our drinks. The sinewy, crinkly man comes in, his face as remote as if he's spent his life gazing just beyond the shoulder of the Sphinx. Audrey and I smile at him, trying to express gratitude and to distance ourselves from Jimmy, but Roni doesn't register anyone besides his employers. He is barefoot, downcast, and hunched. Where Jimmy is puffed up, Roni is hollowed out; where Jimmy is glacial and cold-blooded, Roni is parched and birdlike.

Jimmy and Selma usher us into their mahogany-paneled dining room, which is outfitted with five-tiered crystal chandeliers and table linens that glow like moonlight. Each china plate is flanked by heavy silver flatware. Four settings huddle together at the center of a long, icy glide of table. Audrey and I sit, timidly sneaking our chairs into the table. We gaze at the emptiness around us, the high, bright ceilings. Apparently we are the only ones invited.

Jimmy might be mythically wealthy, but he is miserly. And unlike Bachelor-Uncle, he does not compensate with other forms of charm or generosity. Roni brings out the *mezza*, which turns out to be a single tomato cut into quarters, a sliced cucumber, a minute plate of coarse salt, and a tiny pitcher of clear olive oil. He places the food at the center of the table, and instantly the table looks emptier. Audrey glances at me, doubtless wondering if this is another of my uncles' little inside jokes.

Aunt Selma picks up her fork and knife, and we follow suit. The utensils feel leaden, as if weighted to trick you into thinking that you're eating something. The knife handle rolls and swells, a full, sensuous shape in the hand. That's the most gratifying part of the meal. The tomato is watery and, for some reason, peeled, while the cucumber is warty and bad natured. Aunt Selma proceeds to dissect her portion of the produce into perfect little cubes, like a conceptual chef. Then I notice that Uncle Jimmy has balanced a still-smoking cigarette on his plate and seized his tomato quarter in his fist, as if to do battle with it. But his muscles are palsied; his hand shakes and weaves from side to side, the skinless tomato practically puréed in his hand. He drops the mess on his plate and returns to his highball.

I begin to sense that we'd better eat our vegetables because there might not be much more to this dinner. I pick up my fork and turn to Audrey, but before I can give her any kind of signal, a terrible noise surges from the next room. It is a cry of inexpressible pain, grief, and dread. It is uncanny, quavering, and sustained, like something from an Edgar Allan Poe story or from the next world altogether. It rises and falls, operatic, made of both a sob and a scream. Audrey's gleaming, labial fork crashes into her plate. Each and every hair on my body stands up. I stop my knife halfway through the cucumber, paralyzed, and for a surreal, hallucinatory moment, the cry seems as powerful and insistent as if it emanated from the walls of the room itself. Then Aunt Selma looks over at Audrey.

"Please mind the china," she scolds. "It's very expensive!"

Audrey gapes at me. The sound has only now started to fall off its crescendo and fade. Then, from the same depths, another high-pitched sob rises up in the wake of the first, this one even louder and more outraged. My gut response kicks in. I think the cry came from the servant, who's finally gone over the edge. I blurt out, "Roni!" But when Roni appears in the doorway, he looks confused and out of sorts, annoyed that the foreigner girl is shouting for him—doesn't he have enough bosses? Then another dreadful shriek blazes up from behind him. The screamer is in the kitchen.

Roni vanishes back through the kitchen doorway, which glows pale orange. I look at this light, and slowly a memory begins to coalesce. There are rumors about a disabled grandchild that some of my cousins were talking about one day at lunch. Supposedly, one of Selma and Jimmy's grown children had left their disabled child locked in a room and slipped a note under the neighbor's door: "We're going to Europe. Please check on the baby." According to the gossip, the child had screamed alone in his room for two days before the grandparents found out and rescued him. My cousins said that Jimmy and Selma now kept this child shut up in a back room, protected from nosy intruders but isolated from the world, like a changeling hunched in a dungeon. Roni and the Sri Lankan servants fed and clothed him, but it was doubtful anyone ever really spoke to him. "But what is there to say?" my cousin Miriam had asked. "He speaks in screams."

Yet another quavering cry splits the air. I attempt telepathic eye signaling with Audrey, trying silently to convey: *Don't panic: They keep their grandchild locked up and we're supposed to pretend he doesn't exist.*

While Selma and Jimmy continue discussing the significance of certain fluctuations in the weather—hard rain is a bad sign, soft rain is a good sign—the dreadful screams continue. I even begin to notice a range of nuances—some screams sound like terror, some like frustration, and some like questions. Through it all, Selma and Jimmy pass the salt, complain about the price of food, dissect their two chicken kabobs. If the screams get louder, they raise their voices. Audrey and I don't say a word.

Gradually, the cries modulate themselves so it's as if someone is standing in the next room, participating in our conversation through a series of nonverbal, strangulated commentaries. Even Audrey and I rejoin the conversation, telling my aunt and uncle about our day in the old souk. We pause for a particularly loud shriek, then debate which stands sold the best falafels. I start to feel so relaxed about the whole situation that at one point I dare to nod toward the kitchen door and say in a light, joshing voice, "Someone sounds hungry!"

There is the most infinitesimal pause in Selma's eating, a minute recoil, as if I'd just belched at the table. No one responds.

As if taking pity on me, Roni chooses to emerge at that moment with a plate of tiny, tender *fetayer*. These savory turnovers are often stuffed with spinach and onion and baked into a delicate golden bread. Usually they are big enough to fill up my hand, and I can make a meal out of one, or perhaps two if I'm very hungry. But the *fetayer* that Roni puts before us—four on an engraved silver platter—are bite-size canapés that give us just the merest taste of green vegetable and flaky crust. Then, in a moment, this small mercy is gone as well.

After our repast of two diminutive chicken kabobs, two dollops of yogurt, and two steamed zucchini quarters each, Roni clears away the dishes and returns with a plate of jaw-breaking, fillings-yanking, elderly butterscotch chewies.

"We know you Americans like your treats!" Selma scolds, chuckling.

As Audrey and I are eager to exit the House of Screaming and go get something to eat, we put a couple of chewies in our pockets, where they will ooze all over the linings, and we begin issuing little sighs of contentment and regret. Oh, my goodness, where *has* the time gone? My great-aunt and great-uncle sit back, twiddling toothpicks and scowling. Clearly, we haven't been dismissed yet, and they've got something they'd like to say.

Jimmy rolls forward and touches the table. "The reason we invited you here," he announces, "is because of the rumors."

"The rumors about us," Aunt Selma adds.

I put down my napkin with interest, thinking, We'll at least find out what's going on here.

"Oh yes, we know everyone's talking about it," Auntie Selma says, examining her French manicure. "You don't have to deny it."

"Well, I might have heard something," I mumble. Audrey's eyes flick up to mine as if to scold me for failing to warn her.

Uncle Jimmy slaps the table. "What are they saying! Who is talking?"

As I recall, it was a few of their own children who warned me about the situation. Not wanting to be a snitch, I try to look innocent and absentminded. I study the wrappers of the nefarious butterscotches, which bear the image of a child in bloomers chasing a hoop with a stick.

"It doesn't matter who says what," Selma breaks in. "The fact is— they're all talking, even the foreigners now," she adds, indicating us. "So we'll tell you what really happened."

"We treated that girl like a goddamned princess!" Uncle Jimmy roars, one knobby finger stirring the air.

I almost say that I thought it was a boy, but Auntie Selma is already waving him down. "Begin at the beginning, Jimmy. Everybody knows that life is like hell for these girls in Sri Lanka—"

Sri Lanka?

"They're no better than slaves there," Uncle Jimmy announces. "They load them into buses and ship them to Jordan, where at least it's a thousand times better if someone catches them."

"He means, you know . . ." Aunt Selma waves one beringed hand around, her long nails gleaming. "Like, adopts them."

They adopted this child?

"We got her from the agency," Auntie Selma says. "You know, they lock the girls in all night with the rats and the bugs, they beat them up with clubs and barely feed them anything. Horrible."

What sort of adoption agency is this?

"That last girl, I tell you"—Uncle Jimmy leans forward conspiratorially—"she stole."

"And she lied and she skipped half the dusting and she sneaked food out of the cupboards! *She ate our food.*"

"She was always showing her legs to me," Uncle Jimmy says in a lowered voice. "She left the bedroom door open a tiny crack always."

Selma pauses, looks at Jimmy, then continues. "Anyway, so we threw her out and went back to the agency and got a new one."

Through my eddies of confusion, comprehension finally breaks through. We are talking not about the screamer in the kitchen, but about a maid.

"This time we think, Okay, we treat this new one extra-double-special. We save her from the horrible slave agency—"

"They beat them every day there, you know, at the slave agency," Aunt Selma interjects. "I saw it. There are cockroaches absolutely every which where."

"We gave this one her own room, her own bed, Selma gives her one of her own dresses, we treated her like a son-of-a-bitch princess!" Uncle Jimmy's lips are white and distended, and his hooded eyes widen. "We treated her like Miss America."

"They say this one can cook good, so we even put her in the kitchen, where it's nicer. But the food she makes isn't natural food—"

"No eggplant, no lamb, no stuffed squash."

"She makes food with rice, grass, peanuts, crazy spices. So many spices! Red sauces—who knows what it is—"

"A mess."

"So after just two weeks, this new girl, she's crying all the time— oh, she's tired, oh, she's hungry, oh, she misses her little baby—"

"Her baby?" Audrey asks in a small, horror-struck voice.

Aunt Selma pokes up her narrow shoulders. "Who knows with these girls? That's how they are there. They have a million and two babies a day, they leave them everywhere—just drop them down and walk away like nothing!"

"Who can keep track?" Uncle Jimmy asks.

"Oh! She is trouble, this one. Always running around, talking to the other slave agency girls in the neighborhood—"

"She tempts Roni with her legs, I seen it," Uncle Jimmy says.

"She is always giving him and the ba—everybody—leftover food and treats, always going where she isn't supposed to go!" Selma adds with a sudden ferocity, grabbing the table edge. "This girl, she upsets every single thing in this house. We start to think she is even going to steal things. . . ."

"I hear her talking to the little one all day, all night," Uncle Jimmy muses. "Why? What is she saying? Neither of them speaks the human language. . . ."

"Talking to who?" I ask in a dwindling voice.

"To nobody, never mind!" Selma snaps at Jimmy, then me. She presses her hand to her chest, lifts her head, and closes her eyes, as if swallowing something bitter. "Okay. Anyway. Things get so bad, I can barely stand the aggravation," she says. "Now I've got this headache all the time that the new maid is going to run out—"

"So we lock her in the bedroom!" Uncle Jimmy says.

"Tch! *No.*" Aunt Selma's eyes roll. "Just when she's not working!"

At that moment, Roni emerges from the kitchen and approaches us at his excruciating pace. Stony silence falls over the table. He carefully picks up each plate, eyes downcast. Neither Jimmy nor Selma stirs, but they follow his every movement with their eyes. When I attempt to hand my plate to him, he doesn't take it but simply waits, motionless, until I return it to the table. Then he picks it up. The screaming has abated to a low, rhythmic gurgle, and when I peek at Roni, I notice that he seems to nod very slightly in time to the sound, as if it is playing inside his head like a metronome. Then he wafts out of the room.

Aunt Selma sighs and rolls her eyes again as soon as Roni returns to the kitchen, as if his very presence summarizes the whole problem. "Okay, so—maybe three, four days go by after we start locking her in, and one morning something funny happens."

"I always check on her at night, just when she's asleep," Jimmy says. "She always has all her clothes on. Why? She always has the door closed!"

Aunt Selma looks at him, then takes a breath. "Right. So this morning we're waiting downstairs for our coffee, and where is the girl now? No coffee! No girl! We call for Roni, because it is his job to unlock her, no problems that way—he only speaks Arabic and she speaks English."

"And some other language," Uncle Jimmy says.

"No chance for them to cook up with some big ideas together— God knows what. The ways servants like to cook things up, you would not believe. Anyway, Roni comes in and tells us—no girl! She's not in her room, not anywhere." Now Aunt Selma's eyes are startled wide, as if she is reliving the shock right then and there. Her hand waves before her face.

"We run through the house!"

"I looked in her bedroom!"

"In the living room! The bathroom! The study!"

"Finally . . ." Aunt Selma tilts her head toward the kitchen. "Roni calls out: 'Mistress, master, come quick, the girl is in the street!' Oh, my God." Aunt Selma grabs her chest, the cords in her throat tight as violin strings.

"We didn't notice her window was open," Uncle Jimmy explains.

The outcome of the story is that the girl jumped out the window and was lying crumpled but still alive in the street. I imagine that she was trying to escape my great-aunt and great-uncle either by running away or by killing herself—which I could certainly sympathize with. But Aunt Selma has a different interpretation of things.

"She planned to break her leg," she says, ticking her nails on the butter-knife blade.

"To shame us," Uncle Jimmy says.

"She thinks that we'll feel sorry for her with her crying, crying, crying. I know the way these servant girls work with their plans and their schemes," Aunt Selma says. "She thinks we'll drive her to the doctor and give her all kinds of money to go back to Sri Lanka and her babies. This was her big plan. Oh, I drove her all right." Aunt Selma smiles slyly, and I see the same yellow-vapor smile reflected on Uncle Jimmy. "When she saw where I was driving her, that's when she started screaming."

"She is pulling the handle. Like she'll pull it off the door! She tried to jump right out of the car," Uncle Jimmy says, his hands and shoulders crooked up near his ears. "Always jumping everywhere, that one."

"Where did you take her?" I croak, doom rising like a mist from deep inside me.

"Right back to the slave agency, of course," Aunt Selma says. "I told them to go ahead and beat her! She was too high in her own mind, not broken down enough. That's the way these kinds of girls get from these terrible countries, I told the agency man. She thinks she is the only girl in the world with a baby? Well, some babies *don't have mothers*!" She dusts off her hands. "And so that's it."

"End of story," says Uncle Jimmy.

"Now you know what happened. That's the entire true story, so you'll know not to believe all the rumors. Thanks to God we cleared that up." A beat of doubt passes over her face as she says this. She frowns at the butter knife as if she senses there is something she's left out, some forgotten word or critical point.

"But . . . what happened to the girl?" Audrey asks.

"Who? The maid? Oh, who knows," Aunt Selma says reproachfully. "These girls, once they get here they always want to go straight back to the jungle."

"Like Ta-ra-zan!" Uncle Jimmy volunteers.

"But they've got no money and no people, so they can't. Now they are in civilization with no way to go home. That is the reality of things. Maybe she will work for some people who aren't so soft as we are. Then she'll start to understand things better."

There's an abrupt thud to the conversation, and silence descends, as thick as the cloth covering our table. We sit with our hands in our laps, unable to meet each other's gazes. No one seems to know what to say, so finally I clear my throat and ask, "Who does your cooking now?"

"We're back to old Roni," says Uncle Jimmy. "At least that one doesn't cry."

Now they seem ready, even eager, to dismiss us. A lilt of something like vindication lifts Uncle Jimmy's chin, his skin tightens across his cheekbones, and his eyes turn filmy. Again, I glimpse something glassy and amphibious that seems to surface from beneath his skin. There is a flat, denatured smile on his face. Uncle Jimmy stretches in his chair and focuses on me for what must be the first time all afternoon. He interlaces his fingers over his belly and says, "So, girl, do you know your father is a real son of a bitch?"

"Oh, uh-hunh, well . . . well." I dust off my lap, petrified that this is the start of another story. "That's interesting."

"A real true bastard, that one. I could tell you all sorts of stories there!"

"Yes, well, thanks for lunch!" I say brightly, and scrape back my chair.

Audrey and I leave our napkins on the table. As we mumble thanks and farewell, the child imprisoned in the kitchen reawakens from his trance, and an inspired, anguished cry rises through the gloom like a red wing.

We step backward toward the front door, faster now. I touch the knob and glance back in time to see the kitchen door open just a crack. At first, all I see is Roni standing there silently. He is holding a vegetable peeler, his fingers slipping along the tiny interior lip of a blade. Then, for just an instant, so fleeting that I wonder if I've imagined it, from behind Roni's back peeps another face—exquisitely formed, tear streaked, glowing black eyes, and open full red lips.

I open the door. Outside, a soft white rain is sifting down like powdered sugar. We leave, I hope forever, this house of crying.

SPINACH-STUFFED *FETAYER* FOR THOSE IN SEARCH OF HOME

A nice snack to take on your journey.

DOUGH

1 package yeast	1 teaspoon salt
1 cup water	½ cup olive oil
1 teaspoon sugar	3 to 4 cups flour

FILLING

1 pound fresh spinach, washed, drained, and chopped	Salt and freshly ground pepper
2 medium onions, minced	Juice of 1 lemon
5 tablespoons olive oil	¼ cup toasted pine nuts
	3 teaspoons ground sumac

In a large bowl, stir the yeast into the water, add the sugar, and let sit for a few minutes. Stir in the salt and oil, then add the flour in small batches, continuing until the dough isn't sticky. Turn onto a floured board and knead until the dough is smooth and elastic, about 10 minutes. Place the dough in a large greased bowl and cover it with a towel. Let the dough rise in a warm kitchen for about 1 hour; the dough should double in size. Punch it down and let it rise again, about 30 minutes.

Next, prepare the filling. In a medium frying pan, sauté the spinach, onions, 3 tablespoons of the olive oil, salt and pepper, lemon juice, pine nuts, and sumac on medium heat. Remove from the heat and set aside. Preheat the oven to 400 degrees.

Pinch off small handfuls of the dough, shape and roll it out so that each piece is a 5 × 5-inch square, about ¼ inch thick. Each square of dough should be 5 inches long by 5 inches wide when rolled out.

Working quickly, place about 2 tablespoons of the filling inside one corner of the dough square and fold the opposite corner over this so the dough forms a triangle. Pinch the ends together, sealing in the spinach mixture. Brush the remaining olive oil over the top of each *fetayer*. Bake on a greased tray for about 15 to 20 minutes; the dough should be browned.

MAKES ABOUT 12 *FETAYER*.

TWENTY

Once upon a Time

A string of sea green beads swings wildly from the rearview mirror as the cab takes a sharp left. All the windows are wide open and the air roaring in from outside is hot as a hair dryer, so loud that I can barely hear the Jordanian rap music blasting from the radio.

Beside me in the backseat, clapping his hands and attempting unsuccessfully to sing along, is my father. Turned to watch him over one shoulder, elbow slung back over the front seat, is my young friend Phineas. Both of them are visiting from America. I'd worried when I realized that they'd planned their visits to Jordan on overlapping dates. Bud would certainly disapprove of a single man staying with me, if only just a friend. Even though I'm thirty-four, my father still calls every week to ask what time I got home the night before, how much money I've saved, and what I've eaten for dinner. But over his years in America, Bud has mellowed on the topics of tradition, honor, and shame, affecting a certain indifference to the whole subject area. Besides, it's almost impossible to read anything treacherous or seductive into Phinny. He's twenty-six years old, but the back of his head looks twelve; translucent, cherry-colored ears fan from his head and, in front, his smile is big and easy, his top lip curling up toward his nose. He is smart, lost, excitable, and sensitive to the point of skinlessness—just the sort of person Bud is always drawn to.

I've known Phinny since he was fourteen years old. When I was a graduate student at Binghamton, he and his mother moved into the apartment next door to mine. Phinny discovered that if he came over with armloads of his favorite ear-scraping experimental music, I would let him play his tapes, sometimes until three a.m., while he slumped, shoulders practically resting on the seat of the armchair, and stared at the ceiling, going over the details of his girlfriend trouble. Even after I moved to take a teaching job in a new city and learned to lock my doors, he continued to send me new tapes every month, along with scrolls of letters detailing in a back-slanting, minute penmanship his latest encounters with heartache.

With no other information than each other's names, Phinny and Bud still managed to find each other at the gate in JFK. They sat together on the flight from New York to Amman, where, Phinny tells me later, Bud spent the first two hours giving Phinny his life story, leaving Phinny very little space to give Bud details about the last girl who ruined everything. After this, Bud pushed back his seat and snored openmouthed for a few hours, then woke and strolled up and down the center aisle, chatting gaily with the other passengers and letting folks know he was going to visit his daughter. And oh, did they happen to realize that his daughter—a *doctora*—is a *Fulbright scholar*? "Oh no? Well, she is! A few more husbands than she needs, and even with all that no babies. But who knows, maybe there's still time, *inshallah*, stubborn like a mule-head, but cute like her sisters, the youngest is still unmarried, by the way."

Bud's plans are to visit me and his extended family. Phinny's goals are a bit more abstract. He'd called me from the States just a week earlier, voice wobbling as he sketched the essentials of his latest breakup. When I'd carelessly suggested he distract himself with a visit to Jordan, he'd said, "Hey, okay!" and by that evening had charged an airline ticket on his mother's credit card. Now the cab is taking the three of us directly from the airport to Uncle Danny's house. He and his wife live in a simple, chic country house flanked by open-air, three-quarter rooms with partially crumbled, whitewashed walls dating from the Roman occupation. There are soft stone floors and a slick, glassed-in patio that overlooks this lushest, blackest, most ancient of Jordanian nights. It has been nearly ten years since my father's last visit to Jordan, and his brothers can't wait for him to unpack—he must be brought straight from the airport to the table. Franco, Uncle Danny's tawny, almond-faced Romanian servant, comes to open the gate for our taxi. We drive up the meandering gravel path with

Franco running barefoot behind the car. The land is cleared and bustling with fruit trees and flowering bushes, acres of velvety land-scaping reaching deep into countryside, bisected by a sleeve of road. The wind bends the soft branches and enriches the night with the scent of jasmine and orange blossoms.

Tonight everyone is here. My father is the prodigal one, the long-lost American brother, everyone's current favorite. His brothers and uncles and cousins have made a point of complaining about him and telling me unflattering stories about him all year—about his short temper, inflated pride, goofiness, and loose ways with money—as if he is some sort of wacky character in a book I've never read before. Now his elderly older brothers laugh and clap his round face between their hands as if he is six years old. Tears run down the creases in their faces, and they kiss him loudly, over and over, on both cheeks. Many of them haven't seen him in ten years. "You look so old!" his brothers howl. They lift his arms and turn him around, checking every line, pointing out his gray temples. But he's been following the healthy American lifestyle—eating fresh foods, exercising, occasionally show-ing restraint. His brothers, who roast in the desert sun, steep in the cigarette smoke that fills every public space, eat too much, and drink more, are the ones who look decades older. Their bug eyes bulge, bloodshot and permanently forlorn, but they're used to one another's faces. They remember my fifty-nine-year-old father as he last ap-peared on visits ten or twenty or forty years ago.

My aunties complain that he's terribly, frighteningly thin—though he's probably forty pounds overweight. Aunt Yusra cries for Franco to bring the *mezza*. Hurry! Hurry! as if he is about to vanish.

"Ghassan, you son of a bitch," Uncle Hal says ferociously. "Look at you! What the hell have you done? What the hell have you done to me? How can you be so goddamn old? What has that American done to you?"

"That American" is my mother, whom no one will refer to by name, as if doing so will incur the wrath of her evil eye. Mom has this fearsome reputation because, out of all the brothers who immigrated to America, Bud is the only one to have actually stayed on. So Mom, teacher of third graders, is acknowledged to be a sort of diabolical mastermind, which seems to make more sense to them than imagining that there might be something inside of Bud himself keeping him in that lost place that is not-home.

There's time for a few more complaints about my father's age before Franco appears with a big tray of *mezza,* which he fans across the picnic table with plates and paring knives. The brothers sit at their places, expectant and distracted as birds. Uncle Frankie starts drumming on the table with his fingers, and they launch into a bawdy song about the prophet Muhammad and a variety of fruits and vegetables. They sing with gusto, clapping and improvising a new vegetable with each refrain, which isn't that difficult since the song is the Arabic version of "99 Bottles of Beer on the Wall." The song is also another dig at my father, since they consider his boyhood conversion from Syrian Orthodox to Islam another one of his screwball childhood misbehaviors. But Bud is in an undentable good mood. He is the happiest I've seen him in years, as he's kissed and stroked, teased and fawned over. He claps and sings along, and when Phinny asks him to explain the lyrics, he purses his lips into a little drawstring smile and says, "It's something about salad!" and then kisses Phinny on top of his head.

Dishes are passed. The hummus goes around, the bread, the olive oil, the stuffed tomatoes, the candied walnuts, the wavy strands of unbraided cheese, plates of tiny grilled lamb chops and chicken yellow with turmeric. But then the aunties start murmuring: Their heads swivel, their eyes cut down to narrow, evaluative glances; then they turn back, heads inclined into more murmuring. It's been noted that the foreigner-boy, Phineas, who's been sitting slanted back in his chair, brightly observing everything, is not eating all of the food the uncles heaped on his plate. Instead, he has been asking Bud about the contents of each item and ignoring every dish containing meat.

The relatives don't know what to make of this extraordinary behavior. A murk of Arabic and English muttering subsumes the table. Everyone cranes around to observe for themselves and report to the person next to them.

"He's not eating—this Phin-Phan—" Aunt Jasmine shreds the odd, un-Arabic confluence of syllables in Phineas's name. "Phanaman doesn't like the food?"

Phinny opens his mouth, but Uncle Jack says, "Phanamian is skipping the meat part, you see?" He picks up Phinny's plate and displays it to the table. "He is a little backward, I think."

Bud takes the plate from his brother and gently repositions it at the middle of the table like a centerpiece. "Phoneos is allll right! He's my friend, Phanny." He thumps Phinny a few times, and Phinny falls forward and then eases back, face hopeful.

As if making a suggestion, Phinny says, "Phin-e-as."

"Phoney," Bud echoes, nodding.

Uncle Danny holds up his knobby, great-knuckled fingers. "If this little boy doesn't eat his meat, he won't be able to produce babies."

A couple of the uncles agree on this point. Bachelor-Uncle says, "For sure he won't enjoy the part that comes before having babies."

Phinny looks disoriented and glassy-eyed; he has been sipping a glass of white *araq* that was placed in his hand as soon as we arrived at the house. The uncles refill it with every few sips that he takes, and now his eyes look a bit loose in their sockets and his face is a mottled coral color. As he drinks he looks younger; his skin takes on a faint translucence. I haven't heard him say much of anything since our arrival. Suddenly I'm worried. "Phinny? You feeling okay?"

He waves me away. "No, I 'joy making babies," he says, raising his glass. A number of the uncles automatically raise theirs. Phinny's glass dips and swings as if he is conducting a marching band. "Meat's murder. I make babies, not war." Some of the glasses clink, an accidental toast.

"Well, he might enjoy it, but definitely he won't have sons," Uncle Danny says as calmly and firmly as if he's just read up on the topic.

Rich-Uncle Jimmy cracks a slanting smile and says in Arabic, "Maybe we should ask Ghassan about that," and sneaks a glance at my father.

"Never mind, never mind!" declaims my father, who's also getting a pink *araq*-bloom across his cheeks. "Fattoush is allll right! He's perfect. In fact, Fattoush is like a son to me!" He slings an arm around Phinny's shoulders and neck and drags him in close.

Phinny nestles his glass into the center of his chest and settles inside Bud's elbow. "Sh'like a fadder t'me," he says, tipping another sip of *araq* into his mouth.

Fattoush means "bread salad" in Arabic, and everyone can pronounce Fattoush, so that is Phinny's name for the rest of his stay. The aunts and uncles begin calling Bud "*Abu*-Fattoush" because *abu* means "father of." And Bud has always wanted a son. Thirty years ago, we fought over whether my mother was carrying a baby girl or boy. I was four, barely to his waist, shouting up at him, "Girl! Girl! Girl!" He leaned forward and ranted back, "Boy! Boy! Boy!" But that was then, and I've had half a glass of *araq* myself and feel muzzy, mellow, and generous about everything. It's just fine that Bud finds a replacement for me the moment he gets to town. It's only right, I reason, that Bud should claim an American son for himself, and even better, this may take some pressure off me.

Bud and I are still pals, sure, but he continues to imagine that his discontent comes from the world around him—as do I. Perhaps I inherited this trait from Bud. My mother, the eternal American, knows that we are inescapably responsible for our lives and are the masters of our own futures. She has no chronic need to keep moving, trying on houses, countries, jobs, looking for the perfect fit, at which point everything can finally start. No, with Mom, what you see is what you get, plain and simple. But with Bud the answer is "out there." There is eternally something he wants me to do, or not to have done at all, and that something flits ephemerally from topic to topic, from my selection in husbands to my choice of careers. Something should have been done differently—if only I would listen! "Listen to what, Dad?" I might ask. Even he doesn't know, though deep in his consciousness he senses that he used to know what to do and that he told me, but that as usual I wasn't listening—in fact, I *never listen*—and now we've both missed it. Our one chance at getting things right, always floating just out of reach, like trying to look at a dust particle on the surface of the eye. Never mind, he will say, rolling out the broad, satisfying vowels in "never"—never you mind.

FATTOUSH: BREAD SALAD
Which everyone loves and everyone can pronounce.

½ cucumber, peeled and diced
1½ loaves of pita bread, cut into pieces
¼ cup olive oil
1 tablespoon lemon juice
1 garlic clove, crushed
Salt and freshly ground pepper

½ red bell pepper, diced
1 tomato, chopped
¼ cup sliced scallions
2 tablespoons chopped flat-leaf parsley
3 tablespoons chopped mint
Inner leaves of head of romaine, chopped into chunks

Preheat the oven to 350 degrees. Sprinkle the cucumber with salt, drain for 30 minutes, and pat dry.

On a cookie sheet, bake the pita pieces, shaking occasionally, 18 to 20 minutes, until crisp.

In a large bowl, whisk the oil, lemon juice, and garlic with salt and pepper to taste. Stir in the bell pepper, tomato, scallions, parsley, mint, cucumber, and pita. Toss with the romaine leaves to combine, and serve.

The moon comes up, emanating a halo of light, and all the grandchildren fall asleep draped over their mothers' laps. Fattoush lies bonelessly arrayed in a teak chaise longue in the corner, sleeping off his glasses of *araq*. I idly eavesdrop on the brothers' gossip. It's easier for them to talk if I don't understand Arabic, so I try not to register any reactions. I don't have to pretend much—there is a flux of insider jokes and family history in the room that I will never understand anyway.

"So after his manufacturing business bought out all the competitors, Sami, that damn poet, is suddenly practically everything but a saint by now. . . ."

"For the amount of money he gives the church, he should be a saint and a half."

"He's trying to rent his soul back from the devil."

"Yes, but he wants it at half price."

"With a free pair of shoes thrown in."

"He needs them for all his running around at those funny-boy poet bars."

Someone raises his eyebrows. They twitch their eyes in my direction. "Is she listening?"

"She's listening, but she doesn't know what to do with it."

I listen, but the brothers don't reveal anything. They lean together as if they are the last true brothers in the known world and are plotting something big. Look, there is Uncle Hal with his soft, round nose, hazel eyes drifting at half-mast, dreaming of the splendid, brutal Ottoman Empire. There is Uncle Jack, with his secret diplomatic smile. There is crazy Uncle Frankie, eyes bloated, jowls drooping, claylike and dull; but when he looks up, his features flicker with light, quick and timid as a sparrow's.

I can see them individually, but together they make an ineffable algebra, a matrix that I can hardly imagine to be *family*.

Here is family: My father has a round, waxy scar like a knothole in one arm from a childhood knife fight with Uncle Frankie. When Bud was away in the Jordanian air force, Uncle Jack sold Bud's dog. Why? "Just because he could!" says Bud. Uncle Jimmy stole the knife Bud inherited from his father. Bud's cousin Sulieman set fire to the schoolhouse while Bud and most of his brothers were inside attending class. "But he was only nine," Bud says, chortling. "So how could you blame him?" There are a million resentments in this room over land, money, and power, epic family grudges that go back decades. There are brothers here whom Bud has cursed, threatened, or thrown punches at, brothers who've literally robbed him, brothers he's refused to see or speak to for years at a time.

And they can't stop kissing one another, big kisses on the cheeks, head, neck, squeezing one another's hands. They weep over one another, crying brilliant, poetic tears. In just a couple of weeks, Bud will be furiously cutting his visit short, which happens on every single trip he makes back to Jordan. He will be shaking his hands at the wall and shouting at the ceiling and stomping as though to squash flat the very idea of "family" forever. Even though he never remembers about this part of his visits home, it is essential to his ritual of return.

Tonight he laughs, backhands the tears from his cheeks, and says over and over, voice wobbling, "My brothers, my brothers."

"Hooray for *Abu*-Fattoush and his son, Fattoush!" Uncle Jack cries out after upending his glass of *araq*.

Then he gets everyone to lift their glasses and cry, "Hip, hip, hooray!"

Fattoush snores temperately in his corner.

Fattoush and Bud share my guest room with its matching twin beds. I wake that night to a limpid blue starlight and the sound of Fattoush weeping. Beginning the next morning, he starts writing a series of long, accusatory letters to his faithless girl, Stacy, back in the States. These missives are full of demands and confessions, which he reads to us before sealing them into envelopes. Each night, after they turn out their light, I can still hear his voice fluttering through the bedroom wall, pouring his heart out to my father. I walk past and catch a glimpse of Bud lolling back on the bed, listening with a bemused, fascinated air: *Is this what sons are like? Much more entertaining than daughters!* Bud takes me aside after one of their sessions. "This Fattoush, he is extreme," he says approvingly. "He feels everything there is to feel. He reminds me of myself."

Each night, Fattoush wakes after a few hours of sleep, wanders into the living room, and sprawls on the hard couch that smells like the inside of an old elevator. He watches whatever he can get on Jordanian TV at three-thirty a.m., and we find him asleep there in the morning, static rolling across the TV screen. Then my father makes him a plate of what he calls special wake-up eggs, over easy fried in butter with chili paste, which Fattoush eats propped up on the couch, slightly flushed and damp skinned.

After that, they dress and one or another of my uncles arrives and whisks them off for another roundelay of lunch and visits. Even though I've assured him this isn't necessary, Fattoush appears to have no objection to spending his days in the company of my sixty- and seventy-year-old uncles. I'm exhausted by the parties myself and will usually opt out in order to stay home and stare at the yellowing notes of my unwritten novel.

That's on the sunny days. But it's December, the wintry season, when rain and sleet will suddenly plummet from the sky. On such days, the uncles like to be received at my apartment, which they've started referring to as "Ghassan's house." They wedge themselves into the punitive, hard-seated, chrome-legged chairs that came with the place—twenty-two chairs that my landlord had arranged in a big, tight circle around the perimeter of the living room, the chrome gleaming like a grin—and the one dust-spewing, sprung-shot couch against the wall.

The brothers crowd me out of the living room with their thunder-wheezing laughter, their curling gray worms of cigarette ash, and their wild-horse eyes. I have a few friends who know to come over on these rainy days of uncles. We set up the bootleg version of Monopoly on the dining room table. Fattoush wafts away from the uncles, attracted by the cinnamon skin and topaz eyes of my friend Mai. Mai's friend Dabir also comes along. Dabir is twenty-four, droll, bored, irritated, and probably gay and likes to be called Dobby. He cradles his chin in his palm and watches, intrigued by Fattoush's helpless enchantment with Mai. Fattoush pulls out a chair for Mai, scrupulous as a flight attendant, and asks if he can bring her any-thing. Dobby says, "I'd love a ginger ale." But Mai just smiles archly and shakes her head, so Fattoush floats down into the seat beside her.

In my apartment, with its windows open to the city soot and desert air, if I don't dust every morning, the furniture will be shrouded in a gray film by noon. The game board slides around in the tabletop dust that has gathered there since the last dusting a few hours ago. I purchased the Monopoly game at the souk in Aqaba. While the board looks the same, the place names are all Jordanian, switching Amman for Atlantic City, Shmeisani Circle for Reading Railroad, the Cave of Sleepers for Broadway. Dobby translates the community chest cards, which are filled with legalese that seems to have been written by someone playing another game. The cards demand things like "Restitution in three parts of 200 dinars to the offending party for trespass on Abdoun Way," or "10 dunams of land payable to the Master of the Port of Aqaba."

Mai, who works in a royalty-funded environmental conservation office, refuses to translate because she says that Monopoly is yet another bourgeois capitalist West-centric scheme. That doesn't stop her from playing, however. In fact, she uses the game as a method of flirting with Fattoush. Honeying her voice and lowering her lashes, she says, "Mmm, you think you've caught me, you devil. I'm not afraid of you," as she tosses a few funny-money dinars of baksheesh at him.

The tips of Fattoush's ears turn scarlet. Thrilled and stupefied by the unexpected flirtation, he refuses to take money from her, legal or not. "How could I expect payment from one so lovely?" he asks. "Here, take some houses," he says, pushing the little game pieces at her.

Dobby pouts and fumes that they're not playing fair. "Man, this is totally outrageous," he says in his mellifluous voice. Dobby attended two years of design school in London, which seems to have instilled in him a heightened sense of irony and impatience toward Jordan and his life here. He shoves himself out of the chair, slides through a crack in the uncles' circle of chairs, snaps up a tan cigarette from one of the packs on my coffee table, and returns already smoking. He clicks his head back in the uncles' direction. "What are all those fat boys doing in there?" he grumbles. "My God."

But Fattoush isn't answering. His chin is propped on his fist as he drifts in a waking dream of Mai.

I am limited to playing in distracted little bouts, perpetually on call to bring my father and his brothers cookies, coffee, nuts, pressed apricots, nougat, seeds, and oranges. The Jordanian rains thunder against my windows and turn them waxy and veined. When it builds into hailstones, I go to the windows and row in the long, oarlike metal poles attached to massive iron shutters. They close out all daylight and some of the wind, and the stones roar against them like the Last Judgment. After the hail, phone lines won't work and sometimes the electricity all over town goes out. The drivers are transformed as they ease their way beneath dead traffic lights, roll down their windows to wave one another ahead, or offer lifts to soaked pedestrians.

It's crowded, but the uncles are happy here at their brother's house. It's like a snow day for them. Their own children and grandchildren are cooped up back home. Here, they can gossip with abandon, smoke cigarettes, and eat everything that their wives don't let them eat—pastries, candied chickpeas, Turkish delight, sweetened milk with rosewater, ice cream. They present these items wrapped up in pink and silver papers like house gifts to me at the door; I in turn am to present them in attractive bowls. Then they eat whatever they brought. They smoke, balancing the cigarettes between their second and third fingers in the same hands they use to lift demitasses of sugar-spiked black Arabic coffee. They sit with one knee crossed over the other, their feet bouncing with caffeine.

My uncles open with the usual bad-tempered political debates about Israel and Palestine, nuclear weapons, Israel and Lebanon, Saddam Hussein, Saudi Arabia, too much oil, not enough oil. There are no solutions to any of these problems, only opinions and grief and exasperation with the world, the terrible world—which is code for America—where nobody will listen to them and nobody asks for their opinion. Why is it, they wonder, that America gets fatter, that American TV shows get louder, and that TV contestants win millions with a single answer, while the rest of the world gets leaner, hungrier, sicker, angrier? Can this be right? What can be done? Gradually these frustrations make way for intimate revelations about their own disappointments. Frequently their confessions have to do with the way their children are turning out and all the unsatisfactory people they are always finding to marry.

"He could have been a prince! I told him so—a goddamn prince! And then he had to go and get an art degree. . . ."

"I told her fifty thousand times: Don't marry that bum. And did she listen? What do you think?"

"What the hell does anyone do with a so-called art degree? Is he going to eat the art? Is he going to feed it to his family?"

"I said, That bum doesn't know how to comb his own hair, you think he knows how to get married and raise babies?"

Outside, the drumming rains soften to a sizzle, then silence. We crack open the shutters. There's a wash of sun that turns the streets as gold as something ripe. The call to prayers rises from just behind the city horizon and whitens the sky.

"It's time!" Uncle Frankie says. He snaps on the TV and there it is—*The Bold and the Beautiful,* a TV show that I wouldn't have glanced at in the States. Now, however, I know the theme music by heart. I know the names of all the characters, the actors, the writers, the producers. I know where it was shot.

My Russian-made TV is propped up on four pointy stilt legs. It hums as the ardent theme music swells up in a burst of static. The uncles murmur their approval and lean in toward the screen. The American soap opera, with its thieving patriarchs, lazy, weak sons, and conniving, vindictive matriarchs, pleases the Jordanians. After *Baywatch, The Bold and the Beautiful* is one of the most popular shows in the Arab world. This is how America represents itself in other countries: cheesy programming, soap operas, and canceled shows. Selling off bad jokes, one-dimensional characters in skimpy clothes, and flimsy stories is a quick way to run a profit. And of course, when everyone tunes in to *The Bold and the Beautiful* at four, they assume they are watching life in America.

"What is that Ridge up to now?" says Uncle Hal, indicating a cleft-chinned man lurking in some shrubbery. "Why is he fooling with the bushes?"

"He is a bad son," says Uncle Frankie. "God save me from a son like this."

"But you can't blame him, considering what Eric and Grant and that Brooke did to him," says Uncle Hal.

"He will come to no good," intones Uncle Jimmy.

"Never mind about all this psychology," says Uncle Jack. "Ridge is this way because of the Gypsy curse."

"What Gypsy curse?" Uncle Hal says.

"Quiet!" Dobby scolds. "I can't hear a word, you people."

Eventually the show draws to another cliff-hanging close. Breathlessly spoken promises and threats trail off in midair, lips tighten, and eyes narrow. After chattering through the whole program, the uncles sink back in their seats and fall into a postchurch trance. They sigh and drink down to the thick dregs of their coffee. The last rain puddles have vaporized in the streets. We push the heavy shutters all the way open on their iron poles, and the city is steaming with fiery mist.

The uncles brush off their trousers, mutter, and begin preparation for the grown-up business of getting home for dinner. They revert to their older, heavier, and more serious selves. The remains of an afternoon of snacking and complaining are dusted onto my floor and furniture cushions.

Mai abruptly stands to go as well. Caught off guard, Fattoush stumbles to his feet, his chair dancing backward. He pats at his pockets, asking if he can have her number and wondering if she'd like to get a drink sometime, just the two of them. His hands search up and down the front of his shirt for a pen. But Mai, who'd been twirling her hair, pouting, and saying things all afternoon like "You want your big bad rent money, handsome, you'll have to come over here and get it!" has returned to her usual reserved, good-Arab-girl self now that the Monopoly game is back in the box. She pulls back and gives him a look as cool as a splash of water. He follows her, astonished, all the way to the door, which she closes with a crisp click behind her.

Dobby, who works in the same office as Mai and has known her, as he says, since before he was born, scrutinizes Fattoush, who is still standing with one hand frozen on the doorknob. He turns and mumbles to me, "This Fattoush has a lot to learn."

After a long string of sighs, Fattoush goes outside to smoke Jordanian cigarettes. Dobby stays behind and helps me wash the dishes.

THE UNCLES' FAVORITE *MEZZA* PLATTER

Reminiscent of Spanish tapas, a mezza course is designed to stimulate hunger, not satisfy it. It provides the segue from greeting the arriving guests to the full-scale meal. So be careful to strike a balance: Tease the palate with little tastes and simple, small dishes, and don't let anyone spoil his or her appetite! Certain dishes are perennial favorites for a mezza, though all cooks have preferred selections and may decide to rotate in new ones to keep their guests alert. Here are a few of the classics:

olives with chili paste
lebeneh
braided string cheese cut
    into long segments and
    partially unbraided
sliced radishes
roasted peanuts or
    pumpkin seeds
roasted chickpeas
fried falafel balls (p. 171)

peeled, sliced cucumber
raw, peeled scallions
hummus (p. 125)
ripe tomatoes, sliced in
    wedges
hearts of romaine
tabbouleh salad
    (p. 143)
pita bread sliced into
    wedges (p.136)

I am known to the night, the desert, and to horses.
—al-Mutanabbi

We roll down the windows of our big rented Jeep as the four of us—Bud, Fattoush, Mai, and I—make ourselves known to the night. The desert air sways around us, and the stars crack and craze the sky overhead. On the desert highway, we pass the muted shapes of Bedouins, of restless horses, of drifting, swan-necked camels. It is one of the nights that I walk past all the refracting mirrors of homesickness, disorientation, loss, and see myself in place.

We approach the little hillside village of Yehdoudeh, but the Bedouins who work the lower portions of the field are already asleep or moodily sipping their black coffee in the dark. They sit on goat-hair blankets on the ground, gazing into the middle distance, their small lamps glowing on the hill like fireflies. There are far fewer Bedouins than there used to be, as cars and trains and modernity have crowded them out—and the Bedu's hillside is darker than it used to be. There is a suggestion of hidden, grazing animals. We wind our way up and around in the dusty Jeep. Yehdoudeh—fertile, ancient, and remote as the moon—is one of my father's ancestral places.

At the top of the hill is a walled city that was occupied by the Abu-Jabers generations ago. The fortress has been divided into apartments and summer homes. Some people call it the Abu-Jaber castle, but my mother wryly refers to it as "the compound." In Arabic, they call it Khirbet Abu-Jaber, literally "the Abu-Jaber Ruins," and it's hard not to hear this name as a comment on the family itself. The place is huge and labyrinthine, with stone floors and walls and remote medieval windows whose light comes through in shards. I feel I could walk into these high, crumbling walls and never be found again. Voices echo and shuffle and drip or burst out loudly from unexpected places. There is nothing more pensive than looking out from these terraces. Before me stretch miles of plains, desert, and scattered village lights. Beyond that are the unlit corners of the world.

Flinty, bone white roads bearing the names of my ancestors wend across the hill. I haven't been back here since my childhood, when we made special excursions from Amman to "the country." The country was where we'd find my tall great-granduncle, the sheikh. He was a magnificent man, poised and stately as an old tree, who still wore his Bedouin robes and sword. I reflect on the marvelous day years ago when we drove to the country and all ate together in the Bedouin manner, standing in a circle about a platter of food. The sheikh lived out of walls with his tribe in the hilly land behind the fortress, and he would point at the fortress and say, "That was where we kept the horses."

But even though the fortress is so adamant and venerable, and time itself seems distilled, hanging like a humidity in the air here, something is different since I last saw the place twenty-five years ago. The four of us begin wandering its enclosed pathways, its hulking pale rock walls and polished stone floors. The air is moist and cool inside, though we're surrounded by arid land. In the open courtyards, the night has a pure lilac cast. The rooms swim with tea-colored light shed by brass lamps suspended on chains, and the walls are covered with tapestries that shimmer with arch-backed dogs and gazelles. It is a grand, spectral place.

Bud steps into an empty stone chamber made sapphire from the filtered light of two lamps. It's like a private chapel. He turns toward the lanterns and the slope of his back seems softened with an irreducible longing. He looks back, hands open like someone in prayer, and says to me: "You see? This is what I've been talking about."

We leave the room and walk together in a clutch, listening to our footsteps echo. I think again: Something is different here. We turn a corner and the sudden glow of electric lights is jarring, too yellow. I squint, momentarily dazed, my fingers shielding my eyes.

"Is that a shopping mall?" asks Fattoush, his voice struck halfway between hope and disbelief.

I lower my hand. It is. It's a corridor filled with old-timey desert craft shoppes filled with possibly authentic crafts like embroidered dresses, glass bottles layered with colored sands, and mosaic-etched china. There are T-shirts that say, "I ♥ King Hussein," and "I Kiss Camels," as well as plastic key chains, porcelain figurines, and coin purses embossed with amulets against the evil eye. Curious, we turn down a short flight of steps and discover that the lower level is occupied by a glassblowing operation selling earrings, bracelets, tumblers, and bowls. We watch a sweat-soaked glassblower operate an enormous bellows and raise the temperature in the room to scorching. The currents of heat fan us back up the stairs.

"Where did all this come from?" Bud asks. "No one told me about these stores before. . . ."

"This is too perfect," says Fattoush.

"Well, there's no escaping Western capitalization," Mai says. "*Viva* American-style democracy! *Viva* commercial exploitation!"

Fattoush buys a stuffed camel with spinning, heart-shaped eyes and gives it to Mai, who gazes at it in dismay and manages to bury all but its crazy head in her purse.

We poke along the collection of shops, stroking shawls, twirling mobiles, and reading T-shirts. Around another corner, we see a huge red-and-blue canvas tent is set up inside on the stone floor.

"Well, well, well," Bud breathes. His eyes are intent, his nostrils flare.

He moves toward the tent with his hands out and open as if he is about to start flying, and the rest of us follow. I realize as we approach that the red tent is actually an elaborate entryway leading into a vast, open courtyard full of tables and people.

It's a restaurant.

"Kan Zaman," Fattoush reads the English half of the English/Arabic sign hung over the interior doorway. "What does that mean?"

"Once upon a time," Mai says, a beat of irony stringing out her words.

Bud echoes her, his eyes raised.

It is the restaurant of restaurants, here in the heart of the heart of Abu-Jaber country. On exactly the spot, I later learn, where long ago the family kept the horse stables.

The restaurant looks natural among the stone walls and medieval light, as if such a place has always been in business in this location. It makes a kind of historical sense. My drunken, wantonly generous grandfather used to invite whole neighborhoods to his house for dinner, and Kan Zaman is an extension of those invitations. There's a brisk hubbub, the big round tables are crowded, and a rear wall of arched windows faces out over a driveway filled with steaming, rumbling tour buses.

Bud touches his palm to his chest as if about to sing an aria. "Do you see this?" he implores, as he had back in the blue-lit chamber, as if I'm refusing to open my eyes. "This is it. This is exactly what I've been trying to tell you!"

While the rest of us hesitate in the doorway, he walks right into the restaurant and strolls around the tables, muttering: "Good, good, very good." Diners glance up from two-foot-high tasseled menus as he passes, assuming, perhaps, that he is the maître d'. I watch him amble through, chin tucked, hands clasped behind his back, taking possession of the place.

"*What* has he been trying to tell you?" Fattoush asks me, his voice low. Mai turns her plush gaze from Fattoush to me, and it seems we've all fallen under a believer's spell, each of us wondering about Bud's special, private truths.

I open my hands, shrug. "He's always saying things like that."

But it is a very simple reality: Bud is finally in place. His history spirals directly from this wind and desert, where distances dip into pools of shadow and the only sign of life is the pulse of camels stalking their shadows. A long time ago, the people here learned to give food, water, and shelter to anyone who needed it, before they needed it, because that would be the only way to keep one another alive in such a hard place. Such an imperative, repeated so many times over the generations, insinuates itself into the genetic code, becomes a drive or instinct. I watch Bud scrutinize the dishes on one family's table, observe as he puts his hand on the back of another man's chair and leans in to ask if everything is to his liking.

"Look at your dad." Mai turns to me, her face bright with astonishment. "Does he own this restaurant?"

Bud nods to another couple who've come in and points toward a nice table, then waves to a waiter, who hurries over with an armload of menus. Bud inspects a fork and sends it back for a fresh one.

"It would seem so," I say to Mai.

After a few minutes of impromptu ownership, Bud dusts off his hands and turns to go. A waiter approaches him, I assume to ask what on earth he thinks he's doing there. Instead, the man says, "Sir—they don't like their lamb at that table!"

Bud looks the man over a bit critically, then says, "What don't they like?"

"They want it *Engleesi* style, with mint jelly, but we don't have mint jelly. I don't even know, what is mint jelly?"

The table in question is filled with pink-cheeked tourists in shorts and knee socks. Bud nods at the waiter. "Never mind. I can already tell you, they won't like the lamb. Get them a nice plate of mixed grill and tell them it's on the house. Remember, they're our guests."

The waiter thanks him and runs off. Bud watches him push through the swinging doors to the kitchen. His face is dignified and his back upright. One hand rests formally on his midsection; he looks a bit like Napoleon in repose. As we turn back at last, I notice Mai still lingering, backlit, in the doorway, ducking her head toward Fattoush as he moves toward her, as if the mood of Bud's dream is catching. The silhouette of her hand barely grazes the back of his. For a moment I feel a surge of affection for them, as if they're an actual couple.

This evening, it seems, contains a small warp, like a ripple in its fabric, that shows us another way that things could have gone. Our alternative lives emerge in bas-relief: a life in which Mai falls in love with Fattoush; in which Bud owns and runs Kan Zaman; in which I live contentedly in Jordan and understand exactly where in the world I belong.

Soon, I know, we will be walking out of this curved night, back into the regular lives we've set in motion, the old familiar pathways. But for now, it is very lovely, and oddly satisfying, to think that there are always other possibilities, hidden in the blue-lit chambers.

GARLIC-STUFFED ROASTED LUXURIOUS LEG OF LAMB

4- to 6-pound leg of lamb,
trimmed of fat
8 cloves garlic, peeled and
slivered
3 tablespoons olive oil
1 small onion, grated
1 cup vinegar

1 cup water
6 carrots, peeled and
chopped
½ pound mushrooms
Salt and freshly ground
pepper

Cut slits all over the lamb with the tip of a sharp knife and insert the garlic slivers in the slits.

In a large cooking pot, heat the oil until it sizzles, then sear the lamb, browning on all sides and taking care not to burn it.

Add the onion, vinegar, and water to the lamb, bring to a boil, and then reduce to a medium-low heat. Simmer, covered, for 1½ hours. Turn the meat, add the carrots and mushrooms, and simmer, covered, for another 1½ hours. Try to resist lifting the lid to peek into the pot. It will smell divine. When done, add salt and pepper to taste.

SERVES 6 TO 8.

TWENTY-ONE

Just a Taste

Mai and I loll in the leather chairs of her government office, clicking spoons in glasses of American-style iced tea. During one especially long, glistening afternoon, our friend Dobby taught Ziad, the office driver, to make iced tea in his free time, when he wasn't driving Dobby and Mai around to bakeries and cafés. It is a lovely, golden iced tea, delicately brewed with cardamom and brightened with sugar and lemon and whole sprigs of mint. Ziad hand-chipped the ice from solid blocks in the office sink.

Like iced tea in Jordan, Mai is a bit of an anomaly, a hybrid of older and newer worlds. Mai's parents are unusually liberal and cosmopolitan; her dignified, frowning father is one of the king's personal advisers, and her American mother, Katy, in her gleaming cashmere suits, is the founder of an organization dedicated to preserving the ancient buildings and historical sites of Amman. This is why Mai at thirty-two has so far not been required to marry anyone. Dobby, who also works in Mai's office, who was born and raised in Jordan and who, ever since his sojourns in Paris and London, groans regularly about his distaste for Jordanian food, music, clothing—in fact, all things Jordanian—says the problem is that Mai's parents are too sophisticated for Jordan. They prefer that Mai find her own suitors, without their intervention. But Jordanians do not share in the American institution of dating—at least not publicly—so it is very difficult for someone like Mai to meet anyone.

From what I've observed, this situation seems to suit her just fine. Mai and I have been friends since French-Catholic-Jordanian grade school, back in the days when I was engaged to Hisham. Twenty-five years ago, she was a little girl with a stern expression, polished shoes, and an immense cloud of black hair. Even then, Mai informed me that she found boys unsatisfactory and had no wish to marry one. Since childhood, she has had a dignified equanimity about her, of exactly the sort that has always eluded me; her eyes are dark and level, and her physical beauty seems predicated on a sort of emotional distance. If Mai secretly pines for a suitor in the hidden nights of her dreams, I'd never guess it now, watching her roll her big leather chair back and forth behind her burnished desk, stabbing buttons on the intercom and ordering Ziad to bring us more ice, fresh mint, sliced oranges and limes.

I admire her fierce manner. Like my aunt Aya, Mai was the only daughter in a family of sons, which has rendered her unflinching and indomitable. Her cheekbones are high and straight and suggest something of a ship's prow, and her eyes have a dauntless clarity. She has the presence and loveliness of a film star but there is also a deep vertical line between her eyebrows; Dobby is always fussing over her hair and nails and tries to smooth out this line with his fingertips, scolding her to "stop glaring." But she continues to glare.

"He really has a thing for you," I say, underlining the obvious.

"Fattoush?" She swivels her sheer gaze to me. "No—he's a child."

Fattoush has sent me to Mai to plead his case. I'm meant to act as his "cultural attaché," to tell Mai all about his "talents," and to get a sense of her level of interest. "He's not so bad—he loves music and . . . he's studying art history, you know," I say haplessly, drawing a blank on his list of talents.

"Oh yeah? Like in grade school, you mean?" She snorts with satisfaction, her teeth clicking on the glass of iced tea.

It occurs to me that some part of Mai's scorn may come from fear—of losing herself, her independence, in a relationship with a traditional man. More than one Jordanian woman has told me of an easygoing courtship period with an Arab fiancé that abruptly comes to a halt after the wedding—the sweet suitor suddenly insisting that his wife quit her job, produce babies, and wait on both himself and his mother.

Mai's little greenish gray cat, Lonely, curls between my ankles like a puff of fog. He stares at me in perpetual astonishment—perhaps at

his good fortune. In parts of the Middle East, cats used to be vener-
ated, but in modern Jordan they're bums, forever spilling out of
garbage cans, trailing a foul reek.

But Mai found Lonely when he was tiny and newly abandoned
under her windowsill; now he is pampered, fluffed up as a powder
puff. He leaps to Mai's lap, slinks into a coil, and begins kneading her
thigh. Mai strokes the crown of his head down to the base of his
spine. Lonely's eyes lower to wet slits as she strokes and strokes. "No,"
she finally says in a new, formal voice. "I've got a cat in my life. Which
is plenty. And I'm afraid that Fattoush isn't a man. Give me a man—
then we'll talk."

His ears gleam and his cheeks are fiery with exertion and sunburn.

Fattoush is doing the twist while Mai embroiders the air over her
head with intricate, diaphanous hand movements, dancing at her full
length.

Fattoush invests himself in his dance, rolling and swiveling and
elbowing the air. Mai stays an eternal half step out of reach, like a jinn
or a mirage. A distant, neutral smile floats on her lips.

The rest of the family ignores them—they're eating *mezza*.

Last night, when I tried gently to dissuade Fattoush from his infatuation with Mai, he brushed aside my concerns. Even when I finally
blurted out, nearly verbatim—in exasperation—her request for "a
man," Fattoush seemed only mildly bemused. "A man, eh?" he said,
chuckling and puffing out his chest. "So she wants a real man?"

The record player's arm slides up and down over the Fayrouz
record, and music bounces off the stone walls of the fortress ceilings
and arched doorways. Bud's cousin Haroun and his wife, Sandra, live
in one of the ancient apartments in the Abu-Jaber compound at
Yehdoudeh. Uncle Haroun went to the States long enough to not finish a degree in engineering and to collect his Wisconsin-born bride,
Sandra, who was as ready to go as if she'd been standing at a bus stop
all those wintry years, waiting for Haroun to arrive. "Where did she
appear from?" Bud asked when he heard about his cousin's engage-

ment. "It's like a magic trick." They married, returned to Jordan, and settled into one of the apartments of the medieval fortress, where Sandra began having daughters and cooking esoteric Arabic dishes as matter-of-factly as if she'd been doing it all her life. Sandra, with her long, thin nose and small, regal head, is the unacknowledged reigning queen of Abu-Jaber cookery. None of the family can bring themselves to admit that an American could outcook them, but there are always friends and family lined up in orderly rows along her table, their faces clear and open as those of a congregation at services, waiting expectantly at their plates. Before each meal, Sandra always pauses, platter in hand, to claim her moment of recognition before placing the food on the table. She reads slick American gourmet magazines and visits the tiny, bubbling kitchens of the local old crones, studying the ways they blend their spices and balance their sauces. She guards her recipe for bitter *mulukhiyyah* greens as jealously as if it's the polio vaccine, and even her adult daughters complain that she deliberately leaves crucial ingredients out of the recipes she gives them. Today, she frowns at the music over one shoulder, unhappy with anything that might interfere with the experience of eating her cooking.

Fattoush and Mai are dancing in the clearing at the center of the main room. The stone floors make a fine dance surface, and the singer's elastic Arabic notes bound through the air. A long table is set up against one wall and servers bustle around it, laying out heavy platters piled with roasts and rice and vegetables. Occasionally, the relatives call to Fattoush and Mai to sit and eat, but every time Mai turns to go, Fattoush snatches her hand and begs her for another dance. Mai makes a show of relenting each time, but I know she must want to dance. Mai does only what she wants.

"Look at her play with her little mousy." Dobby nudges me, slitting his eyes and making his smile very sly. "She's toying with him."

At that moment, Aunt Sandra emerges from the kitchen carrying a small tray of glistening stuffed grape leaves that she says are the "vegetarian special." She takes the plate right up to Fattoush on the dance floor and waves it under his nose so that the rich aroma softens him and his dancing falters. He sneaks a delicate glance at Mai, who shrugs, and he follows Aunt Sandra back to the table like a man in a waking dream.

The atmosphere is feverish, the air humid with conversation and drinking. Sandra has proclaimed that this meal would be an American-style buffet. She has hired a man who claimed to be a professional bartender—a dusky-eyed young Bedouin who takes all sorts of orders for mixed drinks, beer, and wine but serves everyone tall glasses of *araq* instead. Fattoush, Mai, all the wives, and I are seated at one table. Most of the uncles prowl the buffet table, eating directly from the serving platters with their hands.

"They're standing up like wild Bedouins in a tent!" Sandra complains, glaring at the bartender as if he is responsible. But her husband, Haroun, is the leading culprit, calling his brothers over to this or that plate, brandishing chicken legs, and encouraging them to tear the lamb pieces directly from the skewers with their teeth.

Haroun materializes at Fattoush's left shoulder and gestures at his plate. "Come on, boy, let me give you some real food. Enough with the leaves and twigs."

Fattoush pays no attention. He is glazed from his joyful exertion and sheerly buoyant beside Mai. He hunches over his plate of vegetarian grape leaves and guards it with both arms, as he's learned to do so the uncles won't try to pile on more food, and he eats with evident appetite. He's lost about ten pounds during his weeks in Jordan, with all the meat dodging he's had to do. This is the most I've seen him eat in one sitting.

Haroun brings up the recurrent concern about Fattoush's child-bearing abilities. "You know, you can't have a baby from just dancing around and eating leaves like a monkey," he observes.

Sandra waves her husband away with her long, imperious fingers and seats herself to my left. She complains, "These Jordanian men can't fathom anyone deliberately turning down meat."

Fattoush grins as he eats, nodding at Mai, Aunt Sandra, me, back to Mai, and so on. Sandra, who never eats when she is feeding others, pulls her elbows into her lap and asks, "How long have you been a vegetarian?"

Fattoush chews and bobs and scoops more grape leaves onto his plate. "Ever since I was eleven years old. I've been a vegetarian for more than half my life now. I saw a TV show on the way they slaughter cows and that did it for me," he confides to Mai in a tender way.

Sandra contemplates him with a fond, abstracted smile, clearly enjoying his pleasure in the meal. Like Bud, she doesn't have a son, and she looks as though she'd like to try rubbing her hand along the shorn, downy nape of his thin neck. "Do you like the grape leaves?" she coaxes. "I made them special."

He nods with his whole upper body. "I've never had anything like these. I'd eat them every day if I could—I don't think I'd ever get tired of them. They taste incredible."

"Oh, well . . ." Sandra brushes modestly at her sleeves. "After all, we want you to grow big and strong."

It is not so much what she says as the way she says it—sharply, disjointedly. I slowly turn toward her and think I see in her eyes the coppery glint of a secret arsonist or poisoner. There's an odd set to her lips, and the angles of her jaw don't quite match up. I glance back at Fattoush, and then I slowly return my gaze to Sandra. She's holding so still, she doesn't seem to be blinking. All at once, a great fizzing rush comes over me. My spine unbends. My fingers close around the silvery handle of my fork. I reach toward Fattoush's plate—is that Sandra's chilly white hand rising to stop me? No, she lowers it. Without asking permission, I spear a stuffed grape leaf from his plate. "I just have to try one of these special ones," I say, and then bite in. It is delicious, of course—there was no question of that. I taste the moist sweetness of rice and fresh oil, the faint brine of the leaf, a luscious node of onion, garlic, currant . . . and there, quite subtle, nearly transparent yet unmistakable, is the flavor of lamb.

My eyes fly up to Fattoush, who is devouring the tightly wrapped packets in single bites as he fans one hand through the air, describing his skateboarding exploits to Mai. Do I tell him what he's eating? I look back to Sandra, who is watching me, her eyes amused. She puts her hand on mine—it's surprisingly warm. "There's just a little in there," she says. "For flavor."

Fattoush smiles at us as he forks up another helping, chewing and rocking.

My lips part. I hesitate. Fattoush notices my expression and lifts his eyebrows.

"And quite honestly," Sandra says in her drowsy, flat American voice, "I'm not that sure that what they're saying isn't true—" She tilts her head at Fattoush. "You know, he really *might* have trouble having babies otherwise. For heaven's sake, you can't literally cut out all the meat. Look at Haroun—he always ate so much milk and ice cream, and you see? All we had were daughters!"

Fattoush stops mid-chew, his mouth a tiny circle, eyes filmed with the intimation of panic. He covers his mouth with his hand. He swallows.

His skin takes on a pewtered sheen, slick with sweat. He stands, slightly lopsided, and says, "Oh. Oh."

Mai eyes Fattoush's plate, then indignantly snaps in Arabic at Aunt Sandra. Sandra regards us placidly in turn and says, "Oh now, what's all this fuss about a little taste of lamb?"

I find Bud standing over a platter of sumac-roasted chicken with Uncle Frankie. They appear to be having some sort of business meeting. I interrupt to point out Fattoush, who is still standing but is now starting to crumple, clutching his stomach. Mai crouches beside him, trying to fan him with a napkin.

Dobby and Bud half carry, half drag Fattoush outside, where he totters and sways and then vomits weakly down the center of the driveway. Mai watches from a window. Uncle Haroun comes out with a garden hose while Aunt Sandra stands in the doorway. Her neck and shoulders are erect as an empress's, and her hands are squared on her hips. She is supremely annoyed. "Now what on earth?"

"I can't digest meat," Fattoush says meekly. He is mortified and apologetic and wrings his hands as if begging for mercy. "I haven't eaten it in fifteen years—I don't have the enzymes for it."

"Oh, God in heaven," Sandra says, flinging her hands in the air before going back inside.

Fattoush vomits out the window on the ride home, speckling himself. At one point, he whimpers about disgracing himself in front of Mai, but I say that she likes him far too much to mind a little vomit. I tell him to think of it as a bonding experience. He then spends most of the night moaning on the floor of his room, occasionally crab-walking to the bathroom for more retching. Bud hovers at the bathroom door with mugs of soup, tea, and ginger ale, all of which are waved away by Fattoush's limp hand.

I keep vigil with Bud, both of us upright and unblinking at late-night TV, an eye-scalding buzz of ancient westerns that I've never heard of.

"This reminds me of when you and your sisters were the littlest girls," Bud says as we nibble Fattoush's broth and crackers. The toilet roars and shudders one wall away.

"Whenever somebody was sick, your mother and I would sit up just like this, worrying about you." He gestures toward Fattoush shuffling miserably back to his room. "Do you remember those times?"

It's true—there is something about this cave of light in the dark, the glass of ginger ale, the scent of soup, the waiting to get well, that reminds me of childhood and a time when my parents were practically still children themselves. Our lives were something we went into together, in quiet living rooms, waiting up past bedtime.

"I think Fattoush could use someone to take care of him," Bud says, his voice low.

"Do you think this is all in his head?" I ask Bud.

He shrugs. "Maybe yes, maybe no."

"Maybe he could take better care of himself."

Bud pooches out his lips. "That sounds like something an American would say."

As dawn is turning to a bronze glow in the windows, Bud has fallen asleep in a chair and I'm uncomfortably kinked on the couch. Fattoush appears in the living room entryway. "I think I'm better now."

I wake up a little and squint at him in the dimness. He looks as hollowed out as a parenthesis, and his eyes are wells. My voice doesn't work yet, so I wave at him. He smiles wanly and waves back. He starts to head off to bed, then stops and returns. He sways once, lightly.

"Phinny?" I boost myself onto my elbows. "Do you need something? Some aspirin? Another blanket?"

"Well, it's just . . ." He props himself against the wall and lowers his head as if ducking a ray of light. His forehead wrinkles as he lifts his eyes to mine. "I was just wondering—do you really think Mai likes me?"

One week later, I come home after a day of errands and find my father and Fattoush sitting around in the living room, the air turgid with the feel of a broken-off conversation. Their faces, as they turn to me, are colored with guilt. Fattoush stands, putting out both hands as if to hold me in place. "Now—okay, don't get all upset," he says, measuring his words.

"What?" I stand still. The breath pools in the bottoms of my lungs, and the TV image freezes. Outside, the birds hold their last notes.

Bud smiles a wide, unnatural smile. "Hello, Ya Ba," he says.

I study his smile. "What happened?"

"This wasn't a plan or anything."

"Please—just tell me."

Bud grins and shakes his head the way he does when it's someone on the phone he doesn't want to speak with.

"*What.*" My voice goes an octave higher.

They both look alert now. Fattoush nods and swallows and finally says to me, "Your father—okay . . . he . . . he bought a building today."

"He—"

"See, what did I tell you?" Bud says to Fattoush. Bud bats at an invisible crumb on his sleeve, then looks up with a flash of inspiration. "I bought it for you, honey!"

I carefully set my bags of groceries on the coffee table, then I drop onto my hard couch. A flume of dust goes up.

"It's for the whole family." Bud sits forward into his excitement, warming up now. "We can all live on the first floor, the restaurant will go on the second floor—"

"The place was a steal," Fattoush enthuses. "Two hundred K!"

"Two *hundred thousand dollars*!" I white-knuckle the arm of the couch. "Where are you going to get that kind of money?"

Bud bunches up his lips as if concocting an answer. Finally he says, "I have some retirement money saved, for your information. And who likes to retire, anyway? No one! You know what happens when you retire? You go crazy! For your information, I have a *plan.* I will make a restaurant that my family can all come and work at! Besides, your mother always has some money hidden somewhere, in the cupboards, under the rug. She loves doing that."

"So you told Mom about this?"

More batting at invisible crumbs. "Not a hundred percent exactly yet."

"Diana, listen, listen, this is a totally amazing, awesome, incredible deal," Fattoush persists. "Frankie's house is huge. There's more than enough room for everyone on just the first floor alone—"

"Or maybe we should put the family on the second floor and the restaurant on—"

"Okay, wait a minute—" I put out my hand. The sun in the windows, usually so clear and light, seems to thicken and liquefy. "You mean you bought *Uncle Frankie's* house?"

Both of them look at me. Bud rubs his eye with the flat of his palm.

Among my rascally, troublesome, sly uncles and cousins, Frankie is the most rascally, troublesome, and sly of all. Aside from occasional, half-joking stabs at employment, he has lived most of his life like one of the lilies of the valley, neither toiling nor reaping. He survives by shaving off pieces of the land he inherited and selling them at exorbitant prices. He has also recently invested in a small franchise that embeds holographic images on pendants for necklaces. This business, he tells any potential investor, is a "gold mine." But for the past decade, he has largely augmented his lifestyle by renting out the floors of his five-story, squared-off house while he and his wife retreat to an ever shrinking space at the center. The house no longer has a kitchen because Frankie tore out the stove and refrigerator to sell to some Bedouins who didn't have access to electrical outlets. He rented the flat roof of their house to a family that wore bright scarves and gold earrings and cooked over a rooftop campfire. Most recently, he rented his first floor and his fourth floor to two opposing political parties to house their campaign headquarters. The front of the house is draped with two thirty-foot banners proclaiming the names of the two warring factions, and there are constant skirmishes over which banner is to be draped higher than the other. Sometimes both banners hang straight down in parallel tatters. All day long, middle-aged men run out of one or the other campaign headquarters, up and down the steps of the house with bags of takeout food, throwing their garbage wrappings and melon rinds at each other's doors. The entryway reeks like the dumpster behind a bowling alley, and refuse clutters the staircase.

"You bought that building for two hundred thousand dollars," I say, squinting hard, as if I could bring it into better focus.

Bud smiles, holds up his hands, smooth and even as a wave. "Ya Ba, let me explain real estate to you. Real estate costs a great deal of money. . . ."

Fattoush rushes in. "Really, Diana, you don't know! Frankie says he could get double what he's asking for this place. Even triple! It's a gold mine."

"So why's he asking for so little, then?"

Bud frowns, concentrates, rolls forward in his chair. This is a lesson he wants me to learn: "Because that is what family does. They help each other."

"Dad!" I strangle the word in a half scream, then place one hand over my mouth and look up at him. "Dad, it doesn't matter—you can't afford it."

"What—it's no problem. I've got fifty thousand saved up, your mom's gotta have the same amount, easy. And then once we sell our house it's no problem. Of course, it's not the whole building, but at least—"

"What do you mean, it's not the whole building?"

Bud and Fattoush look at each other. Is that a small glimmer of awareness struggling to emerge? Liver-colored streaks appear in Fattoush's milky skin. Bud clears his throat. "It doesn't include the roof," he mumbles.

That's when I go into my bedroom and lock the door. I sit on the bed and examine the intricate swirls in the plaster ceiling and attempt to assess the situation. I think: Bud is about to give away their life savings and house.

Then the thought comes to me—distantly and quietly, like a person shouting from the horizon—that I am partially to blame here. I put the idea of Jordan back into my father's head. After Bud had managed to live for several years in relative serenity in America, his daughter moved back to the homeland and stirred everything up again.

My own fault.

I rub my hand over the coarse grain of my bedspread. My life has not been uncomfortable here. True, the elderly bed in my furnished apartment is so slept-in that the mattress has a furrow that I roll into every night. True, the landlord has installed a permanent red light fixture in my office, for reasons known only to himself, so my work glows nightly in an angry, accusatory crimson. And true, I cannot walk by myself in the streets of Amman without hearing sweet nothings from strangers like "Hello, you sexy Russian!" and "Meow, meow, Miss Pussycat!"

But Jordan has turned out to be more familiar, socially lush, and deeply welcoming than I'd ever expected it to be. I knew as soon as the airplane door opened onto the clean desert night, the scents of jasmine, dust, and mint weaving through the air. Through my bedroom window, I can see fluted minarets and domes made incandescent by the sun. The call to prayers lifts from the three closest mosques, coming first in delicate slivers, then rising full throated and silvery as the olive trees that shine along my avenue, calling me back, as if to say *Here it is, the place you were meant to be, at last.*

Wouldn't it be wonderful to run a restaurant in Jordan with my father? For a second I don't let myself think about money, or my writing, or the practical reasons to do or not do anything—including the fact of who Bud is and who I have turned out to be. Instead, I think about a warm room full of people eating, the air damp and rich with the aromas of roasted garlic and olive oil, braised chicken, stuffed squashes, grape leaves wrapped tenderly around their delicate fillings. I think of all of us together again.

But then the call to prayers fades back into the cityscape, and I am left staring at the bed that slips every night from one end of the room to the other because the floor is tilted. I am back in my apartment, where I haven't cooked anything besides scrambled eggs in over a month because the kitchen reeks of sour wood, mold, and insecticide.

I go to my door and touch its smooth grain. Bud's and Fattoush's voices are lowered, discussing how to talk me into seeing how wonderful everything is. I walk out and once again there's that swoop of silence. I stand in the doorway, staring at their upturned faces. "So, Dad," I say, "I'd like to speak to you about this."

Fattoush dusts off his knees and straightens up. "Fantastic. You know, we were really hoping that once you sort of calmed down and had a chance to—"

"Dad." I fix Bud with an X-ray eyeball. "Let's you and me go get a coffee."

"Great, I could use some caffeine." Fattoush starts walking toward the door.

I point at him. "Okay—you? Stay here."

Fattoush shrinks down on the hard couch. The axis of my gaze shifts to Bud. I wait.

Just a few blocks away from my apartment is a tidy little café called Babiche that serves French pastries, Italian cappuccinos, and hummus. Both Bud and I already feel depleted by the conversation we haven't yet had, so we sit quietly at our oversize window table, our fingers trailing over the silly, colorful plastic menu, reading and rereading, both of us distracted and unhappy. We've forgotten how to fight with each other. Almost without noticing it, our natures have matured and formed, so that here we now sit, without a way to speak.

The shop owner watches us, concerned, from her glass pastry case at the front of the store. Bud and I are so obviously struggling and failing to talk about something that she sends over what she feels will best help us in our difficult, metaphysical state. For Bud, that is a steaming pot of dense black Arabic coffee; for me, it's a long, silver dish of strawberry, vanilla, and chocolate ice cream under a drizzle of hot fudge—a Neapolitan.

I dip a slim, swan-necked spoon into the ice cream and taste the ripe sweetness of berries, the exotic, resinous twist of vanilla bean, the formal purity of the chocolate. Something sentimental reawakens in my nature and softens my resistance. But when I look at Bud, it seems that the coffee is reviving some unwelcome consciousness in him. He studies my ice cream a bit gloomily, then shakes his head and makes his "no one understands me" gesture, tossing up one hand. He contemplates the procession of chattering teenagers swinging in and out of the glass doors. Then the door to the restaurant ticks open and in comes a big, busy family—babies wallowing in the arms of harried parents, several giddy-grinning children, and a couple of take-charge seniors. They immediately start pushing tables together and re-arranging the furniture. I see Bud jealously taking all of this in. Back in the States, he was in the habit of pointing at strangers' babies and saying to me and my sisters, "There, girls, I would like some of those."

But now he is contemplative, sunk in meditation. He turns his saucer slowly, then takes an expansive, dark, philosophical breath and says, "Who knows what anything means in this whole world? Why does the sun rise in the morning, why—"

"Dad, no."

He looks up from the coffee, his eyes flat and plaintive now. "I miss you," he says. "I miss my girls. This isn't how it's supposed to go, everyone running in a million directions. Look at you—back in the States, you live out in the wilderness somewhere—"

"Portland."

"Suzanne in the Deep South—"

"San Francisco."

"And the baby living in that pit of vipers—"

"New York City."

"What kind of a family is that? In Jordan this never would have happened."

"Dad—we're happy. We all like where we live. We're Amer—" I don't say it. I turn the spoon in my fingers.

"I can't take it, I just—can't—take it." He presses down on his heart. "So, yes, I buy a restaurant! Yes, I did it. I buy a restaurant because finally I see that it's time. Just like I always tried to tell you. Didn't I try? We can live downstairs and the restaurant will be upstairs. It will be more than jobs—you and your sisters, you'll all be owners. You'll all be part of the big family again. You'll be living here and your babies won't be foreigners. We can run it together and it will be perfect—don't you see that?" His expression is so clear, direct, and fierce, I have to look away.

Instead of speaking, I eat ice cream. While Bud talks, I take slow, melting spoonfuls, the hot fudge dense and dark with a burnt-sugar edge, the metal spoon cool in my mouth. My father's words dissolve in a place beneath my throat, a lost, forgotten location I feel only when certain old songs come on the radio.

I want more than anything to be able to say to my father: *Of course, yes, your splendid dream will come true at last.* But the cold spoon clicks against my teeth. There are too many things I know for sure: My sisters will not move to Jordan; they have lives of their own now. And I'm not staying on in Jordan once my grant is finished; I miss the States too much. Uncle Frankie's building doesn't have a kitchen in it. Bud doesn't even have the nerve to tell Mom that he bought the building. And we would all end up fighting with one another all the time anyway.

Bud has forgotten about the rambunctious family sitting a few tables away and is staring at me, as if I am now the one who can grant his wishes. "Don't you see?" he asks again, as if it is just a matter of changing the expression on my face. "This is our last chance to be a family all together again. That's all. That's all I'm saying." His hands open and then curl shut on the tabletop. He adds in a quiet, desperate voice, "I told Fattoush he could be a manager."

I slip the spoon into the muddled remains of ice cream, sweet and sad as a last glance, a blown kiss. The late afternoon light fills the windows. I wait, then tap Bud's hand and nod. "That's good, because he needs a job."

Some people have a genius for convincing you that their dreams are the deepest, truest, finest of all dreams, even as some part of you knows they're crazy. Perhaps some people dream better than others. If such a thing could be true, then I'd have to say that Bud is a first-class, grade-A dreamer. His dreams are elaborate, enduring, and so lovely to look at. They're the sorts of dreams that could make you angry because you can see how much you might start to want them for yourself, and you know that for some reason, you won't be able to have them.

That night, Bud finally gets up the nerve to call Mom. I hardly breathe in the next room, where I am standing over the stove, stirring and staring down into the round black eye of a pot of Arabic coffee. The scent of the coffee and cardamom rises into my face and mingles with the sound of Bud's voice talking about everything and revealing nothing. He talks about food, restaurants, family, angling in from a hundred directions. Over and over, it seems that I hear him approaching his true topic, only to veer away from it again. "You know, I've been thinking about restaurants ever since I got here," he finally says. A pause, then, "Oh no, nothing special. Just, you know, about restaurants in general, how I like them so much. Is it raining there?" At the end of an hour, he has told her nothing.

The next day, I get a phone call.

"What's this I hear?"

"Uh . . ." My voice wobbles.

"I couldn't believe my ears."

"Aunt Aya?"

"I hear your father is buying Frankie's house for three hundred thousand."

Three hundred thousand? "Auntie Aya! I thought you were in the desert."

"I was. Does he know it's infested with centipedes?"

Centipedes! "Are you coming to town?"

"And the stench and the garbage at that place—I wouldn't put a monkey in there." Her voice snaps shut like a change purse.

Now I'm nodding, tugging on the phone cord. "And he hasn't even told my mother!"

"What? Oh, this is ridiculous! Why doesn't he have sense by now? Some of the brothers you can trust a little, and some you can even trust a little more. But Frankie . . . ?" Her voice teeters ominously toward some unnamed precipice.

"I know!"

She sighs so intensely into the receiver that it's as if the phone catches fire. On my end, I sigh as well. And I think for a moment that we must be feeling the same thing, wondering what could possibly drive these brothers like this, instigating one another, striking up against one another, rock and flint. Finally, she says, "Okay. Never mind. I will fix it. Don't let your father go out with any of his brothers. Today I am coming to get him."

Auntie Aya arrives wearing an elaborate, silver-embroidered ankle-length blue dress, jingling gold bangles, and silver shoes with heels as long and supple as Bedouin daggers. I can hear Aunt Aya's jewelry in the hallway before she gets to my door. Bud hears her, too, and it takes him a moment to register what that familiar sound is. His mouth opens and he folds his paper and slowly touches the arms of his chair as if they are talismans. Fattoush looks over lazily from the TV, the screen washed white from the sun. Aunt Aya bats at the door and walks in, calling, "Hello, I am here. I have come out of the desert to see you. Where is my boneless niece? Where is that brother of mine?"

The sun hits her as she enters, and all the little bits of jewelry and tiny embroidered mirrors on her dress flare with light. Even her black hair, I see, contains a bolt of white that wasn't there fifteen years ago, glistening from her part all the way down past her shoulders.

Bud springs out of his chair, then freezes like an escapee in a searchlight. "How wonderful. Aya is here," he says. He lumbers to her, wraps his arms around her, and for a moment it looks like surrender. But then he straightens and peeps behind her hopefully, saying, "Hal is coming for me any minute now. . . . Yes, I think he'll be here in a second. Then we can all have breakfast together."

Auntie Aya merely smiles and says, "Not today, brother. Today you're with me, and we've got places to go."

Fattoush stands, hand extended cautiously. "We haven't met. I'm Gus's business partner—"

But she flicks her nails at him. "No, I'm afraid you stay here today."

Fattoush watches them go, his features muddled and wary. He's been in Jordan nearly a month but is still often disoriented by the people here. Finally, he retires to the study that he's set up on my dining room table. He says he's going back to work on his business plan for the restaurant. While I sit a few chairs away in the living room and stare at my unwritten novel, a clicked pen in my hand, he leans over the table, mumbles, and moves sheets of loose-leaf notebook paper around in the dust. He's shown me these notes several times already this week. Each page is covered with cryptic rhetorical questions and occasional stabs at answers like "Theme? Middle East? Too obvious. Safari food? Too weird? What is safari food? Steak in a pan?" After half an hour or so of arranging these papers and questions into various piles, he touches the back of his hand to his forehead as if checking for a fever. This is the first day since arriving that he hasn't spent in the company of my uncles; he's usually eaten two lunches by now. He looks blearily over at me and says that he's feeling lightheaded.

We walk into town to the Popeye's Fried Chicken, a white-tiled cubicle of a restaurant, where he orders several sides of coleslaw and French fries; he scrapes out the little mayonnaisy, clear plastic tubs with his fork and smokes a few Marlboros that Uncle Hal left after his last visit to our house. Fattoush casts moony glances at the cashier, a veiled girl with slate eyes, and talks about heartless Stacy back home and the jealousy and remorse she'll feel when she learns that he's become a business owner in Jordan. He speculates hopefully that he may have already settled down with Mai when Stacy comes to beg his pardon. When she asks him if she can come back, he'll be kind but firm. He gnaws at the edges of his bitten-down fingertips . . . but what if she doesn't want to come back? he ponders. Could that happen? He cuts a dark look at me, as if all women are in cahoots. It's not entirely clear to Fattoush what women want. His mother said she couldn't stand being married, and his father said he loved it, both times.

"My dad, he lives in Maryland with this whole other family he started after me," Fattoush says, hunched over the table. "It's like, after he started the second one, the first one didn't count anymore. I was just supposed to vanish. I can tell his wife doesn't like having me around too much, either. I make her nervous."

I run my fingertips over the tabletop, over sparkling chips of mica suspended in the slick tile. I'd never even thought of Phinny as having a father of his own before.

"How come there are people like that?"

I balance my head sideways on one hand. "Like what, Phinny?"

He looks at me a little wildly. "How come my father never cooked me any eggs?"

I try to think of something soothing or funny to say, something about how many people can't cook even the simplest thing. But I don't say anything.

On our way out, he holds the door open for me and prompts me gently but firmly, "And please try to remember—my name is no longer Phinny."

FATHERLY FRIED EGGS

2 garlic cloves, thinly sliced	Chili pepper flakes to taste
1 tomato, seeded and diced	Salt and pepper to taste
1 small onion, diced	2 tablespoons olive oil
1 teaspoon ground sumac	5 large eggs

In medium frying pan, sauté the vegetables and spices in the olive oil on medium heat, letting the juices dry up a bit. Break the eggs over this mixture, and fry sunny-side up or scramble together, according to taste. Serve with sliced cheese and bread.

SERVES 2.

We walk all the way down through the spiraling neighborhoods, past balconies filled with the aroma of tuberose and verbena, past crumbling staircases and screened porches flittering with songbirds. We stroll down to the ancient town center—named after the goddess Amoun, a goddess who really didn't care what politicians and generals and roaming tribal bands said about her or her fine, rough space. The streets here wind and welter according to the whims of the earth. The place is so old that the pavement is yellow with dust, the sidewalks cracked and intricate as mosaic tiles. People chatter and circle and bargain, tides move through the streets. This place feels like a point of origin—one of the fountainheads where the human community intersects with the earth. Outside of a tiny antique bookshop, I stop and place my hand against the faded storefront. I can just make out the side of Fattoush's face through the glints in the storefront window as he tries—and fails—to haggle. My head swims a little, and I wonder if it's possible that certain areas exert an additional gravitational pull. For a moment, I think I have a vivid memory of being eight and standing in this very spot. The faces pour around me, colors of wheat and earth and spice; the sky pulses with something like breath. Finally, Fattoush emerges with his books and my hand falls.

Fattoush and I amble through the crowds and go nosing along the endless street of crooked shops, their counters piled up with scarves, carpets, prayer beads, brass pots, embroidered dresses, demitasses, chessboards. We bargain and accept tiny glass cups of strong tea and tell the shopkeepers our names and what country we're from. They smile dazzling smiles, rock forward, and say, "Welcome, welcome!"

Fattoush buys enamel earrings in the shape of little hands for his mother. His hand hovers over a small wood-inlaid box. "Stacy might like this." He glances at me, then lowers his hand. "But I don't want Mai to be jealous."

When we finally walk all the long, hot, uphill way home, Bud is already back, sprawled in Fattoush's usual spot on the couch. He looks as if Aunt Aya dragged him into an alley and beat him for a few hours. His hair is disheveled, his tie loosened, and his shirt unbuttoned; there are gray circles under his eyes.

"Dad . . ." I stand at the edge of the couch tentatively. "You okay?"

"I can't take it," he groans, slinging the crook of his elbow over his eyes.

Fattoush and I pull up chairs and stare at him in dismay.

Bud drags his arm away from his forehead. "Her auntie—" He points at me and shakes his finger. "She killed me." He returns his arm to his forehead.

Speaking through his elbow, Bud describes a day of epic proportions. In her dust-caked Mercedes-Benz, Aya drove him through the sueded hillsides of Amman to look at real estate—building after building, each one brighter, larger, and cheaper than the one before, all of them nicer and less expensive than Frankie's building. "He wants two, three, four times as much as these other places! And they have kitchens!" Slowly and steadily, through the dust-cracked windows of Aya's car, comprehension came to Bud. Wide commercial boulevards, flanked by high-rises, legions of shops, restaurants, and offices streamed past the car windows, his consciousness darkened by disillusion. It was apparent in every FOR RENT sign. The way he describes it, his awakening was less of a rising toward light than a weight crushing down, the understanding that he had once again been duped by his brother, that Jordan wasn't what he thought it was, that his family wasn't who he thought they were, and that the world wasn't what it was supposed to be. Frankie, his brother, was willing to openly, brazenly swindle him out of his own retirement savings: What did that say about the universe? There was no point to buying this restaurant to be closer to his family in Jordan, because family didn't exist—not in the pristine sense that he wanted it to. In the end, they were all just people like everyone else. "None of it is real," he moans into the crook of his arm. "None."

We gaze at him. He looks like the painting of the man on the cover of the *Introduction to Existentialism* book that I read in intermediate French. I wonder if Aunt Aya intended for her shopping trip to bring on this level of crisis. Where another person might have seen all those cheap, available properties as opportunities, Bud could see in them only his betrayal.

Aya calls later that afternoon, after Bud has dropped into a flat, comalike sleep on the couch, and says, "Well, I cured him. I cured him of the family."

I shift the receiver and look at Bud through the kitchen door. I notice the way his wrist is still flopped loosely across his eyes. He takes long, shuddering breaths. "If he's cured of something, shouldn't he be feeling better?" I whisper.

She laughs her black velvet laugh and says, "Oh no, cures are often worse than the illnesses. In my experience, most cures have to have some poison, too."

While this observation has the tang of the truth, I don't like to hear it, and I ask almost petulantly, "Then why get cured of anything?"

"That is the question everyone must answer for themselves. My only advice, *habeebti*, is that you have to take the long view. The poison may not kill you."

That night, I wake from a heavy, sumptuous sleep like a diver rising from deep beneath the surface of a black sea. Slender, silver threads of feelings, associations, and images gather mysteriously inside of me. I hunt around in the still-dark for the pen and stack of bare paper I've kept by the bedside table since arriving in Jordan. And I write down the details for a new novel as they come to me, light as figments, glints in the nighttime of memory. This novel is set in the United States. And after a few hours of work, I drift off to sleep as if I'd never been awake at all.

TWENTY-TWO

Beyond the Land of Duty-Free

Bud is cutting his visit short, returning to America one week early. And Fattoush is going back with him, two weeks later than his original return date. He doesn't want to stay on without Bud, and I don't go to any great lengths to convince him otherwise. The night before they leave, my father hangs on his brothers' necks at an all-night drinking party they've thrown to help him prepare for his long flight the next morning. He seems to have forgotten about being cured of the family.

"My brothers, my brothers," he says in between beers, then hugs Uncle Hal and smears his tear-soaked face into his brother's neck.

"You are the greatest brother of all," insists Rich-Uncle Jimmy, leaning on them both and slapping Bud on the back. "You are my favorite brother."

All remaining seven brothers crowd one another at the bar, throwing their arms around one another's shoulders. They feed one another bites of rice from a tray of food set out on the counter. They lift the steaming hot grains on the tips of their fingers and put them right into one another's mouths. Their reminiscences and jokes are so old and familiar, they barely need to be spoken aloud. They ignore their wives and children and grandchildren. At this moment, they're the only ones in the world. I gaze at them fondly. This is not the way my sisters and I relate to each other. Our relationship is close, but not nearly as wild or uncontainable—and this is a great relief.

On the morning of their transoceanic flight, after a total of two hours' sleep, Bud and Fattoush both lean forward on the hard couch, elbows on knees, wrists and heads dangling, their shoulder blades melted down. There are eggplant-colored shadows under their eyes, their expressions the slack, semishocked faces of insomniacs. Neither of them will eat anything but water and aspirins. I can't even distract Bud by asking questions about his childhood. He flaps one loose hand and says, "Over. It's all—allllll over now! I'm never coming back to Jordan again. I'm old and I'm tired, and that's all I have to say on the subject."

But on the taxi ride to the airport, it's as if the last painful strands stretching from Bud to this place begin to snap. He perks up. He takes off his tie, calls the driver "bud," and asks where he's from. When the man glances into the rearview mirror with a wide, handsome smile and says, "Palestine," Bud chortles, looks out the window at the streaming landscape like a visitor from a faraway place, and murmurs, "That's beautiful, buddy, just beautiful!"

The Amman airport is like all airports—full of resonating tiled floors, overlit and echoing as a mausoleum. Fattoush, Bud, and I glide, lost in the corridors. Fattoush looks back over one shoulder. I know he is nurturing a private hope that Mai will have a change of heart, appear at the airport, and take him in her arms. His eyes are sunken, his lips are chapped to shreds. "Why are we leaving?" he asks Bud repeatedly, as if he can't quite recall the answer. "Why don't we stay a little longer? Maybe we should try starting another business? It doesn't have to be a restaurant. We could start a spa!"

Bud hugs Fattoush's shoulders with one arm, crumpling him into one armpit. "You are such a *fattoush,* you *fattoush!*" he exclaims unhelpfully. Then, "Time to go home."

We get past the narrow waiting area and the one fast-food stand, past the security checkpoints, the ticket counter, the customs office, the pat-down station, the passport checker, and the exit-tax taker. Eventually, the airport telescopes backward behind us as we ride the escalator upstairs into a gleaming horizon.

We are delivered to counters glowing with Swiss watches, spicy French perfumes, and mahogany-sleek Italian shoes—things that are not available in the shops of Amman. A big sign proclaims: DUTY-

FREE SHOPS. It's like entering a neutral little kingdom set somewhere in the Alps. Men and women in chic, fitted Western clothing glide by carrying bottles of Chivas Regal and crystal vases. It is hermetically sealed, staffed by an international conference of lithe young people who carry on conversations in twenty languages.

There are even glass counters where you can buy Jordanian "crafts"—pastries, embroidered shawls, and tea cozies like the kind available in the shopping mall in the Abu-Jaber family fortress. But it seems we've already left Jordan. It's impossible to imagine the wild sun glittering just beyond the walls of this airport.

My father sets off as if into an enchanted forest, hypnotized by the glass counters, buying all the perfumes, bracelets, and scarves he'd forgotten to buy for everyone back in America. Fattoush hangs back, morose and squinting in the bleached lights, his elaborate career and revenge plans shattered.

During the previous night's drinking party, while the reality of departure was still just a wisp in the air around him, Fattoush haunted Mai, hovering at her elbow as if awaiting instructions. When she yawned, picked up her coat, and told Fattoush that she'd be seeing him around, he grabbed her fingers with both hands and stopped just short of kneeling before her. He squatted to his heels, and leaning in the direction of the dance floor, he cried, "Please oh pleaseoh-pleaseohplease . . . don't leave me."

She closed her eyes and asked if he would please let go of her fingers.

But Fattoush clung to her, pleading in an unintelligible ramble. His eyes were as muddled and wet as a child's. Finally, Dobby came over, put a kindly hand on his shoulder, and led him away. At the bar, Fattoush hung his head over a syrup-yellow drink.

"She'll never go for you, man," Dobby said, pitying and annoyed. "It's nothing personal. But you've got to understand—she's a Muslim and you're a Christian. She lives with her *parents*. That's what the girls do here. Nobody *dates* here, it just isn't done. She'll probably just marry the guy they choose for her." He turns to me and mutters, "Or not."

"That's insane," Fattoush said vehemently, eyes blinking hard, lashes spiky with tears. "Why should she do that? It's her life! Besides, I'm not Christian!"

Dobby drew up, vaguely exasperated. "All right, then what are you?"

Fattoush thought about this for a moment. "Well, if I have to *be* anything . . . then I guess I'm a pagan."

Dobby laughed while Fattoush stared at him. Then Dobby stopped and said, "Yeah, okay, but you're a Christian."

There is a little more than an hour remaining before their flight when Bud decides that it is time for them to "nibble on a little something." The land of duty-free has everything but actual restaurants. Across the corridor from the icy countertops is a pallid, cafeteria-style place where we can slide trays along chrome railings and select from a landslide of cookies sealed in plastic or a trough full of reconstituted eggs. But Bud has a dreamlike memory of eating at an actual restaurant here. We ask one or two of the blond duty-free cashiers, but they don't seem to know anything about such a place.

Then Bud spots a Jordanian man in a crisp new skycap uniform sitting in the cafeteria, gazing forlornly into a cup of American-style coffee. The old man's face, a webbing of wrinkles and eyes so deep-set that you can barely make out the pupils, seems to catch and tighten as Bud speaks to him. "Oh yes," he says in Arabic. "The restaurant? It's still there." Then he gives a set of directions, arcane and elaborate as if to Sinbad's cave.

"You pass the restroom with the tarnished door handle—if you get to the one with the shiny handle, turn back! Turn right at the corridor with the strange carpeting, then you have to ride up the narrow escalator . . ."

We begin walking and quickly forget his directions once we're outside of duty-free. We find ourselves in a maze of hallways and escalators like details in an Escher painting, depositing us on floors like ledges, with no rooms to enter. Bud insists that he remembers the way, but it seems clear that he does not. Miraculously, we find the narrow escalator at the end of the longest corridor. At the top, we walk down another corridor, this one like the crack in the rock to the entrance of Petra. Finally, a cavernous room opens before us; metal rotating fans stand posted in the corners like potted palms. The place is all but empty. A man with a thin, disappointed mustache and a man in a stained apron sit tilted on stools, elbows on the bar that runs along one wall, their faces propped up toward the TV showing Bedouin soap operas. The only light comes from a bank of windows lining the back wall; these open out on an arid beige emptiness, blowing sand, desiccated fields, a ribbon of highway.

The place has the dim, after-hours feel of a closed restaurant. But as soon as we appear, vacillating in the doorway and poised to flee, the men spot us and descend from their stools, arms outstretched, crying, "*Ahlan! Ahlan!*" as if we are long overdue but eagerly expected relations.

With great ceremony we are shown to a square linoleum table in the center of the ringing room. Breezes from the fans sweep over our table like trade winds. The man in the apron disappears through a small trapdoor, and the waiter hands us menus that feature an international potpourri: teriyaki, French onion soup, and tortellini. One section, labeled "Everything to make you happy!" could have been lifted from the window of an American diner: steak and eggs, meat loaf, green salads, tomato soup, fried chicken, and spaghetti.

The mustached man stations himself at our table, shoulders back, his body stiffened with a vaguely military bearing. "Yes, yes, yes, my friends," he says in English. "What am I about to do for you?" But as he lifts his pad, his expression sharpens and turns skeptical, as if already expecting to be disappointed by our order.

His glare chases away my hunger. I request just a bowl of Greek egg-and-lemon soup and in so doing seem to confirm something he'd already suspected. Fattoush, who's been growing more morose all morning, now looks downright funereal. He orders only a cup of coffee. Bud, however, busily points all over the menu, ordering a full-blown American-style breakfast. As he lists scrambled eggs and steak, sliced onions and sautéed mushrooms, fried potatoes and chicken, buttered toast and fresh orange juice, the waiter undergoes a meta-morphosis. His brows tick closer together, his eyes rake my father, his mouth goes taut, his little mustache bristles. Finally, he can contain himself no longer and bursts out: "Ghassan Abu-Jaber!"

Bud lowers the menu and cranes his head toward the waiter. The waiter leans in close to my father. I can see Bud's eyes focusing, read-ing the man's face as if it is a tablet of ancient runes; his eyebrows lower, his lips move silently, everything in him is drawn into concen-tration, and finally he breathes a name: "Mo Kadeem."

The man he used to wash the rice and lentils with in the king's air force.

"It's me!" says Mo Kadeem. His face is splendid with a long, crooked smile. He spreads his arms wide and Bud lurches to his feet, knocking over his chair, and the two men swing this way and that in a staggering embrace.

"Mo Kadeem!"

They rub tears from their faces, but more pop into their eyes. Bud keeps grabbing the man's shoulders, checking his solidity. They drag their chairs together and sit pressed closed like boys, holding each other's arms. The room rings like a vault, and I can hear little blips of echoes behind all the questions they ask each other in English and Arabic. "Where have you been all this time? Where did you go? Did you see the world? Did you get married? How many babies?"

Mo laughs but also shakes his head with a heavy downward dip. "What a crazy time. Now I live with my mother. But after the air force, I went to Australia. I tried to ask girls to go out, but they wouldn't talk to me. I went to Venezuela, Bangkok, Canada. You would not believe where I've been!" More of the heavy head shake. "And after two years of traveling, I realized I didn't like it," he says. "Here I was, twenty-three years old, I thought I was free as can be—I thought I didn't need anything. But every single morning when I woke up in Sweden or Mexico, the first thing I thought of was my mother's teapot on the kitchen table. Every night I fell asleep smelling the sweetness of the lemon tree outside my window. I was like one of the pine trees planted in the Jordan Valley. As soon as you take it away from its home, it dries right up." He pauses, curling his fingers under his chin and scratching his throat in a careful, thoughtful way as he studies my father. A crease forms in the space between his eyebrows. "When you came in here . . . I thought you were an American."

Bud's chest rises and his face gleams. "Well," he says mildly, a bit modestly, "I am."

A whole new galaxy of suns, moons, stars, and songbirds pops out of the air and starts to orbit my head. My ears seem to be picking up frequencies from Mars. I look at Bud from three different angles. Finally, I take one of the lacy-edged paper doilies and write: "Today my father said he was an American." I date it and fold it into my purse.

Mo Kadeem is also staring at him. "In all that time, all those lentils, you never said you wanted to go to America, you never said anything about traveling anywhere."

We watch him studying Bud's face. We can see the way he takes it in, the fact that Bud went away to a new place and never actually came back. That Bud has had, in some way, the life that Mo had been meant to have. Bud is the first to look away, his face modest, and even a little embarrassed—as if he has been caught with something that did not belong to him.

"I know," Bud admits. "I never meant to go. It just turned out that way. Although I did marry a nice, tall wife," he says, smiling shyly at the tabletop. "I'm going to see her soon!" he announces, as if this has just occurred to him.

"You were always the lucky one," Mo says peevishly. "I always thought you knew exactly who you were. I was jealous of that, in fact. I think maybe that's even why I came back to Jordan."

"No, I didn't know anything," Bud protests.

Mo straightens then. He takes another long, fierce matador's look at Bud while we all hold our breath. Is he cursing us? Wishing he'd never returned to Jordan? Finally he bows and glides away without a word.

"I think he's upset," Bud murmers. We debate in whispers whether or not he's going to come back.

After several minutes of discussing Mo and then several more minutes of discussing ways to sneak out, we see the trapdoor in the back of the restaurant open and Mo emerges carrying a full tray: Nothing on it is what we ordered. There are thick slices of *halloumi* cheese wedged between freshly grilled sausages, hummus enriched with nuggets of fried lamb, dates stuffed with almonds, *sfeeha* pastries plump with ground chicken and onion, broiled kabobs, roasted fish in tahini sauce, tomatoes stuffed with beef and rice, and, of course, gallons of sweet mint tea. As he carries it to us across the empty restaurant, a space as big as a dance floor, he shouts: "How do you expect to fly to other worlds without a real breakfast?"

My father runs over and grabs dishes off the tray, insisting: Mo has to eat with us! We pull up a chair, then another, because the chef in his white apron has appeared, peeking demurely from the kitchen door, then moving to the table.

Bud compliments him on his wonderful food, and the chef blushes, lowering his head. He tells us in Arabic, "This is the usual breakfast for the staff." Suddenly Mo swings his ferocious glare on Fattoush, who draws back in his chair. "What kind coffee you want? Americano or *gahweh*?"

Fattoush stammers before collecting himself: "May I please have some *gahweh,* sir?"

Mo smiles but doesn't stand up, as if Fattoush just passed a test. He looks us over. "So these are your big American children?"

Bud looks vaguely in our direction, busy piling his plate with *sfeehas.* "That's right."

Fattoush beams, a sweet red flush rising from his neck. He ducks his head toward his plate, which is almost empty.

Mo rolls forward and claps Bud on the shoulder. "Do you remember, my friend? Up to our armpits in lentils?"

"And what about *frekeh*?"

"And crying, crying, with all those onions."

"Peeling, washing, chopping, soaking . . ." Bud's voice rises and falls, as if he is singing a small, brokenhearted song.

"These English," Mo says in a lowered voice, gesturing to the empty room. "They don't eat food, they don't know what food is. They think food is French fries." He says this with a thin-lipped bitterness as he imitates someone daintily consuming a pile of fries. "They come in here, and what do they want? Fish and chips, tea and scones, lamb and mint jelly! What is mint jelly? They take over the whole menu with these terrible things, just like they take over the *whole world*."

We are all relieved there aren't any English eating French fries in the room: They are all still safely down below in the land of duty-free. The restaurant remains uncolonized for the moment, an oasis of intimacy. Beyond the dusty windows is voluptuous sunlight, beige, arid earth, and the smell of wild honey. But inside we huddle, happily, familiarly—five of us eating together at the center of a lost room as wide as the desert, a ceiling as high as the sun.

MO KADEEM'S ROASTED FISH IN TAHINI SAUCE
For impressing that certain someone.

6 fish fillets (haddock is
very nice for this)
3 tablespoons butter, cut
into small pieces
Juice of 2 lemons
6 cloves garlic, finely minced
1 teaspoon salt

1 teaspoon freshly ground
pepper
½ cup flat-leaf parsley,
chopped
1 onion, thinly sliced
1 tablespoon olive oil

SAUCE

1¼ cups tahini
½ cup olive oil
Juice of 1 lemon
1 tablespoon ground cumin

1 teaspoon salt
1 teaspoon freshly ground
pepper

¼ cup toasted pine nuts
(optional)

Preheat the oven to 350 degrees. Place the fish in a baking dish and dot the fish all over with the butter. Sprinkle with the lemon juice, garlic, salt, pepper, and parsley. Bake for 15 minutes, or until barely done.

Sauté the sliced onion in 1 tablespoon of olive oil until translucent and set aside.

In a saucepan, stir together the sauce ingredients and simmer over low heat, about 10 minutes. Adjust the seasonings and add a little water for a creamy consistency.

Remove the baking dish from the oven. Spread the onion slices over the fish, then pour the tahini sauce over this. Bake at 350 degrees for another 20 to 30 minutes. Top with the pine nuts and serve with garnishes of lemon wedges.

MAKES 4 TO 6 SERVINGS.

TWENTY-THREE

HTML

When I finally return to the States a few months later, I'm certain that I am ready to be home again. I've missed America for a year, craved its glowing supermarkets and orderly drivers, its plush movie theaters and its bookstores and rivers and curbs and everything in its sense of imminence—the feeling of expectation, the urgency of rain-slicked city nights as traffic picks up and someone is going somewhere all the time.

But when I return, I discover that I am once again a child, lying mute in a blank motel room and straining for the old smells and sounds of my lost Jordanian neighborhood. After a year of lethally silent soap operas and stately Jordanian newscasts, American sitcom laugh tracks sound jarring and surreal to me. I am disturbed by the billboards radiant with images of people eating and drinking like Vikings, advertising "All You Can Eat." By cars the size of small houses. And in the evening when the traffic packs into a rush-hour snarl, no friends gather on my front lawn, wanting to come up and drink tea or drag me out in the night to see what we can see. I miss them terribly.

I get lost. I am set loose in a wilderness. Jordan has torn me open, and inside this opening are pictures of light and dust-scrubbed air and flowering jasmine. I have trouble sleeping or focusing; people frown as if there is something slightly off-kilter on my face. A friend who has moved frequently between Yemen and America meets me at a Turkish café and, over the demitasses of dense black coffee, tells me that I am suffering from culture shock, that it is a sort of soul-sickness, that it will subside. But I can't imagine that I will ever be whole again.

And I feel so impossibly alone—as if I am the first and only person ever to be unmoored between countries. So I perversely do things to make myself feel even more isolated. I resign from my university position in Eugene. I move to Portland, into a minuscule apartment; I take it for its wall of sliding glass looking toward the Willamette River and for its little kitchen, tight and shiny as a ship's galley. I cook all the dishes that I ate in Jordan, the simple Bedouin flavors—meat, oil, and fire; like Bud, I am trying to live in the taste of things.

I'd published *Arabian Jazz* not long before I'd left for Jordan, and while I was overseas, people read my novel and began to have opinions about it. When I return to America, there is mail waiting for me (not everyone has e-mail yet). College students send me their papers analyzing my characters; there are several generous, heartfelt newspaper reviews; a man in Romania sends me a slender gold ring; people from many different cultural backgrounds—Italian, Russian, Chinese, African—tell me that they come from a family just like the one in the book. I learn that there are Greek, Polish, French, and Dutch versions of my characters—living counterparts; their American-born children write in to tell me this. A newspaper announces that *Arabian Jazz* is the first mainstream novel about the Arab-American experience.

I don't know if this is actually true, but the claim alone seems to convey a great weight of responsibility, because I also start to hear from readers that I think of as "the Betrayed." These are the Arab-American immigrants and scholars and young people who complain that I haven't written their story. One girl protests angrily that her father wasn't nearly as fun or easygoing as the father in my book. An academic publishes a scathing review of *Arabian Jazz* with numbered paragraphs, each enumerating the many "errors" of my novel, taking issue with everything from the type of videocassette a character brings from Jordan to the fact that one of the characters—a Greek Orthodox bishop—is described as having crumbs in his beard. An anonymous person slides a letter under my office door that demands I stop writing "depressing things" about the Arabs and instead write about "happy, uplifting Arab things." One woman writes: "Do your parents know you wrote this book? Naughty, naughty girl!" It seems that a great lament rises up from the Arab-American world and rings in the living room: the sense of being unfairly cast, unrepresented, their unique stories and voices (aside from only the most extreme, violent, and sensational) unheard and ignored. In retrospect, I think that this lament was already in the air, but by publishing a novel, I just happened to provide a name and an address to mail it to. I am their disappointing American child—the one who didn't speak Arabic, who didn't sound or dress or behave in any way as an Arab is supposed to. And I understand why so many readers felt so betrayed, alone in America, where the only media images of Arabs are bomb throwers and other lunatics. But at the time, I too feel shipwrecked—cut off from family, home, and even the idea of a cultural community—the one people I'd hoped would provide me with some sense of connection and acceptance.

That fall, I start teaching at Portland State University. After classes, I read the latest letters from my readers—the accusations and questions, demands and congratulations. Then I try to clear my head of voices. I walk to the International Market—an import store filled with bars of olive oil soaps, barrels of spices, packages of dried noodles. I buy bags of *zataar*, cumin, and sumac, sometimes to cook with, sometimes just to have their comforting scent circulating in my apartment.

So I am alone, alone, alone. But, as I said before, I am also guilty of perversely doing whatever I can to amplify that state, to feel it all the more keenly, so perhaps there is also something delicious and unspeakable in the pain of that aloneness. Perhaps I enjoy feeling judged, criticized, and deeply misunderstood. Perhaps that feeling is also a bit like home.

Since I have nothing better to do than work, I take an extra job through a private college teaching a creative writing class on the Internet. When the school asks if I know how to write HTML, I say brightly, Oh yes, a little! I have actually never heard of HTML. When the school discovers that I don't even understand how to fill out the registration form for their software, they kindly decide to assign a tutor to me. On our first meeting in my school office, the tutor tries to explain a few basic principles of computer language—as I stare at him with an increasingly desperate expression. He finally gives up.

My tutor's name is Scott; he is young and dark eyed, and I can't help but notice that this tutor of mine has a way of looking at me, at times, with great patience, fondness, and delight and other times with attentiveness, steadiness, and certainty. I'm noticing too much, I tell myself, a bad habit of mine. This is just his natural expression. Still, it is disorienting to have someone sitting next to you looking at you in this way, so I can't look back at him too much when we work on the computer together, the cursor blinking between the two of us like a private symbol.

While we work, I learn something that I had already suspected—I am not very good at all at computer language. Scott fills out the registration form for me, as I sit there shaking and simpering. Then he simply takes over. I slump back in my office chair and dictate the class lectures to him. As we make our way through the term, however, for some reason, we need to have more and more meetings, not fewer. My tutor adds increasingly elaborate images, sounds, and graphics to the class Web site; it becomes a multimedia event. We start to meet in cafés, and we talk more about our lives than we ever do about HTML. I tell him about Bud and his love of cooking. Scott tells me about the restaurants he's worked in and the time he'd offered a dessert of flourless chocolate torte to Julia Child in a swanky Boston restaurant. She complained about his description, scolding in her flutey voice, "Why call it flourless when *all* tortes are flourless?"

Then we have a meeting at his apartment, which turns out to be even smaller, and much tidier, than mine. It looks like the inside of a Hemingway story. The walls are covered with nautical charts and boat diagrams. There's also a mounted pair of antique snowshoes, a stuffed pheasant that his grandfather hunted, and a table beside the computer that is covered with fly-fishing and fly-tying accoutrements. I touch a gracefully arched piece of bamboo mounted on another wall. "Is this—a fishing pole?"

"A fishing rod," he says, smiling. He produces a tray of cheeses, crackers, and sliced fruits artfully fanned across a white plate. "I thought we could snack while we work." He places the tray of food in front of the computer, so it will be difficult to read the keyboard, and it finally occurs to me that all these meetings weren't only about learning to speak computer.

The first time we kiss (and this takes months and months to get to—months and months of private lessons and extra meetings, Scott appearing in the hall outside my office, taking my writing classes, forever finding some esoteric bit of computerese that I need to learn, inviting me over for "extra help"), it almost seems to happen accidentally. One second we are sitting on the couch, talking about whether or not the Internet class should have its own logo, the next we are kissing. I stand up out of our embrace and tell my tutor—who is startled, waiting motionlessly for me to return to the couch—that I am going for a stroll. And I go outside on an endless walk. It is raining, of course, as the air of Portland always seems impregnated with rain. The afternoon rain at first is restrained, powdering over the buildings, then it comes down hard. I walk close to the buildings and there's a deep quaking inside of me; I'm warm from walking, but tremors run along my arms and legs. Perhaps I'm trying to return to aloneness, my unknownness. How can I give up such surety? It's the only thing I know anymore; it is the house I've lived in for so long.

I walk all over the city for almost two hours. I'm soaked, stunned with fear. Finally, I return to stand outside my tutor's apartment building, looking up at the rectangle of light where his window is—a patch of light thrown like a white handkerchief down to the lawn. I can't go in. I can see this very clearly. How can I go back there?

· · ·

Interestingly enough, however, I don't want to return to my apartment with its little ship's galley of a kitchen, either. But I have to
go somewhere, I'm getting drenched. So I go to the International
Market. I start scooping up little cellophane bags of amber-colored
spices, some fresh pita bread, braided cheese, a small glass jug of olive
oil, a pomegranate, little plastic containers of hummus, my favorite
Arabic bean dip—*ful mudammas*—and a small bunch of oranges.

With a plastic bag of groceries in either hand, I walk across the park
blocks that bisect downtown Portland, under the tall trees that wag
their leaves free every autumn so the air fills with leaf storms. I cut
between dank, dripping campus buildings, step over quick streams
of curb runoff, inhale the tang of diesel rising from the nearby highway, the steam of decayed leaves, mulch, and dirt, and just the faintest
whiff of something green piercing the soil.

I hesitate for just a moment this time at the lighted lobby of his
building, then swing open the front glass door a bit too forcefully and
wince, worried that I've cracked it, but no. The elevator rumbles and
shakes, and I drip a damp ring on the forest green carpet, and when I
get to Scott's floor, he is already leaning in the door, as if he's been
waiting there since I left. He has a big white towel that he rubs over
my hair. He'd seen me standing outside in the rain; he says he was
worried that I would never come back again. I go into the bathroom
and change into some clothes he's given me: a soft cotton shirt and a
pair of jeans that droop from my hips. My feet are cold, so he puts a
pair of clean socks in the oven before I put them on. And when I
come out of the bathroom, I see that he's opened the bags of food,
placed each item on its own small plate or bowl. "Was this right?" he
asks. "I wasn't sure if you were saving this for later, but you were gone
so long—I thought you must be hungry." His voice fades a bit; he is
looking at my getup, laughing, taking my inventory. He looks at me a
moment longer and says, "You have green eyes."

I feel not captured, but saved—given safe harbor from the raining,
unknown world beyond the windows. I sit cross-legged on the floor
beside the steamer trunk he uses as a table and show him how you
tear the bread with your hands, how you dip the bread in oil, like this,

you see. I tell him, There is a place I want to take you to someday, an amazing country, a beautiful history of mine. But for now we sit on the floor and share a loaf of bread.

FUL FOR LOVE

1 can (15 ounces) small fava
  beans, drained
2 cloves garlic, crushed
2 tablespoons olive oil
Salt and freshly ground
  pepper

Juice of 1 lemon
1 small onion, finely
  diced
1 tablespoon finely chopped
  flat-leaf parsley

In a saucepan, combine the fava beans, garlic, 1 tablespoon of the oil, salt, and pepper. Simmer over low heat about 10 minutes, then remove from the heat. Add the lemon juice and remaining oil and mash into the beans with a fork.

Garnish with the onion and parsley. *Ful* is also nice topped with some chopped tomato. Serve with pita bread.

TWENTY-FOUR

The First Meal

Finally, Bud gets his restaurant.

He comes back from Jordan, announces to himself for the hundredth or thousandth or millionth time that he really and truly lives in this country, this Amerikee, this beauty, place of lost radio songs, unknowable glances, cold blue lakes, of work not family, of facing forward not back, of solitude not tribes, of lightness not weight, and he goes out and he finds the place.

It comes to him through a friend of a cousin of a guy at work, so the purchase—as he explains it later—seems both like a business transaction and like fate. The difference this time is that he asks Mom for her opinion of the place. She looks at it, sees past the destiny, checks the books, and says yes.

Actually, it's not so much a restaurant as a driving range, a long green lawn where golfers go to prop up their tees and practice their swings. There is also a miniature golf course and a batting cage—so the whole thing comprises a "family fun center," Bud explains to me—there's even a big sign out front that says so. He points to it: BUD'S FAMILY FUN CENTER. Attached to all this is a little hut with a window where Bud is constantly giving children free tokens to the batting cages and gossiping with his customers and friends and passersby. Inside the hut, beside the window, is a nice big grill, a deep fryer, a blender, and a freezer. This is my father's restaurant. The heart and soul of Bud's Family Fun Center, serving rows of burgers, sizzling French fries, blistering hot dogs, and grilled cheese sandwiches.

These basic foods recall my father's first meal in America, not at the railing of a ship, but at a table in Cosmo's Malt Shop—a daily regime of hamburger and Coke—that began all his other American meals.

Bud grills the burgers, adds a little chopped onion, toasts the buns just so. He leans into the grill, singing his unique version of the songs on the radio. My youngest sister, Monica, comes in with her husband and their baby and helps scoop ice cream. My mother dispenses tees and tokens to customers. Friends from my parents' square-dancing club sit forward in the metal folding chairs, drinking coffee, elbows on their knees, and talk about one another. In the end, the type of food doesn't matter so much to Bud; it's cooking it and feeding people and watching them eat, keeping them alive in the desert of the world—that is all he really cares about.

My parents have a videotape that the golf pro made of a series of instructional sessions he gave my father to help him analyze his swing and chart his progression. Bud feels it's not enough to cook his chili dogs and grilled cheese sandwiches. The owner of a Family Fun Center should know how to golf. So once a week, he pops a new tape into the VCR player and studies the grainy, silent black-and-white film.

Lesson One: Bud swings. Wildly. Crookedly. The ball dribbles off to one side. Bud grins and shrugs. Watches the ball. Shrugs. It's all in fun!

Lesson Five: Same swing. Same outcome.

Lesson Ten: No change.

Lesson Eleven: Bud scowls furtively at the camera. Evidently the pro is telling him something he doesn't want to hear. The pro comes on camera, keeps his head down, demonstrates a modified swing. Bud tries to imitate this swing, jerks his head back, and reproduces exactly his own original swing.

Lesson Twelve: Palsied swing. Pro tries to come on camera. Bud glares at him. He backs off.

Lesson Thirteen: Bud shouts a few words at the camera. No swing.

Lesson Fourteen: Bud hurls down club, shakes fist at camera while shouting things, face turns very dark. Storming toward camera. Earthquake effect. Sudden veering off camera.

End of film.

After two profitable summers, Bud turns the business over to Monica and her husband. Turns out, after a lifetime of pining for a restaurant of his own, well, this isn't it. He says it's because it makes him tired. He wipes his hand over his face, looks up at the sky, and says, "I can't take it." At the Fun Center, he was surrounded by people in a way he never had been before—openly, constantly, publicly. It exhausted him. With his instinct to serve, to cook, to talk, to welcome, he had no way to ever close his doors, no way to ever say no. Though it was filled with Americans, the shack resembled an overcrowded, talk-heavy Jordanian coffeehouse. But Bud is no longer—not entirely—Jordanian.

My father and his brothers fly back and forth, back and forth, whisking over the oceans and continents. They live their lives in the air, in the ether of in-between, the borderlands. Whenever they see one another, they cook, they scoop the warm rice up in the curve of their palms, bring it to their fingertips, and sometimes they feed one another, hand to mouth, in this greatest of intimacies.

Bud has American grandchildren now from both his younger daughters—babies who've stupefied him with love and pleasure. The youngest one, Jake, adores my father with a wild, free-hearted, clear passion. He and his brother come over every day. Not yet two years old, he cries out: "*Jiddo! Jiddo!* Grandpa!" before my mother has a chance to open their front door. He rushes in, straight to my father, urgent yet shy; he climbs into Bud's big, square lap, presses his nose to my father's, his milky fingers on either side of Bud's big, round head, and croons, "*Jiddo,* happy." It's hard to say if this is a question, assertion, or metaphysical analysis. His conversations tend to go this way—lists of objects or feelings he finds interesting: "Cow, car, table, spoon?" went a recent phone conversation. "Dog, house, truck!" And somewhere in this, I hear traces, like words overheard through a closed door, of my childhood conversation on the desert floor with a group of Bedouin women.

But now, for Bud, Jake has his special word, and that word is "happy." Bud laughs and says, "Yes, Jake, *Jiddo* happy."

Jake grins deliriously and says, "*Jiddo*, eat!"

And I wonder if it is this, the children, that can ever anchor any place enough to make it a home. Once we are grown, we are no longer so porous, our identities don't connect with a place as much as they do when we grow up with a place and the places, in turn, grow into us.

I have recently come to understand something about myself, which is that I am—as my uncle Hilal might say—a hopeless case. Even if I had somehow, down the line, brought myself to have babies and to stay in my hometown in a house with an easy, wide-hipped porch, none of that would have made any difference to the sleepless part of me. Like a second, invisible body, I sit up out of my sleep at night, wander across the room, stop beside a darkened window, and dream my way through the glass. It is more than *looking*: the elements of darkness and distance release my mind like a dash of sugar on the surface of hot water. In the distances between stars, it seems there is no flavor or scent (although I think I might detect the purple black glisten of an eggplant skin within the night air, the slyest reminder of how the forms of life and the physical world are infinite and every-where). *Come back,* I want to say to my second self, *there is tea and mint here, there is sugar, there is dark bread and oil.* I must have these things near me: children, hometown, fresh bread, long conversations, animals; I must bring them very near. The second self draws close, like a wild bird, easy to startle away: It owns nothing, and it wants nothing, only to see, to taste, and to describe. It is the wilderness of the interior, the ungoverned consciousness of writing.

We grow into the curve of what we know; for me, that was my family's rootlessness and my father's control and scrutiny—movement and confinement. I am as surely a Bedouin as anyone who has trav-eled in a desert caravan. A reluctant Bedouin—I miss and I long for every place, every country, I have ever lived—and frequently even the places my friends and my family have lived and talked about as well—and I never want to leave any of these places. I want to cry out, to protest: Why must there be only one home! Surely there is no one as bad, as heartbroken, as hopeless at saying good-bye as I am. The fruits and vegetables, the dishes and the music and the light and the trees of all these places have grown into me, drawing me away. And so I go. Into the world, away.

Acknowledgments

Many people have helped me with this book, helped me think about how to write it, how to feel about it, and how to cook for it. For sustained literary, culinary, and emotional wisdom, personal and professional, I thank my friends Anjali Singh, Joy Harris, Stephanie Abou, Alexia Paul, Amber Hoover, Leah Heifferon, and Michiko Clark.

I offer gratitude to a number of friends in Jordan, for helping me to see its hidden beauties and richness, including Alain McNamara, Kathy Sullivan, Bo Haroutunian, Claudio Cimino, Fouad and Jeanine Abu-Shaykh, and especially my dear friend Aida Dabbass, who is greatly missed.

For insight and support, for shared meals, for shared labor, and for all the good talking that goes with it, thanks to my writing group, Chelsea Cain, Whitney Otto, Cynthia Whitcomb, and Karen Karbo.

For brilliant friendship, guidance, and thrilling eating explorations: Alane Salierno Mason, Lorraine Mercer, Bette Sinclair, and Ellen Kanner.

For the great cooks in my life, my glorious grandmother Grace, my fabulous aunts and uncles both in America and Jordan, and the chefs of Portland, Oregon, who've taught me by their brilliant example, especially Hoda Khouri, Mirna Attar, and Philippe Boulot.

For shared trouble, running away, hollering through the woods, in-depth food experiments, taking risks, and bottomless friendship, for our childhood, Pam Jaber, Tariq Abu-Jaber, Suzanne Abu-Jaber, and Monica App.

For painstaking, middle-of-the-night recipe recitations, grocery store breakdowns, and all manner of culinary adventures and triumphs, and for being my models of social generosity and all-around good times, my parents, Pat and Gus.

For rawhide chewing with gusto and unbridled dinnertime enthusiasm, Yogi.

And most of all, for my best, most patient, and truest reader, taster, and friend, Scotty.

To all the great chefs in my life—of food and of experience—I offer my thanks. I am grateful to everyone who has stood at the stove or pulled up a chair to the dinner table beside me.

IT MUST'VE BEEN SOMETHING I ATE
The Return of the Man Who Ate Everything
by Jeffrey Steingarten

It Must've Been Something I Ate finds Jeffrey Steingarten testing the virtues of chocolate and gourmet salts; debunking the mythology of lactose intolerance and Chinese-Restaurant Syndrome; roasting marrow bones for his dog; and offering recipes for everything from lobster rolls to *gratin dauphinois*. The result is one of those rare books that is simultaneously mouthwatering and side-splitting.

Cooking/Essays/0-375-72712-4

ARE YOU REALLY GOING TO EAT THAT?
Reflections of a Culinary Thrill Seeker
by Robb Walsh

For Robb Walsh, food is a window on culture, and his essays brim with insights into our society and those around us. Whether he's discussing halal organic farming with Muslims, traversing the steep hills of Trinidad in search of hot-sauce makers, or savoring the disappearing art of black Southern cooking with an inmate-chef in a Texas penitentiary, Walsh has a unique talent for taking our understanding of food to a deeper level.

Cooking/Food/1-4000-7716-8

STUFFED
Adventures of a Restaurant Family
by Patricia Volk

Patricia Volk's delicious memoir lets us into her big, crazy, loving, and infuriating family, where you're never just hungry—you're starving to death; and you're never full—you're stuffed. Volk's family fed New York City for one hundred years, from 1888 when her great-grandfather introduced pastrami to America until 1988 when her father closed his garment center restaurant. But as seductively as Volk evokes this food, *Stuffed* is at heart a funny, fresh, and profoundly moving paean to family.

Memoir/0-375-72499-0

IN THE EYE OF THE SUN
by Ahdaf Soueif

In the Eye of the Sun tells the story of Asya, a brilliant young woman who grows up in the luxurious world of the Egyptian elite, marries a Westernized husband, and pursues graduate study in England, where she becomes embroiled in a love affair with an Englishman. But for all her worldliness, Asya remains caught in a struggle between ties to her traditions and desire for independence and sexual fulfillment. Lyrical and honest, sensual and erudite, *In the Eye of the Sun* is a revealing account of cultural collisions—and the plight of women all too often caught in the middle.

Fiction/Middle Eastern Studies/0-385-72037-8

THE STORYTELLER'S DAUGHTER
One Woman's Return to Her Lost Homeland
by Saira Shah

As an accomplished journalist and documentarian, Saira Shah returned to Afghanistan, her family's homeland, cloaked in the *burqa* to witness the pungent and shocking realities of Afghan life. As the daughter of the Sufi fabulist Idries Shah, primed by a lifetime of listening to her father's stories, she eagerly sought out, from the mouths of Afghan refugees in Pakistan, the rich and living myths that still sustain this battered culture of warriors. And she discovered that in Afghanistan all the storytellers have been men—until now.

Memoir/Middle Eastern Studies/1-4000-3147-8

VINTAGE AND ANCHOR BOOKS
Available at your local bookstore, or call toll-free to order:
1-800-793-2665 (credit cards only).